HOW TO MAKE BLOCKBUSTER MOVIES AND DO IT ON YOUR OWN

HOW TO MAKE BLOCKBUSTER MOVIES
AND DO IT ON YOUR OWN

TOM GETTY

THIS IS AN ACROLIGHT PICTURES LLC BOOK
PUBLISHED BY TOM GETTY

Copyright © 2019 Acrolight Pictures LLC

This edition published 2019 by Acrolight Pictures LLC.

Press, Johnstown, Pennsylvania

LCCN: 2019903100
ISBN: 978-0-9974800-3-0

Designed by Tom Getty

All rights reserved. No part of this book may be reproduced or transmitted in any form or by any means without written permission of the author.

FIRST EDITION

ACKNOWLEDGEMENTS

This book is a product of 25 years of research, and therefore spans just as many places and faces. Many thanks are in order.

I want to thank…

My Mother, Sally Hare Getty, for nurturing, supporting, and lobbying for my movie aspirations—and also for reminding me that even Steven Spielberg had trouble "getting the shark to work." Also, major thanks to my Father, Charles A. Getty, for countless years of financial, professional, parental, and emotional support.

Major thanks to Robert V. Crites for decades of support.

I also want to show immense thanks to a network of friends who supported my filmmaking efforts, of which none of my films—and the information in this book—would have ever been possible. Christian Condrick, Bill Lusk, Bruce Barger, Nathan Felix, Matt Meehan, Jocelyn Meehan, and Josh Miller, just to name a few.

Also, if it weren't for the many wonderful and patient teachers and educators in the Westmont Hilltop school district, at the University of Pittsburgh at Johnstown, and the University of Pittsburgh main campus, the knowledge and wisdom in this book would have been undercut and undernourished. If you want to find great teachers, seek out: Ginger Stepp, Carol Morgan, Wendy Kesslak, David F. Ward, Dr. Joseph Dewey, Thomas A. Sabo, just to name a few.

And a professional thanks to the late producer Arnold Kopelson, and agent/producer Galen Christy, of High Octane Pictures.

Thank you to all who supported and encouraged my filmmaking explorations. I hope this book adds something back.

*to a great teacher
and even better listener,*
Ginger Stepp

CONTENTS

INTRODUCTION	11
SHOW ME THE MONEY!	24
WRITING PT. 1	39
WRITING PT. 2	63
CAMERAS	85
IMPORTANT NUMBERS	109
WHAT TO RECORD 'ON'	117
AUDIO	120
TO LENS...OR NOT TO LENS...	134
LIGHTS!	140
RECRUITING	155
PRODUCTION	168
PREPARATION	179
ACTUALLY GETTING LOCATIONS	191
FILMING THE MOVIE	197
SHOOTING WITH CAMERAS	206
HALF-WAY THERE	221
SAVING THE MOVIE	226
FIRST ASSEMBLY	232

MUSIC…	240
SPECIAL EFFECTS	245
EDITING	256
FINISHING TOUCHES	260
THE NEXT PHASE…	275
MARKETING	287
MAKING A POSTER	292
MAKING THE TRAILER	299
GETTING MEDIA ATTENTION	310
LAUNCH	315
FILM FESTIVALS	321
WHEN NO ONE COMES KNOCKING…	327
CONCLUSION	330

1
INTRODUCTION

Having purchased this book, I can only assume that you have more than an interest in moviemaking. A person does not seek out a book on movies—and making them—without at least a serious interest.

It's therefore safe to assume you've seen at <u>least</u> one of the following movies:

INCEPTION	THE REVENANT	MEMENTO
GHOSTBUSTERS	DUNKIRK	LORD OF THE RINGS
JURASSIC PARK	DRIVE	THE ROYAL TENENBAUMS
DIE HARD	RAIDERS OF THE LOST ARK	28 DAYS LATER
THE DARK KNIGHT	FIGHT CLUB	GOODFELLAS
HALLOWEEN	DONNIE DARKO	BOOGIE NIGHTS

Pretty good movies, right?

But for you, one of those movies went beyond good. For you, one of those movies listed above—or perhaps one that didn't make the list—showed you the awesome power of filmmaking.

The awesome power a GREAT movie can have over the viewer.

Like the power in...

TAXI DRIVER	SCREAM	TERMINATOR 2
THE DEER HUNTER	THERE WILL BE BLOOD	BLADE RUNNER
THE BLUES BROTHERS	DIE HARD 3	SE7EN

If you're reading this book, you've also realized that your new favorite movie was in fact <u>made</u>. You don't know how exactly. But you get a sense that it was filmed and edited. At the very least.

Therefore, it goes without saying that YOU could make a movie.

One of those movies made you feel:

"I could make a movie just like [fill in the blank]."

The inspiration.

Being inspired to make a movie like…

THE SILENCE OF THE LAMBS	**INTERSTELLAR**
GLADIATOR	**INGLORIOUS BASTARDS**
THE MATRIX	**UNBREAKABLE**
NIGHT OF THE LIVING DEAD	**THE GODFATHER PARTS 1 & 2**
THE BLAIR WITCH PROJECT	**PARANORMAL ACTIVITY**

Did you ever get that feeling?

But where do you start?

Since you or your family, or someone you know, has a camera, you have the feeling and go straight at it. Maybe you use the one on your smartphone. Should be easy enough, you figure. After all, how difficult could something as fun as making a movie be?

But then it doesn't go as expected. The camera doesn't cooperate. Nor does the weather. The shots are all blurry. A roaring sound plagues the audio. Your friend playing the lead leaves too soon. It rains.

Ultimately, what you've recorded doesn't match up at all with what you imagined.

But you're still curious.

So, you press on. If you were born after the 1990s, you go to Google and type, "how to make movies." A lot of good resources come up. Articles, entire websites. Not to mention all the YouTube videos explaining anything about filmmaking you could possibly want. What a gold mine. Depending on your level of interest, you absorb as much as you can.

And yet, as you read these articles, as you watch these videos, these tutorials, you get a sinking feeling. It's difficult to describe. But all of this helpful information… somehow… feels…

Disconnected?

Incomplete?

Scattered?

It's almost as if the information is being beamed back to you from much older, more seemingly accomplished people who are prescribing a process that is completely at odds with both 1) what you know, and

INTRODUCTION

2) what you have. You see something about a script—but what's that exactly? You see something about hiring actors—but—

Do you know any actors?

I certainly didn't.

You see something about lights—but the ones the experts recommend seem expensive. You see something about cameras—but no two people seem to agree on what's the "right" one or the "best one." You read up on "editing" softwares—but, again, no two people agree on a single application. And if you somehow get a hold of any of the recommended softwares, you're all but sure to be bewildered once you've opened them up. Have you tried editing yet? Did you feel bewildered?

I did.

While well meaning, the information publicly available seems to always parrot the same points:

- You need money (even on a low budget movie [did you know some people consider something like $50,000 dollars low budget?])
- You have to go to film school.
- You have to live in LA.
- You need professionals who know what they are doing.
- You need a great script.
- You need permits.
- You need a good lens!
- You need to think VISUALLY!
- You need GOOD actors!
- You need a good cinematographer (what's that?).
- You need GREAT sound.
- You GOTTA' GET NOTICED!

... and the WORST of the WORST...

- You gotta'—GOTTA'—be ORIGINAL!

When I started learning about filmmaking, none of these rules, of course, comported with anything I was doing—or wanted to do. Neither did I have any money. Let alone a "small" amount like $50,000. When I started out as a kid, $100 bucks was a small fortune.

$50,000!?!

That's still a ton of money to me! And I certainly wouldn't spend it on a movie!

I had a lot of difficulty with all of the "rules."

Especially the "L.A. thing." To me, there was nothing worse than even the thought of moving to Los Angeles, California. Let alone actually going through with it. I was having too much fun living in western PA, surrounded by a loving family, pretty awesome friends, great teachers, and even better memories.

I was too inspired to go anywhere else.

Do you want to move to LA? Smog? Traffic? High cost of living? Does that sound appealing to you?

Or are you inspired enough wherever you are?

You must be if you're reading a book on making movies. You must already have something to say.

Why squander that inspiration?

Don't worry. You won't have to go to LA—or spend $300,000 on film school! Not with this book.

Not with me as your guide.

But who am I?

My name is Tom Getty. I'm, as of this writing, 31, and have been making movies since I was seven years old.

I've been learning about movies since…

Well…

Literally since I can remember.

My first memory is of watching GHOSTBUSTERS.

My second memory is of wanting to be a Ghostbuster.

Perhaps it wasn't any more realistic to later decide to be a world-renowned filmmaker?

Nevertheless.

I caught "the bug," and apparently you have too! And I believe they call it a bug because it truly is a sickness, being obsessed with wanting to spend your life running around with a camera, trying to capture the inspiration of your youth.

But here we are, and we have to play it as it lies.

I've directed 3 feature films, all of which have won lots of awards; two of the films have been released around the world by actual distributors on Netflix, Amazon, Red Box, Vudu, and have made actual money. If you haven't already, look up my film EMULATION and my most "recent," RISING FEAR, which can also be found under the title AMERICA HAS FALLEN. You can buy them both on Amazon (and I suggest you do, as a companion to this book). You might like them, you might not. But they will be of, at the very least, great intellectual curiosity to you and proof positive that you can make your own successful movie.

I did literally every job on them, including…

- Writing (the script)
- Directing
- Producing

INTRODUCTION

    - Editing
    - Special Effects
    - Music

...I even played the lead character.

And I made all of the movies without money.

Or, put another way:

I was once like you—and, once I developed my own methods, once I stopped slaving away trying to conform to Hollywood methods, once I stopped following the filmmaking crowd, I actually got to do the very thing it is YOU WANT TO DO.

I made a REAL movie.

Not a short. Even though I did a lot of those.

Not a script. Even though I did a lot of those too.

A real movie.

Like a movie directed by...

    ...PETER JACKSON   ...DAVID LEAN
    ...CHRISTOPHER NOLAN   ...ALFRED HITCHCOCK
    ...STEVEN SPIELBERG   ...FRANCIS FORD COPPOLA
    ...QUENTIN TARANTINO   ...STANLEY KUBRICK
    ....SAM RAIMI   ...RIDLEY SCOTT
    ...MARTIN SCORSESE   ...WES ANDERSON
    ...JAMES WAN   ...SPIKE LEE
    ...DAVID FINCHER   ...TIM BURTON
    ...DAVID LYNCH   ...JAMES CAMERON

Or...

    ...M. NIGHT SHYAMALAN

These are not people playing around with cameras. These are preeminent artists in our society, paid a king's ransom to do something you already do—or would do—for free. Peter Jackson was paid $20 million to write, direct, and produce KING KONG. Christopher Nolan was paid $20 million for DUNKIRK—plus 20% of whatever the film grossed. Steven Spielberg on JURASSIC PARK—alone—made $200 million. On TITANIC, director James Cameron made somewhere between $50-100 million. A small pay day when you consider that he made $350 million from his duties on AVATAR.

Of course, all of this is loose change when you consider George Lucas ultimately made over $4 BILLION from STAR WARS.

These are filmmakers who create movies that express their own personal vision and entertain millions.

Making movies like…

ALIEN	**THE SIXTH SENSE**
CASINO	**PLATOON**
TITANIC	**BEING JOHN MALKOVICH**
NORTH BY NORTHWEST	**THE SHINING**
PULP FICTION	**THE THING**
AVATAR	**THE PRESTIGE**
BACK TO THE FUTURE	**THE EVIL DEAD**

You want to make movies LIKE THESE.

But how did the filmmakers listed above get to the place where they could finally… finally(!)… make actual, real movies? Like the kind you want to make!

Did they know the right people? Did they come from money?

Luck, maybe?

Of course, that's what people will say.

They got lucky.

They got lucky.

Does that hurt to hear? It certainly always made me feel bad.

I never liked depending on the luck business.

And thankfully, you won't have to either.

I'm not going to tell you the same thing about these filmmakers.

I'm not going to tell you, "it's all who you know."

I'm not going to tell you, "it's all about working a room."

I'm not going to tell you, "it's all about being in the right place at the right time."

I am, however, going to tell you how all of those filmmakers got "there."

And not only am I going to tell you how they "got there," I'm going to show you how YOU can do the same.

Would you like to know that?

Would that be interesting to you?

To know how Steven Spielberg, Martin Scorsese, Christopher Nolan, Robert Rodriguez—all of them, all of your favorite filmmakers—got to "the place" you'd someday like to get to as well?

Because, then, if you knew, then you too would have a path. And you would no longer be at the mercy of all this uncertain advice about "following your dreams" and moving out west.

You would know exactly what you'd have to do to get exactly where you want to be.

INTRODUCTION 17

Would you like to know?

I'll tell you.

Ready?

The great directors all "made it," all became major successes and power players in Hollywood, because they all, every last one of them...

Made their first feature film...

...**on their own.**

No help from Hollywood. No help from anyone with power—or money.

Christopher Nolan did it. Spielberg did it. Scorsese did it. Robert Rodriguez did it. M. Night Shyamalan did it.

Sounds too simple, right?

Seems like it should be more of a mystery, or more complex.

And yet, it isn't.

Of course, no one talks about this. And with good reason!

Normal people only want to hear about glass slippers and winning the lottery. I don't blame them. It excuses them from doing the work.

It's much easier to believe in "overnight successes."

And yet, none of the men listed above...

None of them...

Were overnight successes.

Shyamalan, in spite of being heralded as one, his success was ANYTHING but overnight—and anything but handed to him.

And it wasn't because he went to New York University film school, either.

If anything, his success came in spite of that.

He, like all the other directors, had to go out and make a feature film on his own.

Then he had to make another film.

And then—and only THEN, after learning all the tenets of filmmaking from the ground up, did he have his "overnight success."

Christopher Nolan's story is pretty much the same. As is Spielberg's. Although, he directed his feature at 18, while Christopher Nolan was a late bloomer directing his at 27.

And it's not just them.

It's all of the filmmakers.

They all had to direct their first feature on their own.

I always found it amazing that Quentin Tarantino's success as a filmmaker (and he is a good one!) was generally traced back to him having simply worked in a video store. Imagine that! What you won't hear is that before he "got" to direct his "debut" feature, RESERVOIR DOGS (don't you just love that word 'debut!'), he had to direct a film called MY BEST FRIEND'S BIRTHDAY.

…Which he made on his own.

Of course, a privileged few are spared this trial by fire.

But they're never one of the greats.

They're never one of the masters.

Because it's actually doing the first feature that lays the groundwork for the filmmaker's future greatness—and mastery. Becoming a great director is a skill that cannot be obtained anywhere else—anywhere—but on the battlefield of drilling down and making a feature film from scratch.

Does that interest you?

Or does that scare you?

It sure scared me.

But…

That is why you have this book.

And this book shows you how to make that first feature length film—on your own.

Yes.

That's even if…

You don't have any money…

That's even if….

You don't live anywhere special…

That's even if…

You don't like reading about jargon…

I've kept that to an absolute, bare minimum.

I've written this book to take you from inspiration—whatever it is you want to achieve with the film you envision—to finished masterpiece. I've left out nothing.

Are you still worried about money? You won't be after you read this book. I show you how to answer the money question—even if you are broke.

Don't have any ideas for a film? Not a problem. I show you how to write—even if you aren't a writer. I show you exactly how to figure out what to make a movie about with tools and strategies to beat the dreaded, "oh that's already been done before" advice everyone seems eager to give you when you're most inspired. I'll show you how to get around all that—and—and—do it in such a way that you will ACTUALLY create an original movie.

I show you how to find "the perfect" camera—and all the other equip-

INTRODUCTION

ment you'll need. This is all about the secret politics of camera sales—and how the companies DO NOT make cameras for filmmakers like you! I recommend NOT buying a camera UNTIL you read this section.

Worried about permits? I show you how to get locations.

I show you how to find people to help with your movie—and to help for free. Would you like to know how to do that?

I show you how to successfully prepare an entire film shoot. This isn't messing around with storyboards (unless you want to), this isn't a bunch of complicated little Excel programs and charts.

I show you how to direct—even if you've NEVER worked with actors.

I show you how to actually get your movie "in the can." These are not "movie-making" techniques. This is not "blah-blah" about 'close-ups' and picking out angles; this is a Swiss Army knife of directing tricks even the big movie directors use to ensure the scene—and the entire movie—gets shot. This is "stuff" you won't find anywhere else.

I show you what to do when it comes time "to edit." This section goes far beyond just "mere editing." This is editing—and so much more. This is a comprehensive look on how to actually put a movie together—and make it shine.

I also show you how to get your movie "out there." That is to say, "get it distributed." Don't worry—this isn't the "same old, same old" about film festivals and "being seen." No. This is what to do with your movie once you're finished—and want to actually do something with it.

This is getting paid!

I have written this entire book in the exact order you will need to receive it. That is to say, the ACTUAL way the process will more than likely unfold for you. This is not a conventional book about movie production as done in Hollywood. This is THE BOOK on movie production—period. This is movie production—as done in THE REAL WORLD.

You and I have a long journey ahead of us. A vigorous one. We're talking Bruce Wayne at the beginning of BATMAN BEGINS. Frodo in the first LORD OF THE RINGS. Matthew McConaughey at the beginning of INTERSTELLAR. The Ghostbusters after they discovered the first ghost—and Egon proposed the possibility of a ghost containment unit. We're talking Jake Gyllenhaal at the beginning of ZODIAC when he learns of the Zodiac killings, and his obsession to capture the elusive Zodiac blossoms into a decade-plus pursuit.

We're talking about making a REAL movie!

Are you excited?

Are you ready…
…to make a feature length film…
and become… a legendary director?

If so, then let's begin.

PART 1
STARTING FROM SCRATCH

2
SHOW ME THE MONEY!

An aspiring filmmaker's first two major questions are about the camera and the editing software.

His third is always about the money.

It's as if the aspiring filmmaker instinctively knows that a major motion picture costs major dollars. Just a casual search on Google will reveal the approximate amount.

AVATAR—$425 million.
THE DARK KNIGHT RISES—$250 million.
THE FATE OF THE FURIOUS—$250 million.
TITANIC—$200 million.
WORLD WAR Z—$190 million.
THE DARK KNIGHT—$180 million.
TERMINATOR 2—$100 million.

While the above films are filled with big stars and even bigger special effects, movies lacking those qualities cost a lot too.

THE WOLF OF WALL STREET—a period-piece movie about a stock broker—$100 million. THE STEPFORD WIVES—$100 million. THE PEANUTS MOVIE—a cartoon about Snoopy—$99 million. SEX AND THE CITY 2—a comedy about women going on vacation—$95 million. A BEAUTIFUL MIND—a drama about a math genius—$78 million. YOU'VE GOT MAIL—a movie about a man and a woman e-mailing one another—$65 million. MONA LISA

SMILE—a period piece about an art teacher—$65 million. MARLEY & ME—a comedy about a dog—$60 million. THE SOLOIST—a drama about a homeless violinist—$60 million. TWILIGHT—a drama about teenage vampires—$37 million. THE HANGOVER—a comedy about drunks on vacation—$35 million.

Even a supposed "low-budget" film about a Wal-Mart cashier cost $8 million (THE GOOD GIRL).

It begs the question: where are you going to find that kind of money?

Investors? A bank? Friends? Relatives? Does your family have $8 million to burn? How about raising that $8 million on Kickstarter or Go Fund Me? Feel up to the challenge? How about $4 million? A million? $500,000? $100,000? $10,000?

Of course, an even better question is, "what would you even spend the money on—once you got it?" Do you know? How would you spend $10,000, let alone $80 million? Surely that must give you pause.

For as much bellyaching that goes on about movie budgets, few filmmakers even know how they WOULD spend whatever money they could find—let alone WHAT exactly they would spend the money on. The need for money is usually an unquestioned forgone conclusion.

Before we even get into all the business about "budgeting" a movie, and finding money for that budget, we have to take a step back. We have to look at the question of money and budgets from the perspective of...

...*the audience*.

You've heard it before: someone watching a movie will say, "wow, this is really big budget!" Or, they'll grouse, "wow, this is really low budget!" Of course, you take this as an assessment of the movie's quality, and therefore equate budget with quality—or lack thereof.

But have you ever considered how the audience is even going about making these assessments in the first place? How would they know what's high budget and low budget? If you don't have a concrete idea of what you'd spend millions of dollars on, how can an audience member even begin to assess how much was spent in the first place?

Is it something he or she sees? Hears? Feels?

Of course, it's all three—and nothing more.

They see expensive actors, they see lots of stunts, explosions, big sets, exotic locations—then it must be high budget. If there's a limited range of movement in the film's activity, if the film seems to linger around one location, if there's no recognizable stars, if the movie seems "quiet"—then it must be low-budget.

However, they might look at a movie like FUN WITH DICK AND JANE and be surprised to learn that a film about a man and his wife becoming bank robbers would cost $120 million dollars. What's to pay for? Sure, Jim Carrey—but that's, what, $20 million? Audiences would have a similar surprise with HOW DO YOU KNOW—a comedy about Reese Witherspoon having to choose between Owen Wilson and Paul Rudd—which ended up costing $120 million. What cost so much?

Until I did some closer research, I thought the same way. Take the film SIGNS, for example. It's about an alien invasion of Earth—yet, it's told through the perspective of a family living on a farm in Bucks County, Pennsylvania. It's less INDEPENDENCE DAY and more NIGHT OF THE LIVING DEAD. No monuments blow up. No explosions erupt. You only see one, maybe two aliens the entire film. And they're not exactly H.R. Giger's Xenomorph. The biggest set piece is a fight in the living room, climaxed by a spilt glass of water. I was inspired with this movie not only because it was really great, but because it "looked" like a movie I could actually make at 14 years old. I too could find a house (probably my house!), gather up a few of my friends, put some costumes on them, get the ol' camera out, do a few night shoots—and boom: have a film like SIGNS.

The inspiration was in recognizing that I already had the same resources Shyamalan ostensibly had.

The reality was that SIGNS actually cost $75 million to make.

I would have initially guessed $25 million. $20 million for Mel Gibson, the star of the film, and $5 million to actually film the movie.

To the average person and myself when I was younger, money—a "budget"—as we're defining it—is something that goes toward actual, working resources.

In other words, what is seen on screen.

In reality, a "budget," money, generally doesn't end up on screen, or anywhere near it. The truth is, money isn't spent on a movie to supply the needs of what will—or should—end up on screen. Often why a movie was even "budgeted," given money in the first place, has very little to do with the film itself.

You have to understand, Hollywood power players green-light and "budget" movies like a person who is looking to invest in the stock market. And when someone invests in the stock market, they first log onto Morning Star, an investment research firm, and seek out a ranking of the top performing stocks or funds. The person, not wanting to do the research, looks for whichever fund has a five star rating, and then ploughs every last dime into it.

It's called wishful thinking.

It's exactly what Hollywood execs, at all levels of power, are paid for.

SHOW ME THE MONEY!

Wishful thinking.

They are not paid to seek out the best ideas or the best scripts. They are paid to paint a rosy picture for Wall Street.

To do this, they have to be able to point to some kind of empirical data. Usually, that's a movie star's last hit. Which is the real reason stars are hired again and again. Execs want the movie star (or star director, or star franchise such as Batman or James Bond) not because they're so in love with the actor (or director, or franchise), but because the hiring of that actor or actress gives the top brass a seal of approval, a certification of credibility that they themselves were thinking clearly.

It gives them someone to blame when the movie crashes and burns.

It's an insurance policy, a hedge, against failure.

Because unlike the average stock investor, the top brass, the people who green-light movies aren't investing their OWN money. They're investing other people's money—chiefly, Wall Street/conglomerate money. The executive's decisions can't come from the gut or heart. The choices have to—and can only—come from empirical data. This means box office statistics.

This means:

A great idea for a movie would be one starring Jennifer Lawrence.

And if Jennifer isn't available, "let's try for Scarlet Johansson."

Or, if it's not stars, it's intellectual property:

"THE AVENGERS did great. Let's make THE AVENGERS 2."

Or, more rarely:

"THE SIXTH SENSE was great. Maybe the director can turn the trick again?"

Movies are financed and budgeted—given money—based on past performance. NOT based on what has ended up—or will—or needs to—end up on screen.

However, as an aspiring filmmaker even attempting to pitch your idea for a movie, even attempting to look for financing, you believe that the key to finding that financing, to attracting it, to raising it, to whatever you plan on doing to generate a budget for your motion picture, is based on the quality of your idea for the movie.

You, like the average audience member, believe that money spent on a movie actually has to do with the movie itself. And therefore it must be the movie's content that will dictate and shape what money is raised, funded, allotted, or "budgeted."

But it works like this:

A bad idea for a movie would be, "a bank heist told in reverse."

A good idea for a movie, however, would be, "a bank heist told in reverse—and Harvey Keitel is interested."

That's worth about $1.2 million—the budget for RESERVOIR DOGS.

Or, in another example:

"It's about a guy who can't sleep and has to solve a murder in Alaska." Sounds like a cozy time. But it'll never fly.

However, if you re-phrased it as: "Steven Soderbergh, who made the mega hit ERIN BROCKOVICH (**$256,271,286**), and is now currently working on our OCEAN'S 11—which we really need to succeed because it's got about 85 million dollars worth of movie stars including George Clooney, Brad Pitt, and Matt Damon—really likes a movie about a guy with no memory, and the director of that movie is interested in doing this new movie about a guy who can't sleep—and Soderbergh will be executive producer—and Al Pacino also liked the movie about the guy without a memory and wants to work with the guy who is doing this new thing about the guy who can't sleep—oh and the guy who can't sleep solves a murder."

Now, that's a GREAT idea.

Of course, it coincidently ended up being a great motion picture (INSOMNIA, directed by Christopher Nolan). But that's *after* the fact. And the fact that it ended up being a great motion picture is completely and totally incidental.

Here's a few more examples.

"Dinosaurs run amok in Disneyland?" This is a terrible idea.

"Dinosaurs. Disneyland. Spielberg." Say no more.

"A chainsaw wielding maniac?" A cliche (***chin raise***)!

But…

"Reboot TEXAS CHAINSAW MASSACRE?"

That's inspired thinking.

"An invulnerable Philadelphia security guard takes on criminals." Huh!?

But…

"Guy who did SIXTH SENSE wants to do a movie about…" Brilliant.

You get the gist.

It's all about WISHFUL THINKING.

It's important to understand this point because you need to shift your lens on how a movie is budgeted, why it's given even dollar one—to understanding why you will have an impossible time even trying to get ANY money to direct your movie; <u>no matter the quality of your idea—or script</u>.

Take a deep breath and say it with me….

Quality...quality...
Means nothing.
Nothing.
Let's repeat it again.
Quality... means... nothing!

Because there's your opinion. There's my opinion. There's his opinion. There's her opinion. Take any finished movie, and you'll see that its quality, its perceived quality, can be bickered over, argued about, picked on, lied about, negotiated with, rationalized over, until the end of time. You know what I'm talking about: these little differences between, "Oh, THE DARK KNIGHT was way better than DARK KNIGHT RISES," or, "Ridley Scott's work on PROMETHEUS isn't as good as it was with ALIEN," or, "Shyamalan's THE SIXTH SENSE was great, but SIGNS—man, that was the beginning of the end." Personally, I really disliked the movie RESIDENT EVIL: APOCALYPSE when I first saw it. I mean, I really, really had a visceral revulsion/frustration with it ("Nothing like the game, man!"). For years I trashed it, writing about it, analyzing it. Then, as day followed night, like the crack of the sun's morning light, I had an epiphany: RESIDENT EVIL 2: APOCALYPSE is a great movie!

In other words, I'm fickle.

As you are too. As 100% of movie critics are, as the film-going public is, as every single person who invests money in movies is. ESPECIALLY those people. Because what's hot today goes cold tomorrow. What was derided yesterday as misogynist garbage is today ennobling and powerful now that it stars a woman. What was just a "fun time at the movies" 50 years ago, is now considered the de facto classic of all time. Some films get a 10% on the Tomato meter, some get a 100% (you could say, there seem to be a lot of movies these days getting 100% on the meter).

Quality... what a "budget" or "financing" will supposedly increase... means nothing.

What does mean something, what you should REALLY be focused on when looking for money for your movie, is competence.

Competence, NOT quality, not a BIGGER movie, not a GLOSSIER movie, is what you're looking to finance.

Competence is what you will find in whatever movie you see that makes it to a movie theater. Competence is the lighting of the picture looking good, the edits working smoothly, the dialogue coming through clearly and consistently, the shots coming in sharp, the story being told in a coherent way, the audio sounding crisp. Competence—and competence is nothing to sniff at—is what you'll find in the movie RESIDENT

EVIL: APOCALYPSE. It might not be all that true to the game, but man, that is a competent movie.

It's competent because it's PROFESSIONAL.

RESIDENT EVIL: APOCALYPSE has to be one of the most professional looking movies I've ever seen. The edits are sharp, the shots are clean and crisp, the color design is perfect, the make-up on the actors is perfect, the sound is perfect, the actors hit their mark every time, the sets are great (driving a motorcycle through a church, I imagine, is no easy feat [and they didn't film in a real church]), the lighting is perfect, the music is on point, the explosions are front and center, on and on and on.

When you think in terms of "budgeting" your movie, finding money for it, you have to think NOT in terms of quality but in terms of COMPETENCE. What is the maximum level of professionalism you can put up on screen? What is the closest you can come to emulating the COMPETENCE you see demonstrated in every single movie that makes it to a movie theater near you?

When you realize that it's competence you have to fund—and not quality—it becomes a WHOLE lot easier—and a lot more doable—to find money for a movie. Because looking solely at competence will eliminate more than 80% of a typical film's budget.

Why?

Because in Hollywood, a movie's budget is divided into two categories: "above-the-line" and "below-the-line."

"Below-the-line" is money spent on the crew, costs, and materials to actually make the movie. The so-called "above-the-line" costs go to the film's "talent." The writers, the producers, the director, the actors, the creative people.

As the distinction denotes, they also receive above-the-line pay.

Of any given Hollywood budget, upwards of half—sometimes even more—goes to paying for the people who "guide" the creative influence of the film. So, the people who generally whine in the media about "pay gaps" and "gender gaps" are the ones who actually vacuum up the bulk of a movie's budget. Star 1—$20 million. Star 2—$25 million. Supporting star 1—$2 million. Supporting star 2—$2.1 million (just to edge out supporting star 1). The director—$7 million. The producer—$4 million. The executive producer—$2 million. The OTHER executive producer—$900,000.

This is even before we get to the spin-off costs, which the late screenwriter William Goldman called, "adding a third for the shit." Because the stars all need to be pampered, tempered, nurtured, transported, fed, clothed, housed, medicated, and otherwise treated like royalty. Star 1 wants a bigger trailer than star 2, until star 2 catches wind and wants one that's commensurate of his or her years of experience. Then, star 1 refuses the production's make-up artist, so the production has to hire—in addition—the star's makeup artist. That goes the same for the star's pet writer, trainer, cook, drivers, assistants, assistants to assistants, groomers, and chauffeurs. These things aren't cheap. On one movie budget, the transportation of the film's star cost $100,000 dollars!

Star 2 was only allocated $80,000.

Meanwhile, the "below-the-line" people get what they get. And get to work with what's left over.

This is why movies cost so much money:

Much of the so-called "above-the-line" spending doesn't even end up on screen.

Yes, the $20 million dollar actor's face does end up on screen. But most times—8/10 times—it was overkill to even hire such an expensive actor. 8/10 times—literally—literally no one cares. Take one of your parents to a movie sometime (or watch one at home), and, throughout the movie, ask them, "hey, you know who that actor is?" 8 out of 10 times—I promise you—8 out of 10 times, your parent will shake their head "no." To your parent, that person up on screen is just another faceless blur. To a Hollywood executive however, to a director, to whomever paid for that certain actor, that faceless blur—

—Well—

"That's so-and-so, and such-and-such magazine says they're great, and they won an Academy Award for Best Supporting Actor last year, and so-and-so critic says they're a 'breakout star', and John Whose-it's is dating her…"

When your parent shrugs, just think…

That's 20 million that didn't need to be spent.

There's countless movies you and I could list, whose actors and actresses could have been switched out with more economical talent—perhaps even better, more suited to the roll. I know this goes against the sacred screed that it's all about the star, and that you'd do well to hire one (and to a large extent, I'd agree with this), but in most cases it's completely unwarranted and unnecessary.

The reality of filmmaking is that a film's core value, its competency, the value audiences actually take away, is to be found in the "below-the-line" aspects of a film. Not in the more expensive "above-the-line" spending. Because while the "above-the-line" so called "creative types" can be hit or miss, the people, the crew, the professionals, the craftsmen lumped below are always, always, always, always, always, always, every time, on target.

They work with what they get, and they do so brilliantly.

And while we can't hire the top tier tradespeople and craftsmen who work "below-the-line," the skills demonstrated by most of those people CAN be learned, if not slightly emulated to a passable result. Additionally, the resources they work with, can be found ALL around you.

These resources and skills are obvious.

The recognition of them, separate and a part from a movie, however, not so much.

So, when thinking about money for a movie, budgets, whatever you might call it, remember that the bulk of a Hollywood movie budget is not its physical resources—but of the attached talent.

Talent.

I believe it's possible to make a great movie for next to nothing—because you don't have this problem of saddling the production with talent.

Not because you don't have any.

But because it's talent that, in truth, you're developing. The film you will make… *is about developing YOUR talent.*

And yes—you already have the talent to develop. If you bought this book then you obviously have something yearning to get out. Buying it was a huge step. Actually reading it, another. According to the Huffington Post, 47 percent of Americans in 2013 had NOT read even one non-fiction book. That's 150 million people not even attempting to develop what talents they have.

If you're reading this book you already "have it." At least, you have it just as much as Spielberg and Scorsese "had it" when they began.

Look up—and see—if you can—the following films:

MY BEST FRIEND'S BIRTHDAY	**ERASERHEAD**
THE WEDDING PARTY	**EL MARIACHI**
WHOSE THAT KNOCKING AT MY DOOR	**MONSTERS**
FIRELIGHT (IF YOU CAN FIND A COPY)	**FOLLOWING**
BAD TASTE	**SLACKER**
FEAR AND DESIRE	**PI**
DARK STAR	**CLERKS**
IT'S MURDER!	

While you've probably never heard of or seen any of these movies, I can guarantee you'll know their directors:

- **Quentin Tarantino** — MY BEST FRIEND'S BIRTHDAY

SHOW ME THE MONEY!

- **Brian De Palma** — THE WEDDING PARTY
- **Martin Scorsese** — WHOSE THAT KNOCKING AT MY DOOR
- **Peter Jackson** — BAD TASTE
- **Stanley Kubrick** — FEAR AND DESIRE
- **Steven Spielberg** — FIRELIGHT
- **John Carpenter** — DARK STAR
- **Sam Raimi** — IT'S MURDER
- **David Lynch** — ERASERHEAD
- **Robert Rodriguez** — EL MARIACHI
- **Gareth Edwards** — MONSTERS
- **Christopher Nolan** — FOLLOWING
- **Richard Linklater** — SLACKER
- **Darren Aronofsky** — PI
- **Kevin Smith** — CLERKS

While this is a powerhouse listing of Hollywood's greatest—and highest paid—movie directors, none of the films above, save for maybe CLERKS and ERASERHEAD, are celebrated, or, for that matter, even known, when the resumes of these directors are considered.

These films, so important to the respective director's later success—and so illuminating to their powers—are often closeted and omitted from the official rosters.

But all of the films listed represent exactly, down to their last frame, the maximum level of talent and ability their respective directors had at the beginning of their careers.

THESE are the films the directors listed above, left alone, and left without money, would still be making...

...If not for the "below-the-line" craftspeople and the millions of dollars that only begrudgingly follow such a scopic demonstration of managerial abilities.

As you watch the above listed movies, notice that what you—and everyone else—recognizes as their talent, their genius...

...**was not always there**.

You may see some flourishes. Signatures, maybe.

But the truth is, they had yet to command the help and services of the competent, so-called "below-the-line" professionals in Hollywood.

Don't get me wrong. The above listed ARE great movie directors. And yes, their skills as a director probably did improve over the years, and they probably would make an even greater movie now if left alone. But when you compare Christopher Nolan's FOLLOWING to THE DARK KNIGHT—two films made less than a decade a part, you will see exactly what $180 million dollars can do for a great movie director.

THAT'S what makes those directors great. Their ability to maximize and manage available capitol.

They know how to spend money!

It is absolutely, positively, NO coincidence that all of the truly revered directors started EXACTLY where you are now: at the bottom, having to pull it all together for yourself.

This is what creates a master film director. The determination—and the will—to be resourceful.

The great film directors know one single truth: greatness doesn't come from opportunity. <u>Opportunity</u> is made by the determination to be great.

Take Academy Award winning Martin Scorsese for example. Arguably THE best and most accomplished movie director of all time. Having both massive critical and box office success with such legendary films as TAXI DRIVER, RAGING BULL, GOODFELLAS, THE DEPARTED, SHUTTER ISLAND, THE WOLF OF WALL STREET, and too many more to list. Today his name commands top billing, the attraction of Hollywood's highest paid talents like Leonardo DiCaprio, Robert DeNiro, Al Pacino, and he is often awarded some of the highest budgets of any working director today.

But if you study his career, spanning from the late 1960s to current day, a different insight emerges. You will see his career was one of constant battle.

It generally went like this: He would make a hugely successful film like TAXI DRIVER, and then, the powers-that-be would say, "Marty's a genius."

Then, given carte-blanche to do whatever, Scorsese would make a movie like NEW YORK, NEW YORK, which didn't do well commercially or critically, and suddenly those same powers-that-be would say, "Marty who?"

Suddenly, it was back to Square One. And it was back to Square One many times throughout his career.

Square One means less money than the previous film.

After the box office disaster of THE KING OF COMEDY (a great, great movie by the way), the funding for his next picture, a biblical epic titled THE LAST TEMPTATION, was suddenly pulled. To understand why this was a significant time in his career—and therefore would be of great insight to you—I highly suggest you track down a movie called AFTER HOURS. Watch the movie, then watch the documentary included on the DVD. It's titled *Filming For Your Life*. In it, the crew talks about how the movie AFTER HOURS was Scorsese re-discovering his love for movies and his love for making them. But if you read between the lines, you'll realize it wasn't his love for making movies that he found again—

It was finding his own competency.

With the film AFTER HOURS, Scorsese made a great, great film—both financially and critically successful—for far, far less than what he'd become accustomed to. It's here where the powers-that-be in Hollywood got the real message: Scorsese doesn't need us.

Which is the kind of message I'd like you to ultimately signal to the powers-that-be. If you follow what I have to say in this book, you will figure out the truth Scorsese learned: you have it within YOURSELF to legitimately lead some of the world's most talented craftspeople and artists. And that leadership is earned through your will, through your determination, your passion, and your love for the craft itself.

This is the true skill of a director.

Leadership.

The master filmmakers will only ever be the people who started from the bottom.

Therefore:

You're not going to make a low-budget movie; **you're going to make a NO-BUDGET movie**.

Yes, forget money.

In fact, the less money… the better.

Because the moment you spend dollar one, you'll be in for a hundred more. For every dollar you plan to spend, times it by ten. Why? The Pareto principle—which states that only 20 percent of something will produce 80 percent of the actual results. Expenditures increase for this reason. If you pay Peter, you have to pay Paul. And once you pay Paul, then Mary, Jane, and Sue will wonder why they're not making the same—or more. If you don't believe me, look at what happened to Mark Wahlberg when everyone found out he "got" more money than his female co-"star" on the film ALL THE MONEY IN THE WORLD.

And that's before the unions catch wind.

For every dollar you plan to spend, times it by ten.

Money, past a certain point—and that point is a lot closer than you think, is an expensive commodity.

Of course, you will be tempted to go by the way of Kickstarter or "Go Fund Me" or whatever crowdfunding platform is going on in the future. Again, ill-advised. Avoid it. Crowdfunding operates on the principle of offering "rewards" to early investors—and so, therefore, you'll spend the great bulk of your time and money on fulfilling those rewards.

DVDs, t-shirts, early viewings of the movie, thank-you cards (and you'd better send thank you cards to whomever even donates a single dollar!), signed scripts, whatever knick-knack junk that's invented to make the investor feel like their getting something for investing, all costs money and time. For every dollar you make, figure you'll have to spend at least 80 cents of every dollar on managing, returning, and making good on getting that dollar.

Unless you're using crowdfunding as a clever guise for marketing, it's best to just focus your time and efforts on making the movie. Because that's what a successful crowdfunding takes—time and effort. And money.

Don't take it from me. Just look to Zach Braff, the star of the hit show SCRUBS and creator of one of my all time favorite movies GARDEN STATE. In spite of famously raising an astonishing $3.1 million dollars via crowdfunding on Kickstarter for his film I WISH I WAS HERE, the writer and director vowed he would never use the method again. He said, "The onus was on me to now not only try and direct a movie in 26 days and take care of 47,000 people who had backed it, but sort of become a politician and explain crowd-funding to the Earth."

You hear the subtext?

The money ended up costing too much.

Because money, in truth, is the SECOND most expensive commodity on earth.

The first being, thankfully for us, time.

And while we're all in finite supply of it, I'm guessing you have plenty of it on hand.

This is how you make a movie for no money.

You recognize that money is simply a negotiation of time.

Because while the average low-budget movie usually takes about 16 days to shoot, the real cost in making that low-budget movie is in negotiating those 16 days be strung together. That is to say: it's not so much that it costs money to create those 16 days of shooting a film, it's that it costs money to have those days repeat one after another in succession.

Instead of shooting day 1, and then, the following day, shooting day 2, you will have to make due with shooting day 1, and then waiting weeks, maybe even months, to shoot day 2.

You will get your 16 days to shoot the movie—and those 16 days are precious gold—but you will pay for it, you will budget your movie NOT WITH MONEY—

But with time.

You will pay in time.

By doing so, by legitimately putting your heart and soul into getting those shooting days (and realistically, that's really the only time you need other people in production of a movie), you will convince, you will inspire others that what you're pouring so much time into may just be worth them sparing a few hours of their life to be a part of. Like the crew recognized with Scorsese on the set of AFTER HOURS, the people who you get to help you will recognize your passion not in your words or exuberance, but in your determination, resilience, and patience to stay with one single thing across a landscape, across an ocean, of time.

That is what it means to inspire someone.

That is what it means to be a leader.

This is what it means to be a movie director.

And what with your time will you do?

You will survey your world for each and every segment of capital in immediate reach. You take note of the house you already live in. Your friend's house. The house down the street. The house up the street. You note cars, rooms, furniture, props, public areas, parks, the woods, anything—and I mean ANYTHING—physical in reach. Your entire town. Who do you know in it? Where can you go? What do you have access to at this point in time? A good rule of thumb of access is: "Can I actually get my hands on this thing or person within a few hours max?"

The challenge is that everything in your world, every person, is governed by a set of rules, routines, and politics. No, not left wing/right wing politics. But politics in the way Robert McKee describes it: power. Who controls what, and how?

Take your friend's home, for example. Who exactly controls the household? Mom? Dad? Your friend's sister? What rules have they set? Both explicit and implicit. You might think people always eat at 5 PM, but this family, because of the sister's soccer practice, must always wait until 7 PM. That's helpful for you to know because there will be no filming here, at this house, at 7 PM and after. It's helpful to know because it means his Dad doesn't get home until a certain time, and since Mom is the more friendly person to the arts, your friend will feel more comfortable allotting you a space of time from 2 PM to 4PM to run rough shodden over the house, filming to your heart's content.

That is, until Mom figures out what shooting a movie is really like.

Because when your friend asked his mom if you could "shoot" in the house, she envisioned you and her son, running about with a video camera, "shooting a movie." What she didn't envision was all the banging around of equipment, all the close calls with family heirlooms, and all the scratching of her hardwood floors.

She didn't know that "shooting a movie" has all the grace and finesse of moving into a new home, of remodeling the kitchen, of installing an air conditioning system.

In essence, moviemaking has a lot in common with moving furniture.

How will you integrate that reality into the world you live in?

From here, you super charge your resources. You maximize and combine. You improvise.

You become MacGyver.

If you're not familiar with MacGyver, then I want you to put the book down, go look him up, and watch the series (Seriously, you haven't seen MACGYVER?). MacGyver, as is known in popular culture, can solve anything with a piece of duct tape and chewing gum. But his actual genius, what really made him the maestro of the Swiss Army knife, was his practice of a concept coined in 1970 by Edward De Bono called "lateral thinking." Wikipedia defines this as, "solving problems through an indirect and creative approach, using reasoning that is not immediately obvious and involving ideas that may not be obtainable by using only step-by-step logic." In other words, MacGyver had a genius for looking at things in a different way than the rest of us.

In episode 4, titled *The Gauntlet*, for example, MacGyver has to infiltrate a terrorist compound to steal a super secret map that if the terrorists keep, will mean the end of western civilization. How MacGyver goes about breaking into the compound, escaping, fighting the terrorists, fleeing the terrorists, and ultimately escaping to safety, is a masterclass in brilliant improvisation. I highly suggest you watch the episode just to see how many things he's able to do with a simple map.

Of course, some might argue that some of what he does is improbable, and impossible, and unlikely. And I might agree. But the point is for you to embrace that spirit of turning nothing into something, of looking at an item or a person, and envisioning a completely different use or combination of uses in order to solve a problem that you've clearly defined.

Watch MACGYVER, absorb the spirit of MACGYVER, learn to love improvisation and the actual creativity it requires (not the Andy Warhol, fou-fou artist kind), and make your movie!

Be MacGyver!

Realize you don't need any money to make a movie. At least, that is to say, the movie you're GOING TO MAKE.

The movie you HAVE to make. The movie ALL the greats HAD to eventually make.

3
WRITING PT. 1

What is your movie going to be about? A person? Your father? Your mother? Your grandfather? He's seen some interesting times. Sister? Brother? You have a good friend whose life is just begging to be made into a movie.

How about a place? You're thinking about your old college where you met the friends you keep to this day. Those were some special days; so special, you want to make a movie "about it."

Your hometown might work. You know a lot about it. You know the people, the buildings, the feeling. It's another special place with a lot of history.

How about your country? Your fellow citizens will latch onto that. Everyone is always interested in something that features their home country. To boot, you also managed to stay awake in social studies class—so you're well versed in the material. Nothing like a great movie that takes place in the good ol' US of A!

How about a certain time period? It's been a long time since someone made a great movie "about" the 1970s. ZODIAC and ALMOST FAMOUS come to mind. Those two really seemed to evoke that period of time. How about the 1980s? STRANGER THINGS did an excellent job portraying that. An excellent job. Is that what makes it such a magical show?

Or, maybe you want to—and this is a wild guess—make a movie about your high school hockey team. You and your team had a great year—an unprecedented one. You went all the way to states.

You get really excited when talking about this idea for a movie:

"Yea, yea!" You grit your teeth, eyes lighting up, "It'll be about that year—and about all the events leading through it—and fighting with the coach, and all that, and there will be a girl, and she'll be based off such-and-such girl I had a crush on that year; and oh, that one time the team went to Canada for that tournament—crazy—and the movie will be long; none of this hour-and-a-half high school comedy crap; it'll be be big, big, big, Anamorphic, like CASINO; *we're talking 2 ½ hours MINIMUM, 3 hours if I can do it; it'll have all of this great music like Fleetwood Mac, The Rolling Stones, and David Bowie, and there will be this whole sequence, like, the movie will just stop like how Paul Thomas Anderson—you know him, right!?!?—well, like how he does in* BOOGIE NIGHTS *where the last half hour just kinda lingers on this one night. So basically, this is* GOODFELLAS, *but about high school hockey!"*

Sounds like a good movie, right?

But what about your high school hockey team going to states? Do they win? Do they lose? If the team wins, then "what about" them winning? If they lose, so what? What's gained? What's lost? What's learned?

In other words, "who cares!?"

It's as if a movie has to be more than just a collection of shots, sounds, edits, special effects, and music. As if it has to be something larger than just a summary of pictures depicting activity.

It's as if it has to be, alas, about something.

And so, if your movie has to be About Something, then what is Something Worth Being About? How can you compromise between your inspiration, your desire to rush out and film images that evoke your inspiration, and bridge it with a complete movie that will be of interest to...

Society.

Ugh.

Well, what's important to society? War? Peace? Politics? Global warming? Gender inequality? Ah(!)—social injustice! That's always a winner. It seems the news is never short on the seemingly endless grievances of this or that political faction. People really seem to be All About Social Injustice. At least, it seems to be pretty popular with the people who hand out Academy Awards.

But somehow, none of THE ISSUES, as much as the news hypes them, as important as the top-flight celebrities make them out to be, as much gravity as everyone around you seems to grant them—THE ISSUES—well… they just don't really light you up.

You should be ashamed!!!

No, just kidding.

They just don't match…

That fire and excitement, that insane obsession, that need to talk, and talk, and talk, and talk about whatever it is until your friends just can't take it, that impulse to stay up late and write, and write, and write in search of making sense out of what's driving you; that time-defying passion, that, that, that notion that…

"SOMEBODY'S GOTTA MAKE A MOVIE ABOUT MY HOCKEY TEAM!"

So with that, you roll the dice.

People be damned, you're an artist!

You write a so-called script, and miraculously—miraculously—garner millions in financing; you assemble your crew, your actors; you hold that huge nation-wide casting call to find The Girl, the one who reminds you of your original crush, of HER; you pick out all the original locations, convincing the studio to film in your home state; you preach and preach about authenticity, making sure to aptly re-create the time period the story takes place in; you get the RED camera with the Anamorphic lenses—you get two; you film and film and film, encouraging improv—but not too much—capturing every possible nuance, angle, and moment; you get the shots of the guys cackling in the locker room, waxing DeNiro, waxing Paul Newman, waxing Joe Pesci; you manage to get some really funny stuff; you go and edit, edit, edit, edit; you edit for an entire year—hell, you edit for two years, like you heard Scorsese sometimes does; you put in all the music, all the Rollings Stones you can stomach, all the David Bowie your budget will afford (that stuff isn't cheap, by the way); you finish it, miracle of miracles; you send it to Cannes (your production has a guy on the inside); you send it to Sundance (one of the financiers is friends with Redford) you get everyone packed in the theater, you get everyone settled down, you show the movie—

and poof.

Nothing.

The film goes nowhere.

Not a blip on the radar.

Least of all, with you.

Because deep in your heart, after all the opportunities, after all the Anamorphic lenses, after all the music, after all the perfect close-ups of The Girl, after all the articulated editing, after all the people who told you it was an interesting film, you know the truth:

The movie sucks!

I mean, it really sucks.

It's so bad, it doesn't even get the distinction of being a "bomb."

Because it just... vanishes.

What happened?

It's easy, really.

You filmed a movie.

You didn't film... a story.

While you technically "made a film," while you had the visuals and the sounds, and the acting, and the music—you failed to film... a story.

...and putting something on film (or video, as it were) <u>does not make it a 'film!'</u>

A music video is not a film. A 'short' is not a film. A demo 'reel' is not a film. Someone sleeping is not a film. Giving directions to teens on how to best apply make-up and eyelashes is NOT A FILM.

Because while all of those prosaic activites utilize the medium of the visual, while they all involve a camera, while they're all filmed using a camera... that is the exact point where any similarity with actual film-making completely derails.

Filmmaking—real moviemaking—is one thing, and one thing only: TELLING A STORY.

Yes, you can argue that a 'short' is telling a story; yes, you can argue that a 'music video' is telling a story; yes, you can argue that whatever it is "is telling a story."

But you would just be getting in your own way.

And doing so to avoid the real problem:

Filming an ACTUAL story for an ACTUAL film/movie is the most difficult of all the arts.

It's more difficult than composing music, more difficult than mixing, singing, acting, dancing, painting, designing, editing, "dropping a beat," sculpting, or doing any single individual facet of the arts.

Because not only do you have to film a story—you have to actually create the story.

And to create a story—

You gotta' stare at the page until your forehead bleeds.

As Brando in APOCALYPSE NOW mutters: "The horror. The horror."

What's your movie about?

It's about a story.

It's the safest bet you have of actually engaging a sizable audience.

WRITING PT. 1

The further you get from telling an actual story, the less interested *most people will be. There are exceptions, of course.

But you can't bank on being a 'viral' sensation.

You can't bank on people being so stupid.

Because they're not.

At least, not most of them.

Because while society may seem to be going way of the IDIOCRACY, while it seems as if attention spans are ever contracting into the pinhead of a needle—

Few people will sit two hours in the dark for anything other than an actual story.

Any story.

Movies—actual real, honest movies—unlike art and experimental films, and shorts, HAVE to make money. Because unlike filming a short, or an experimental film, or an art film—an actual, real, honest movie can cost hundreds of millions of dollars just to make—never mind to market.

And if it's not putting millions of dollars in jeopardy—it's the time.

Let me say it again.

It's the time.

A motion picture—a legitimate, honest movie—takes upward of a year to produce. And that's a big, Hollywood blockbuster movie.

For a backyard production, it could takes years.

At least.

At some point, either the economics of money or the ruthless economics of father time will demand your movie engage an audience.

But what about—I can hear you already thinking—all those films you've seen that don't seem to really have "a story," didn't seem to have "much of a plot"—and yet were very captivating none the less! What about a movie like SLACKER, a movie that seemingly meanders from one character to another, again and again, until, at the film's climax, the audience is left uncertain of the plot?

Is that a real movie?

Here's where we have to do a bit of a gut check as filmmakers.

One—even that movie is telling a story—although, it's telling many, many stories, all of them unified by one subject: a generation on the road to nowhere. Hence the title, SLACKER.

Two—I'm not—and you're probably not (although I have no way of knowing and you might very well be!) a genius like Richard Linklater, the director of SLACKER and other prosaic movies like WAKING LIFE (a favorite of mine) and DAZED AND CONFUSED (a masterpiece). He has a knack for zeroing in on the mundane, lingering with it, captivating interest, and leaving the audience with a resonance that is not found in other films—simply because other film's can't hold the interest in the way HE can.

We can't bank on having the same level of talent.

You can try.

Personally, I revere Richard Linklater's work. I admire, aside from his brilliance, his (actual) bravery. Because it's bravery that's required to take years of your own life to produce a film like SLACKER, like WAKING LIFE, to find the millions of dollars to create a motion picture like DAZED AND CONFUSED, and believe that whatever you cast your camera upon, it will be totally captivating.

And it might just very well be.

But remember: those movies all had a tough 'go' at the box office. They all had a tough 'go' on home video. Those films required awards and the prestige of critical recommendation to find the audience they eventually did. I personally only ever saw WAKING LIFE because Roger Ebert raved about it. And I'm thankful he did. Seeing it was one of the great movie-watching experiences of my life.

I single out the movie SLACKER for one reason. It suggests to the aspiring filmmaker that a movie can be about anything, and that it can be riffed into existence by just filming talking heads.

Not so.

At least, not so for your purposes.

And that is this:

You want to make a film that has a safe bet of giving you not only a steady career—but also a little money.

No, scratch that.

A lot of money.

If you follow my advice in this chapter, and in succeeding chapters, you will make a movie that will bring you a LOT of money.

You have to film… a story.

COMING UP WITH IDEAS

So, where do you get an idea for a great story? Ugh, it seems like we're back to square one, right? You'll find, as you go on making movies, that a great deal of time is spent in and around finding, coming up with, a great story.

Perhaps you already have a so-called "idea" for one.

WRITING PT. 1

But ideas, at least in my opinion, are always, always misleading. Because not only do ideas come in a vacuum, not only do they come seemingly unattached to anything, they also leave the person who came up with the idea nowhere else to go but putter around and pester everyone with, "I gotta' helluva' an idea for a story."

Ugh.

Ideas—especially an idea for a story—ideas in general—are something else entirely. In the case of storytelling, they are usually just a single piece of a puzzle that has yet to exist.

I trust ideas about as much as I trust inspiration.

Perhaps you have an idea for a zombie story/movie.

I suggest that idea because it's a common one among young filmmakers, including myself. Like moths drawn to the flame, there isn't a beginning filmmaker who ISN'T inspired to make a good 'zombie movie.'

You consider George A. Romero's DAWN OF THE DEAD the Sistine Chapel of not only 'zombie movies,' but of movies in general. You loved NIGHT OF THE LIVING DEAD, DAY OF THE DEAD, LAND OF THE DEAD; you really admired Danny Boyle's 28 DAYS LATER and thought they really took it to the next level with 28 WEEKS LATER; you were surprised by the hidden gem of THE RETURN OF THE LIVING DEAD; you relish ALL six of the RESIDENT EVIL movies; and you're enamored with TRAIN TO BUSAN, DAWN OF THE DEAD (2004), DIARY OF THE DEAD, I AM LEGEND, PLANET TERROR, NIGHT OF THE CREEPS, NIGHT OF THE ZOMBIES, and NIGHT OF THE COMET—just to name a few.

There's something about the collective imagery in all these films that grabs you.

But you develop a quiet dread:

It's all been done before.

The "zombie movie" has been done—and excuse the horrible pun—"to death."

Of course, this doesn't dissuade your enthusiasm. Your "zombie movie" will be different. Yes, it will have all the staples, it'll have all the guns, all the barricades, the gore, the tension, the violence, the haggard heroes armed to the teeth, thrashing through the woods, barricading the farmhouse, hammering the nails into the barricade; it'll have the overcast skies, the lurching corpses, the groaning—it'll have THE MUSIC—The MUSIC!!!—with some John Carpenter synths, or maybe a little Goblin, or maybe something like Hans Zimmer would do—or, maybe, maybe—you'll do it straight, with strings, brass, winds, real classical—not too classical—but something like Marco Beltrami's WORLD WAR Z score.

Yours will be different because YOU will be doing it.

So you spread the good news to friends and family.

First, there's Dad. He's a chummy, intelligent, sensitive and compassionate sort of fellow who encourages your work and loves to hear your ideas—but man: he hates, hates, hates zombie movies. Soon as he hears, "zombie movie," he spins his eyes and turns a cold shoulder; if you press further, you know he'll spit nails. Then there's mom. As soon as she even hears the the first syllable, "zom," her faces mangles into a tessellation of bitterness and rancor. "Oh, I hate that crap!" Except she doesn't say 'crap.' Then, your sister, who is hip and with the times, liberal and more 'open minded'—she's fast—and I mean, fast—to bunch her face and remind you there's already a show called THE WALKING DEAD. Even your friends give the usual, helpful and clinical, "yea, no, that sucks."

"But," you squeak, "this one WILL be different."

"How?" They all snap.

You muster a small voice, a peep really: "Well, I'll be doing it."

Then they pelt you with the hot garbage.

With that, your dreams and enthusiasm for a zombie movie wither and die.

Fine!

You look at other kinds of kinds of movies / stories people might be more friendly toward.

Maybe an 'alien' thing?

"Been there," one friend says.

How about 'vampires?'

"Done THAT," says another.

Ugh.

You begin to wonder if Spielberg has to go through this. The humiliation, the frustration, the rejection! Surely, if Spielberg wanted to, he could make a zombie movie! No questions asked!

And you would be 1000% correct in your assumption. And not only could he get it made, it would be given millions to produce. And it would be heralded as the return of "classic Spielberg."

What gives!?

Why is it that when YOU come up with an idea, and when an established artist dreams up the same idea, it's met with two radically different outcomes? Of course, the answer may seem obvious: You're not Spielberg. You're not David Fincher, Martin Scorsese, Christopher Nolan, George Lucas. You're what they call a "nobody," right?

I would suggest the answer lies somewhere else.

Before you despair you're not Spielberg—or any of the masters—I want to point out one simple thing:

Even Spielberg would have to go through the same frustrating process you have to go through. He would, like I just described, have to go hat in hand, and explain to everyone that he wants to make a "zombie movie."

He too would have to do the dreaded 30 second elevator pitch.

They all do. Nolan, Fincher, Tarantino, Scorsese.

Not to the studio executives, of course. Not to the people who green-light movies.

But rather to...

The audience.

No matter how powerful the director, no matter how accomplished, he or she always, always, always has to clasp their hands and waddle on bended knees to an audience, any audience, and sell them the "idea." It's no coincidence that a movie's TV spot is about the same length it takes from an elevator to get from one floor to the next—30 seconds.

The masters, in other words, all of them, including you, have to to—and I mean have to—take the idea for their story/movie and classify it as 'something.' In fact, they, just like you, would rather throw up their hands and say, "I'm making a movie, damn it." Some filmmakers do choose this route. And leave it up to the marketing department to figure it out.

But then, even the marketing department has to classify it as 'something.'

Someone, somewhere, has to take your movie/story, whatever it is—and it IS 'something'—and say, "this, definitively, is THIS kind of movie."

Someone has to put it... in a box.

I know, I know. You've been told your whole life to "think outside of the box."

No.

You MUST think inside the box.

THAT'S where the real skill in movie-writing, in moviemaking, comes from.

I know, I know. You're different. Or, you might be different. Might. You're an original. Therefore, you don't want to, just can't, make movies that can be so easily categorized.

You might want to make a movie like David Fincher's FIGHT CLUB.

And that one is not so easily categorized, right? Is it action? Drama? Thriller? Is it all those things? To you, perhaps, it's simply a great, stirring, of-the-times movie with great actors, great writing, great source material, great music, great symbolism, and great everything. Unclassifiable. It's what they call a CLASSIC.

And yet, it completely bombed on its initial release.

In spite of the movie having Brad Pitt, in spite of it having Edward Norton, in spite of the movie being a prophecy of 9/11 and a generation of disaffected millennials, FIGHT CLUB opened September 21, 1999 to mostly empty theaters, ultimately only making $33 million dollars.

No one, audiences and critics included, knew what the hell it even was.

Least of all 20th Century Fox. The top executives were reportedly mortified—and confused—after the first screening. FIGHT CLUB producer Art Linson diplomatically offered to the executives that the film was "a comedy."

The head of marketing balked: "That's a comedy!?"

Yes, FIGHT CLUB did eventually find success on home video, making millions in rentals and sales. But that was only after the few guys who saw it in theaters told everyone and their mother that they just had to see it.

The movie generated massive word-of-mouth.

But even those early-adopters-turned-evangelicals had to scramble about their daily lives, at home, at the workplace, in the classroom, in the locker room, spouting the same script: "Oh, you gotta' see this crazy movie. It's really sweet. Just crazy. It's… like… it's like—oh, man. It's just messed up. Like, Brad Pitt is in it. And he has this 'fight club,' and, like they fight other guys in secret. But that's not the sweet part, because there's this other guy—the whole movie is about him—and well—alright—well this is kinda ruining it—but dude, there's this amazing twist at the end of it…"

Make no mistake, FIGHT CLUB is classifiable. It is, and always was, in a box: one day, a powerless, emasculated, disenchanted, corporate wage-slave is lured into a secret organization that promises a fulfilling life. But, when this everyman hero moves through the ranks, he discovers that this is no ordinary organization. This is a secret <u>terrorist</u> organization bent on bringing about the end of western civilization. Suddenly, this everyman hero, this little guy, must not only stop the organization, but he must also match wits with the powerful, omnipotent Brad Pitt character who leads the fight club—that is, if he's to save the society he's already so disenchanted with.

FIGHT CLUB is… classifiable.

It is a <u>psychological thriller</u>.

Which is a story where a powerless person is menaced by a powerful evil. FIGHT CLUB is the same story as the Tony Scott film, ENEMY OF THE STATE. FIGHT CLUB is THE GAME, David Fincher's previous movie. It's THE FUGITIVE. It's MINORITY REPORT. It's THREE DAYS OF CONDOR. It's THE RECRUIT. It's REAR WIN-

WRITING PT. 1

DOW. It's Hitchcock's NORTH BY NORTHWEST. It's VERTIGO. It's, believe it or not, Steven Spielberg's JAWS. Yes, FIGHT CLUB is just as much JAWS as it is any of the other movies I've listed. Instead of a shark though, it's the all powerful Brad Pitt character.

What makes it a "psychological" thriller, instead of just a run-of-the mill thriller, is that the "bad guy" only has the power because of a weakness in the hero's psyche. In THE SIXTH SENSE, itself another "psychological thriller," the hero's psychic weakness is that he's actually—literally—dead. In THE MANCHURIAN CANDIDATE, the Denzel Washington character's psychological weakness is that he's been brainwashed by an evil corporation; the psychological weakness is what gives the corporation power over him. In Christopher Nolan's MEMENTO, the Guy Pearce character suffers from re-occuring memory lapses—making him vulnerable to a host of opportunistic villains. In SHUTTER ISLAND, the character, himself a detective searching a mental hospital for a missing patient, doesn't realize HE, himself, is the mental patient. His mental illness is the very power he must fight against.

In the case of FIGHT CLUB, the hero's psychic weakness is in being easily dominated by the Brad Pitt character. The twist, of course, is that he himself IS actually the Brad Pitt character. The real villain, ultimately, is the hero's own schizophrenia. It is what lays down the gauntlet of the "fight club" that the hero must ultimately battle through.

Look, I resisted this idea of classifying movies, of putting them in "a box," for years. And I mean years. When I was 15 years old and first read *Story* by Robert Mckee, I completely blew past his chapter on the concept of "genre" and classifying movies. His adage to "master your genre" smacked to me of wasting my already limited time (sleeping in class, playing hockey, and fruitlessly chasing girls). Just the idea of sinking so low as to classify my work—blegh.

Either you'll see the light now, or you'll see it later.

Without some sort of categorizing of your movie, some sort of, "this is it what it is, this is the idea, this is the thing," you're left resorting to vague points of references like someone circa 1999 trying to pitch the movie FIGHT CLUB.

The early categorization of a movie yields many benefits.

Chiefly, it will almost virtually guarantee some kind of sale of your motion picture.

The first thing a movie sales agent looks for is: "what kind of movie is it?" He does this because HE will need to know when he tries to go and sell it to "the buyers"—that is, the people who finance distribution companies. The buyers do this because soon THEY'LL have to know when they in turn try and go sell it to general audiences.

"What is it?"

The question must be answered.

Why?

One word:

Expectation.

This is why people either hate a movie or love it. It's because they walk into the theater or they hit 'play' with very defined expectations—hopes, dreams, fears of what the movie will be. When you go see Christopher Nolan's newest movie, you're already "picturing" what it's going to be like. You're thinking about his THE DARK KNIGHT, INCEPTION; you're thinking about his THE PRESTIGE, the emotions MEMENTO left you with; you're thinking about all those things and projecting it onto the film you're about to see. To the extent that the movie meets or exceeds those expectations—or dashes them—will be to the extent you perceive the quality of the movie. This holds true for you, this holds true for the audience.

Audiences have pre-conceived notions.

In spite of constant warnings against it, audiences—human beings(!)—everywhere, every time, always judge a book by its cover.

This is the real reason why your friends and family offer only disgust and rejection at your idea for a zombie movie. They already know what to expect. They hear "zombie" and their mind pulls up a reference grid of every zombie movie they've ever seen, and compare it against what they think YOUR zombie is going to be.

But what about Dad? He's never even seen DAWN OF THE DEAD! Never even seen ANY of the great—or even bad—zombie films.

Don't worry. Even HE knows the story: the dead rises, people run, they scream, they get eaten, and—whatever. What else could possibly happen?

But. This is a good thing.

Audiences having pre-conceived notions, believe it or not, is a GOOD thing.

Because really, do you want someone like my Dad showing up at your zombie movie? Do you really think, ah yes, this time, he'll really warm up to yet another movie about the undead. Trust me. If my Dad sees a movie—doesn't matter if it's like THE FUGITIVE or RAIDERS OF THE LOST ARK (my Dad's favorite movie)—if a zombie shows up, if there's any HINT of a zombie or the undead rising, or anything relating to that kind of subject matter, he hates it. Anything, really, that reeks of the supernatural, that smacks of "horror," he just refuses (although, somehow the very supernatural ending of RAIDERS did somehow pass him unnoticed).

I don't want my Dad watching your movie about zombies.

And you don't either.

I want people who like zombie movies showing up.

But what about the people who DO like zombie movies, who DO like DAWN OF THE DEAD and all those films, and who react negatively to your suggestion of doing "yet another" zombie film? How do you beat their expectations—or at least, meet them?

Do you want to know a secret?

You've been mislead.

There is no such thing as a "zombie movie."

I'll prove it to you.

Go and find every single so-called "zombie movie" or what you think of as a "zombie movie." Buy or rent DAWN OF THE DEAD (1978 *and the 2004 remake), NIGHT OF THE LIVING DEAD, 28 DAYS LATER, 28 WEEKS LATER, THE RETURN OF THE LIVING DEAD, DAY OF THE DEAD, DIARY OF THE DEAD, all of the RESIDENT EVIL movies—all of the great zombie movies, far and wide. Then you track down their screenplays, if you can.

Then you get a massive package of 3x5 notecards.

Then you sit down with the first movie (and the script, if possible), and with each scene you write down what happens. You write how the scene builds and turns.

Let's go through an example with DAWN OF THE DEAD (1978).

Your first attempt at this exercise might have you REALLY describing the first scene in painful detail, and so your description might look something like this:

> Lady is awoken by friend who tells her things are really bad. We find out she is some kind of supervisor who works at a news station. On one of the monitors, the broadcasters are talking about how bad things are getting. Chaos. She patrols the television studio, talking with one of the techs, discovering that they're broadcasting incorrect information about out-of-date rescue shelters. She fights with the other techs, demanding the information be taken off screen—in spite of management's protest. More chaos. She sees two of the broadcasters engaged in debate about

> how to best handle the zombie apocalypse. The one guy explains how the zombies work—"Every dead body that is not exterminated becomes one of them. It gets up and kills! The people it kills get up and kill!" She goes here, she does that. She sees this, says that. The broadcaster bemoans this, he bemoans that. She fights on air with the manager about the rescue stations; he wants them on because he wants people to keep watching, the crew is disgusted, they leave; then the broadcasters continue.

Don't write out your descriptions in this way.
It's unnecessarily wordy and distracts from what's really occuring.
When I ask you to describe the scene, I'm asking you to try and boil down all the activity, all the action on screen, all the information you receive, into *two or three sentences*—max.
Yes, it takes a lot of skill to boil a scene down to only a few sentences. It's hard, but essential. **_Essential_**. Doing so forces you to really grasp the "essence" of the scene, and therefore makes understanding the entire film easier. Doing so restricts and limits you to only observing how the scene "builds" and how it "turns."
What does this mean?
It means exactly what it says.
How the scene… builds… and then how it turns. Meaning, what is the moment that gets the characters through to the next scene?
Let's look at the DAWN OF THE DEAD example again. After training yourself to really see the relevant "stuff," instead of squeezing out tons of irrelevant details, you'll simply write:

> Fran wakes up in a TV studio fueled by chaos, the news anchors fighting over how to best handle the zombie epidemic. Her boyfriend proposes a plan for the two of them to escape tonight via the station's helicopter.

That's how you write out your descriptions.
You see the difference between this shorter version and the previous longer one? In the shorter version, the two sentences capture exactly what's important. Which is how the scene builds and turns. And it

builds with her wandering the studio, taking in the chaos—and then it TURNS with her boyfriend telling her about the plan. The turn is what propels us deeper into the story: the couple steal a helicopter and find refuge in an abandoned Pittsburgh shopping mall.

Yes, there's a lot of activity going on in the scene. And it seems really important. And it is. But it's actually just "exposition." Which is just information the audience needs to follow the story. And you don't need to worry about that as you go through all of these movies.

You're just looking for the events.

The scenes, in other words.

The difficulty is separating the exposition from how the scene moves the movie forward.

Then, you go to the next scene:

> A SWAT team raids a housing project where the residents are defying martial law by hiding their loved ones, who are turning into zombies. The violence gets so bad that the one SWAT member, Roger, is completely hollowed out.

Then, the next scene:

> Roger races off to be alone, and ends up meeting a fellow SWAT member, Peter, who is teetering on a similar disillusionment. Roger lets Peter in on his plan to escape away with his helicopter-pilot friend.

Then, the next scene:

> Roger and Peter are summoned to dispose of the zombies that are stored in the basement. Killing the ghouls is an exercise in cruel mercy—it ends up hollowing out Peter, making him realize it's time to abandon this crumbling society.

You keep doing this for each subsequent scene. I promise, this exercise will completely reveal the actual "plot" of the movie to you—warts and all. It'll show you why the movie gets exciting, it'll show you why it feels slow at times, it'll show you how the story stalls, and how its kicked out of that stall.

Then, you go to the next movie. And the next, and the next, working your way through all of the "zombie movies." If you have the scripts: read a scene, watch a scene. Yes I know; none of your writer friends are doing this. None of the other film students are doing this. Yes I know; this seems like an unholy amount of unnecessary work. <u>But it will elevate your story-writing to a mastery few writers ever achieve</u>.

You're searching for patterns.

Patterns.

These are the underlying conventions, commonalities, similarities that unify a particular kind of film.

For example, the first pattern you'll notice, of course, is "the zombie." These after all are "zombie movies."

Obvious, right?

Not as much as you would think.

Because the "zombie" isn't always a zombie. As you'll find in 28 DAYS LATER, the so-called zombie sometimes "runs." It runs because it's not a monster of the undead—but of a viral outbreak.

Big whoop, yea?

The more commonalities you look for, the more differences you'll note. Some zombies, for instance, can communicate. In LAND OF THE DEAD, for example, the ability of the zombies to communicate greatly impacts the story. Sometimes the difference is to be found in the zombie's origin: sometimes the zombies just show up, unexplained (DAWN OF THE DEAD); sometimes their appearance is the result—maybe—of a radioactive space probe (NIGHT OF THE LIVING DEAD), sometimes, a viral outbreak (RESIDENT EVIL). And sometimes, the zombies don't even "eat" people; they just go crazy on their victims (28 WEEKS LATER, THE CRAZIES).

In fact, the deeper your research into the zombie film, the more each subtle change tempers your initial enthusiasm for this particular movie. In your research, for instance, you'll comes across what many call the first zombie film ever: WHITE ZOMBIE. If you're a fan of all the other "zombie movies" up to this point, WHITE ZOMBIE, a 1932 horror film starring Bela Lugosi, will more than likely leave you indifferent. Its zombie is not the shuffling, rotting, cannibalizing ghoul fans of THE WALKING DEAD have come to know. Rather, this zombie is just a woman in a trance, directed by a voodoo master. This change in origin, motive, behavior, profoundly alters the story. A hypnotized woman wondering about an exotic island just isn't going to imbue the same resonance as thousands of rotting ghouls overrunning New York city. Finding this out signals to you that there is indeed a limit to how much of the "genre" can be changed.

But a change in what?

A change in the convention.

And the convention here, the principle that unites all of the other zombies on your list—but **excludes** WHITE ZOMBIE—is that of the mob. The horde. A large enough mass to destabilize whatever society the film takes place in.

This is what unifies the "zombie movie."

This principle, in other words, is what you're actually interested in.

Not the zombie.

But rather, the mob. The horde.

The destabilization of society via an uncanny or supernatural force.

The use of a "zombie" is incidental.

It's what's called a "cliche." Its continual and repeated use is exactly WHAT makes your friends and family reject your efforts as "just another zombie movie."

A 'zombie' is a cliche.

Of course, this wasn't always the case.

Most fans credit George A. Romero as the grandfather of the modern zombie film. It was, after all, his 1968 film NIGHT OF THE LIVING DEAD that spawned countless imitations.

However: writer George A. Romero's innovation with his classic film has more perspective when you begin to understand the REAL creative leap he made.

Like George Lucas originally wanting to remake Kurosawa's THE HIDDEN FORTRESS and THE SEVEN SAMURAI, and instead having to settle for coming up with his own STAR WARS, George A. Romero originally wanted to produce a film out of the story *I Am Legend*.

No, not the Will Smith film, but rather the 1954 novel penned by Richard Matheson. THAT was actually the first of its kind, telling the story of an entire world overrun not by zombies—but by VAMPIRES.

Romero never wanted to make a "zombie movie." He simply just shared the same fascination Matheson had:

The end of modern society.

From the Antonine plague wiping out a third of the Roman Empire, to the Black Death killing off an estimated 400 million souls, to the Hiroshima and Nagasaki detonations that concluded World War II, to the genocides of the 20th century, human history is a blood soaked canvas marked in epochs of holocaust. The resetting of mankind seems to be around time's every corner. The entity wearing this harbinger, this grim reaper that welcomes it in?

Ourselves.

Your interest doesn't lie with the zombie. It lies in this terrible truth: Every few hundred years it seems, a plague—in one form or another—sweeps the planet, as if nature herself were seeking to restore the balance.

The fear is: we're about due for another one.

The fascination with this kind of film is two-fold: how will the apocalypse happen, and...

Will I be one of the lucky ones to survive it?

You don't need a zombie. **You need some kind of force that will collapse society**.

Knowing this, consider for a moment that it's the mid 1980s. Even now people are getting a little tired of the whole zombie meme—Romero's DAY OF THE DEAD is coming out shortly and its already in direct competition with THE RETURN OF THE LIVING DEAD, itself a knowing derivation and reference to the original Romero film (SCREAM wasn't the first movie to start rattling off its inspirations in the film's dialogue). So, you want to do something a little different.

What's different?

How about something... less supernatural?

The destroying force, you realize, doesn't always have to be of the supernatural. EARTHQUAKE, THE TOWERING INFERNO, THE POSEIDON ADVENTURE, Hitchcock's THE BIRDS, and WHEN TIME RAN OUT were all excellent examples that mother nature has a penchant for destruction. But the natural disaster doesn't light you up.

How about vampires? Ugh. C'mon, you can do better. Werewolves? Ehh...C'mon—you're not Neil Marshal, and it'll be another 15 years before people are welcoming for that masterpiece.

Aliens? Not bad. But James Cameron is literally doing that very film right now—and it's already the original ALIEN meets NIGHT OF THE LIVING DEAD. Plus you're not interested in going to outer space.

So, something uncanny. Not quite supernatural, but not quite familiar either. KING KONG comes to mind, if only because that film had a strange monster that flipped society on its head.

Godzilla also comes to mind. And it strikes a chord with you. The Japanese creation was always good for some serious destruction; and he also, like the Matheson vampires, was a creation of the atomic-era where scientists played god—and ended up only opening Pandora's Box. But Godzilla is also owned by the Japanese, and you can't afford the rights.

Stuck, wanting to improvise, and looking to freshen up the conven-

WRITING PT. 1

tion, you ask yourself, "what exactly was Godzilla?" A lizard? A reptile? After some questioning, you realize he was a sea monster from prehistoric times.

You know, that time when…

Dinosaurs ruled the Earth.

The connection stops you cold.

Dinosaurs.

Remember, it doesn't always have to be a zombie.

Suddenly, you're thinking about dinosaurs and how you could introduce them into a story. Maybe they exist on an uncharted island, a kind of Skull Island as in KING KONG. But that's KING KONG. And LAND OF THE LOST.

You gotta' go different.

But… but… what?

What would be relevant in a world where the corporate re-structuring of the nation, of the globe, is funneling more and more power into the hands of a few faceless corporations, their combined output a mass effort in distracting the working populace from this power-grab with more bread and circuses? Whereas the the Romans erected the the Colosseum and the Pantheon, our greatest minds built Disney World.

If you're Steven Spielberg and you make this realization, you get to make your "zombie movie."

You make JURASSIC PARK.

If you can intellectually leap from NIGHT OF THE LIVING DEAD to JURASSIC PARK, in spite of one story being billed a "horror" film and the other an "adventure" film, you'll never have a problem in coming up with an original story for a movie. The leap, of course, is in seeing both films for what they are: **survival horror**.

Finding its origins in the horror writings of Bram Stoker and H.P Lovecraft and combining with the tenants of the disaster story, the "survival horror" story is the depiction of a society overrun by an unholy abomination. Sometimes it's zombies, sometimes it's the result of genetic trickery—a la, JURASSIC PARK. People die horrible, terrible, grisly deaths, while the survivors, usually people who are NOT trained for such extremes, must match and outwit not only the the abominations—but the surrounding environment. So, instead of an abandoned mall in Pittsburgh, it's Disney World. This environment must not only tax the survivors physically, but also mentally. There should be tons of puzzles for the characters to engage in. No, the puzzle meme is not just for survival horror video games. It's a necessary staple for this kind of story: characters only advance toward safety by literally puzzling their way through the environment. In, JURASSIC PARK, the survivors struggle with a code that is supposed to re-activate the security system. In the film TREMORS (a great entry in this genre), the characters must find clever ways of maneuvering around the ground dwelling "graboids." In DAWN OF THE DEAD, the characters need to find a unique way to empty out the mall of zombies—and seal it for it good.

You're not looking for similar plot points; you're looking for the underlying chords, the underlying conventions, the things that NEED to happen in order for this story to resonate in the specific way it does. For instance, the characters Must Find a Sanctuary. Albeit, a temporary one. Because it's by finding the temporary sanctuary that the protagonists find themselves in even greater danger than before: In JURASSIC PARK, turning the power back on only serves to release the velociraptors.

In DAWN OF THE DEAD, the preserval of the mall only serves to attract a renegade biking gang, who then breach the mall, destroy it, and let even more zombies back in. In RESIDENT EVIL: APOCALYPSE, making it to the helicopter only winds them up against a foe greater than the zombies.

You can run, but you can't hide.

This reversal will force one of the major conventions of the genre: the world of the story must be ended. The characters find that the environment and the force are one in the same—and to destroy one will necessitate the destruction or abandonment of the other. Think about the film ALIENS, where the damaged power plant ends up turning into a thermonuclear weapon; think about CLOVERFIELD and the Hammer Down Protocol that destroys Manhattan. Which is why these stories always, always lead to the characters racing for the last-minute take-off. JURASSIC PARK and DAWN OF THE DEAD end exactly in the same way: the characters taking off in a helicopter, letting go of their paradise on Earth.

This is the obsessive level of understanding I want you to reach when figuring out exactly what kind of story you're telling. This is why it's so important to, as Robert Mckee says, "KNOW YOUR YOUR GENRE." Doing so helps you fall in love with the convention—not the cliche. Or, as far as you're concerned, come up with something that will give you a good chance at vaulting the transom with buyers and audiences—

That is to say you accomplish the two-handed trick of "giving em' the same thing—but only different."

Mastering your genre will guide you from inspiration to masterpiece.

OTHER GENRES

So, what are the other genres? There's the obvious ones: action, adventure, comedy, horror, biography, coming-of-age, sci-fi. Those are the recognized ones, and I personally feel Mckee did a great job outlining them in his book *Story*.

But, while the genres are fairly recognized, I always approach the matter as a way to organize and inspire whatever idea is rattling around in my head.

For instance...

"What kind of movie do I want to make?" I'll ask myself. The word "kind" including anything above—or any combination. I'll think to myself, "I'm seeing a movie where a normal guy gets chased by tons of people. FBI, CIA, covert ops—yea, yea(!)," I think, getting excited, picturing these piping 6'4 guys with beards and tats, garbed in tactical uniforms, lugging the kind of automatic weapons that would make even the most seasoned gun owner blush. "And they want to kill this poor little guy—for whatever reason. And you worry, because this guy isn't Rambo. Nor is he a dweeb, mind you. He's just your average, good citizen who's in the wrong place at the wrong time! And there will be chases, and close calls, and him jumping out windows, and him getting hit by a car, and gunfire, and sweating, and swearing, and his disheveled hair, and cars blowing up, and helicopters, and guys in the helicopter shooting at him—and, and—"

Just having this image, this inspiration can point you in the right direction. Using genre as your guide, you recognize that this inspiration is leaning toward that of the thriller genre.

This is my movie EMULATION: A young college kid is, for mysterious reasons, invited to try out the services of the Emulation corporation; which is a company that provides its clients with the experience of living through a movie.

But why are all these people after this kid? What compelling reason would make the entire world chase after him?

Using genre helped me frame the problem: In every single thriller, whether on screen or off, a crime must happen. You'd think this would have been really obvious to me—yet, it wasn't. I looked at the movies that were inspiring me and, sure enough, they all had a single crime that impacted the world of the character. In THE FUGITIVE, Harrison Ford character's wife is killed—and he's framed for it! In THE GAME, the Michael Douglas character is tricked and robbed of his entire net worth—and then left for dead in Mexico.

In my movie, the hero is summoned to the scene of the crime. It's under the guise of participating in an "emulation." They have him emulating a spy film where he's instructed to assassinate a rogue agent. Only, when he arrives, he finds the person playing the rogue agent is already dead.

And that is, actually, *really* dead.

And the hero is framed for the killing.

This not only centers the movie directly in a crime thriller, but the role-playing, emulation element pulls the story toward that of the psychological thriller. This genre, as we talked about earlier, demands the character suffer from some inner psychological conflict (INSOMNIA, FIGHT CLUB, SECRET WINDOW). In EMULATION, the evil Emulation corporation reveals that their tests on the hero exposed a "split personality" disorder. This makes the character doubt not only himself, but his entire reality.

If you want to come up with an original idea, create a movie-story from scratch, then you have to be honest with yourself about what is actually inspiring you.

It's the genre.

This means looking to other movies. Not to copy, but to compare, contrast, and find exactly what resonates for you in that particular kind of story. Gather up a bunch of of movies you feel are like yours, even if they don't seem so on the surface—especially if they don't seem so on the surface—then, go through each movie, scene by scene, writing down what happens, who the characters are, where it takes place, and how it all ends up. Then, ask what patterns keep happening—and why. This will guide you from inspiration to an actual, good, original story.

WHAT IF YOU ARE ASSIGNED MATERIAL?

Perhaps you are assigned material. You're in a situation where you don't get to pick and choose the material—but instead, it's hoisted onto you.

Your problem is different: you more than likely won't be interested in it.

So, here's how you find the interest.

While unlikely, but just so we're on the same page, say you were assigned the task of re-booting Batman. Let's say this isn't going to be a "sequel," a continuation to a previous installment, but an entirely re-imagined Batman.

While you're going to do something "new," you realize that there are some obvious constraints. Not because you want to enforce any sort of arbitrary limit, but just because without "certain things," this Batman re-imagining will not be Batman. For instance, it'll have to take place mostly in Gotham. You're not about to make the first Batman film that takes place in Boca Raton. Batman will have his toys, of course, his cars, his mansion, his butler Alfred, his allies like Commissioner Gordon, and his enemies like Joker, Bane, and Two-Face.

These things will have to be included.

So, if there are so-called "conventions" that need to happen, if there are things that absolutely have to happen, then what's the point of even making the movie? This material, and its necessary conventions, has already been done many times before.

What, after all, are you going to make the movie actually about?

I certainly hope not Batman.

But then what?

First, you would watch all the previous Batman movies, read all of the comics, the games, all the source material, everything, and then ask yourself, "what about this actually resonates with me?"

You're looking for yourself in the material.

Take what Christopher Nolan did for the film BATMAN BEGINS. On its surface, it's all about Bruce Wayne becoming Batman: His parents are killed, he becomes an orphan, he mopes about, he grows into his 20s and travels abroad, takes up with a rogue organization, trains, returns to Gotham, dons the cape and the cowl, and defeats a plot to destroy his city, cementing his reputation as the watchful guardian, as The Batman.

Beneath it all, however, is something else entirely:

Christopher Nolan and his writers linger a great deal on Wayne's childhood, establishing not just the death of the boy's parents, but his psychological relationship to the father. The film goes to great lengths to show the father's care for his son, the understanding of his son's fears, the father's empathy and compassion, the father's philanthropy, and humility (he doesn't work in Wayne tower, but instead works at the hospital, leaving the running of Wayne Enterprises to so-called, 'better men'). Bruce Wayne's memories of his slain parents are not in relation to the mother, but rather reflections on the influences he gleamed from the father. His future relationships mirror not a seeking of a mentor—but rather the seeking of a father—Luscious Fox, Alfred, Ducard, Commissioner Gordon.

BATMAN BEGINS is not the story of Bruce Wayne becoming Batman. It is the story of a boy choosing which man he will become.

BATMAN BEGINS is a coming of age story.

So, while the tropes of the Batman story were already in place, and were done in all the other Batman films, it is this digging beneath the material and finding the real story that made BATMAN BEGINS a movie worth making—and a trilogy worth completing.

If you're assigned material, and the material already exists in some form or another—a video game, a book, a franchise, an article, a whatever—you have to look past the surface of what makes it that very thing, and discover the actual story below it. That is, the story that resonates with YOU.

In all likely hood, if you are assigned material, if you are given material to turn into a film, chances are it won't immediately resonate with you.

So, for a more likely example, I'll share my own experience in being assigned material. When I was in 8th grade, our class read a story called *Flowers For Algernon*. It's about a young, mentally challenged man named Charlie Gordon, who, through the miracle of science, has his IQ neurologically increased. He goes from a feeble-minded imbecile to a super genius who commands the respect of any party he attends.

Then, the treatment, the increasing of his IQ, causes some sort of tumor. And so, he dies.

I was assigned to turn this into a movie.

In spite of not really caring for the story, something about it made me grit my teeth. His therapist in the story was a kindly, attractive woman. Appealing and lovely. But their relationship was platonic, strictly therapist/patient. Then, when he gets smart—really, when he gets the spoils of being smart—the attention, the popularity, the money, the power—this kindly woman magically, suddenly has the hots for him.

For me, their romance exposed the hypocrisy of everyone's favorite advice: "Just be yourself!"

The real message of the story is simple, if not profound: You are valuable as a human being only to the extent that you fill *other* people's needs. Your feelings, your needs, your hopes and dreams, mean little when matched against the world's. **Your ultimate worth is a value other people determine**.

This resonated with me. This is what I made my film about.

So, look for yourself in the material. I promise, you'll find something great—even if you don't care much for the material!

4
WRITING PT. 2

Now that you've established what you want to make a movie about, your next step is the script.

Right?

No. Not yet.

Professionals might have you believe that successful screenwriting is a matter of starting on page 1 and typing until you reach 110 pages, the average length of a screenplay.

Not so.

The first instinct for a new writer is to get right to the screenplay. Doesn't it stand to reason?

You've probably already done a search on the internet for the screenplay to your favorite movie. Maybe you've found the script, maybe you haven't. But you've probably come across the myriad of sites that host all the available screenplays that are out there. It's an exciting moment when you do find screenplays to read.

This is what movies are made out of.

At one time all of their spectacle and sound was just text on a page. If you're serious about filmmaking, this is a very heady moment.

The first impulse you have is to then write one yourself. This seems completely easy once you see that the writing in a screenplay, at first glance, seems fairly sparse. But what seemed sparse, now appears cryptic.

You see words like "INT" and "EXT" and wonder what they even mean.

You find yourself just a wee bit anxious in reading the descriptions. Because whether or not you've seen the movie—you still find yourself straining your mind's eye to picture what's being described.

It's disconcerting the first time you read a screenplay. That is, if you even read the WHOLE screenplay. Which, if you're starting out, seems like an exercise in masochism. If I were honest with myself, it was years into my own craft that I actually read the entirety of someone ELSE'S screenplay. It took me years to get over the discomfort—and boredom—to discover the value in reading another, established screenplay (established in that it's been filmed).

It took me years to realize the brutal truth about screenplays:

They're kinda pointless.

Not only are they kinda pointless, but they're completely misleading.

If you've ever seen a screenplay, you've walked away with one extremely misleading perception:

They look really easy to write.

You realize, "sure, they're formatted strangely. But if I learned that, if I bought the software that would format the script for me, then it would just be a matter of typing out a hundred pages—and voila: the next DIE HARD."

Not so.

Because while there's only about 11,000 words in the average, finished screenplay—the screenplay itself, the whole spareness of it, the brevity of the telling masks the years of work that went into NOT crafting the screenplay itself....

...But THE STORY below the text.

This is important. You have to recognize that a screenplay—the document filmmakers supposedly film—and an actual, honest story that holds the audience's interest...

...are two totally separate things.

Let me repeat: a screenplay is not a story.

A screenplay is simply a vehicle for a story.

Because whether you were to write a screenplay, a novel, a play—even a video game—you would still have to fill the pages with some kind of content.

And that content is story.

A screenplay is just a technical means of delivering the story. And at that, it's a rather poor means. A script is primarily meant for technicians and the heads of the various departments to communicate with one another. Sure, you hear talk of actors "reading scripts," and the talk about the quality of the script—and this gives you the impression that actors and actresses are "all about the script." But what they're usually referring to is completely different than what is going to be most pertinent to you.

WRITING PT. 2

When an actress or actor says they "love the script," they're actually saying that they love the character they're supposedly going to play. If they do read the script—and, frankly, that's a very generous assumption—they're thinking solely in terms of the character in question, of how they'd look in it, of how they'd come across.

Sure, a producer says he loves the script. But it's because he knows—or has strong connections with—a popular actor or actress who would be receptive to a lead role in the script.

Sure, you'll hear that an agent loves a script. But it's because he knows the character gels with one of his "hot" clients—A-la, "It's a role with some grit," A-la, "It's a strong female role," A-la, "It's a starring role."

The truth is: not many people—even in the industry—understand what a screenplay actually is.

A screenplay is simply a vehicle for a STORY.

Not a character. Not an assortment of clever vignettes. Not a list of quotable dialogue. Not a vehicle to make a movie star look good.

A story.

Because without a story, everything falls apart.

At some point in your career, you have to train yourself to look at a script and be able to see the writing on the wall: "Wow, this really sucks!"

Your ability to make movies will be in direct proportion to not only telling a great story—but in being able to <u>recognize</u> a great story. It's being able to look at whatever the medium of the story is—a novel, a script, a video game—and say, "here's a great story."

But what's a great story?

While an entire book can be written about it—and one, GREAT book, has actually already been written (*Story* by Robert McKee, which I supremely suggest, urge, COMMAND, you grab a copy and make copious notes of)—you have to recognize that writing a story is something completely, completely, totally different than just writing a screenplay.

You've got to realize that before you go any further.

A screenplay is only a limp lattice work that frames hours and hours, months and months, years and years, of hard, mental work. It's only the tip of a vast, sprawling iceberg.

Before you write the screenplay... you have to write the story.

And before you write the story, you have to understand what a story even is.

A BAD SCENE

Allow me to describe the worst scene I ever filmed: Late one evening, a military general (played by Christian Condrick) sits in his mansion, examining folders of "military" documents. These carefully marked "top secret" folders are strewn all over the table. The general picks one up, reviews it—doesn't like it. He flips to another; doesn't like that either. He shakes his head, stands up, goes to the refrigerator—he opens said refrigerator(!)—he looks inside it... and doesn't find anything to his liking. Then, he goes to a cabinet, peaks in; again he doesn't find anything. So he shuts the cabinet. On to the next one. Ah yes—this time, he finds JUST the glass he was looking for. He fills up said glass, walks back to said couch, takes sip of said glass, sets it down, sits, sighs—

And...

End scene!

It takes up about a minute of screen time.

But when I sat in my science class watching the movie with other classmates, the one minute sprawled into an eternity. Arguably, I'm still sitting there, watching that scene, listening to my peers shift uncomfortably on their stools, clearing their throats, hacking and yaking and gargling the phlegm as if subconsciously trying to provide a second soundtrack; there was this beautiful blonde girl, one who I was terribly interested in impressing: she's gazing off at the tiled floor, scratching her hair, determined to root out some imaginary knot; she looks up! But it's only to catch a fleeting glimpse of the janitor out back dumping trash. I can still see the teacher, so kind to allow me this screening for my classmates, slouching in his chair, counting, via his eyes, the laces on his shoes.

Personally, I feel Christian did about as good of a job as any actor could have done, considering the material. You see, the problem with the scene, its failure to captivate, had nothing to do with the acting, or the lighting, or the camera work, or the grainy picture quality, or the lack of a decent camera, or the bad editing, or the lack of budget, or the poor sound, or the poor props. No. It had everything to do, and I mean everything—and please listen up because this is important—had everything to do—

...with the writing.

The writing, the writing, the writing.

And sadly, I was the writer of this scene.

This very bad scene.

WRITING PT. 2

You see, it's a bad scene… BECAUSE NOTHING HAPPENED. It's dead air. And dead air in a motion picture—even a a few seconds of it—even a half a second—is absolute poison, ruin, and death.

So, you could, in a sense, argue that movie-writing just boils down to "avoiding dead air." Does this mean that movies are nothing more than activity, and that to the extent that we, as writers, keep the "activity" up, we hold the audience? No.

If all we needed was activity then I would have been OK in filming my poor friend on his quest for a glass of water. Because that's all the scene was. Activity. Sighing, opening and closing cabinets, opening and closing the refrigerator, yawning (yawning!), sighing, shaking his head. This is the worse kind of activity: the kind that goes nowhere.

What's more, this scene missed the entire point of making a motion picture: to entertain. If this isn't accomplished, then it was all for nothing. At a bare minimum then, in making a movie, we'd like to keep the audience from nodding off.

Let's repeat—the goal of making a motion picture is to entertain. If you keep the audience interested, you've made a good movie. If you do this well, then you've made a GREAT movie.

But that just raises another question.

What holds interest?

Some might argue that it's conflict. I remember often hearing, "make sure you have conflict in your stories." But what does that even mean? What is conflict? Conflict, conflict. I have my ideas about conflict, but so do you. And they're going to be very different.

The word 'conflict' leaves the assumption that stories need to be filled with exploding bombs, sex, gun fights, screaming, yelling, and the usual nastiness that riddles almost every motion picture today.

So, there must be something deeper. Something we can put our hands around. Something that you and I can agree on:

'Change.'

At its heart, filmmaking is all about filming <u>change</u>.

No, not of the 'monetary' kind.

But rather, the change that you and I have known since we were born. Change.

Something begins in one state, it ends up somewhere completely opposite.

A process, in other words. A becoming. Something starts out good, it ends up bad. Something starts out bad—it ends up good.

Change is what sustains the beating heart of filmmaking.

This, ultimately, is why they call them "the movies." They're always moving, always changing.

But, like the word "conflict," we've run into another word that's, arguably, difficult to define. One that yet again seems to demand ever-increasing amounts of violence and chaos, and murder, and war. Like 'conflict,' the word 'change' can also give off the wrong impression.

Perhaps the word 'change,' itself, isn't quite enough to get you going.

Perhaps we should add the word "meaningful."

That is to say… meaningful change is what we must make our filmmaking about.

And what's meaningful change? The general from my movie goes to the kitchen for a drink, opens the cabinet—and this knife-wielding mongo of a guy explodes out—and—

—Ooof.

A banal, violent example, admittedly. But, by this definition, meaningful. My character began the scene alive, merely wanting a drink of water. He tried getting that drink of water—but due to an untimely intrusion, the whole scene leaves him dead. A downer, to be sure.

The key is that it leaves the audience with questions:

"Who was that big dude with the knife?" "Where did he come from?" "How did he get in the house?" "Why did he kill that other guy?" "Will anyone discover the body?" "How will that person react?"

And right there, that's the key to "meaningful change." It's the audience wanting to know "what happens next."

And the way you get them to do this, the way you get them leaning forward, engaged—i.e., entertained—is you play, and hammer, and yank on the chords of their expectations, hopes, fears, and dreams, as they relate to the motion picture they're watching.

However, the scene with the general getting stabbed, left alone, is only one scene. Absent any other context or any other scenes, it's merely a random act of violence that doesn't "come from anywhere," or "go anywhere."

An entire movie needs many of these "meaningful changes." One after another, after another, all of them searing in the audience's mind that all important question: "What happens next?"

A tall order, to be sure.

Thankfully, coming up with the meaningful changes becomes increasingly easy to answer. While each change causes the audience to wonder what happens next, each 'turn' will make you ask the same. Your imagination usually supplies the answers.

The challenge, however, is in finding the <u>FIRST</u> meaningful change.

That is, the change that <u>first</u> pulls the audience forward, and gets

WRITING PT. 2

them to <u>begin</u> asking questions. That change is really hard to come up with. Because while the other changes suggest answers already, <u>getting</u> the audience to <u>start</u> asking questions means you must answer the most compelling question of all:

"So what?"

If anything will make your forehead bleed, it's trying to answer this question. Really. What is it that will initially grab the audience—and shake them out of their daily apathy, fast mesmerized by the telling ahead?

Simple.

It's called "expectation."

The way you "grab the audience," the way you "hook them" (as I'm sure you've heard many a writing teacher advise but never explain), is you play directly on the audience's expectation of the movie their watching.

You do this by first painting a rosy picture. You show em' this nice, placid existence, saying, "Here, see this. Kinda boring right? Just another day in paradise—"

—And then you lunge out—

"When suddenly everything goes to Hell! You thought all was well, huh!? Well, think again!"

You lull their expectation into thinking one thing—and then you give them the exact opposite. It works every time.

In DIE HARD, for example, the writer sedates you into thinking you're going to watch a movie about a guy lugging around a giant panda bear. This guy, John McClane, is just another divorcee wandering post-feminist America, visiting with his ex-wife at her corporation's Christmas party, seeing other guys hit on her; then having to passive-aggressively argue with her about alimony—snooze.

But then!

A horde of terrorists, machine guns blazing, storm the building, taking everyone—including the bullish ex-wife—hostage. Their only hope: John McClane.

Genius!

The audience yanks forward wanting to know what will happen next.

Or, take TITANIC. An easy example. James Cameron paints this lovely mosaic of an ocean liner, and the love that two young people find on her maiden voyage.

Sigh…

Then—WHAM! The ship hits an iceberg—and, well, you know the rest.

Now, this moment doesn't always have to be so blatant. Sometimes your story won't allow such an "in-your-face" event.

Take for example THE DARK KNIGHT RISES, the third and final installment of the The Dark Knight Trilogy.

Christopher Nolan, the film's director and writer, didn't want to make a film where his Batman sees the Bat-Signal, then hops right into action. Instead, he wanted a slow-burner in the fashion of a 70s-era epic, an almost lumbering odyssey beginning with a tremor, and then ending with a bang.

But even Christopher Nolan had to "hook" his audience. How did he and his writers go about the task?

With a robbery.

When THE DARK KNIGHT RISES catches up with Bruce Wayne (Batman) 8 years after THE DARK KNIGHT'S conclusion, we find not a ruthless, cunning vigilante looking for trouble; but rather a tired, isolated old man shuffling into the twilight of his "retirement." It's as if Christopher Nolan is saying, "See. Here. Nothing's happening anymore for this guy. No more fast cars. No more long nights out. Just a long beard and a little depression."

Then, late one night, this mysterious young woman shows up in his bedroom. Interesting, right? Well, it turns out she's there to rob his safe!

But that's not enough to hook the audience.

Why would it? The audience is figuring, "OK. A pretty woman shows up in Bruce Wayne's bedroom. Big deal. Probably happens every night. Oh, she's there to rob him? I'm sure it's not the first time someone tried to steal his money. He'll signal Alfred, signal the police, and that'll be that."

Nothing, it seems, is enough to really shake him out of this funk we've found him in.

That is until you discover what the mysterious young woman has actually stolen.

Jewelry, sure.

But, as Bruce Wayne discovers, she's stolen a copy his fingerprints.

Huh?

What value would a set of Bruce Wayne's finger prints have to a cat burglar?

The question is not only just interesting enough to signal the audience's interest, it's enough to make the retired Bruce Wayne realize something important:

"Something isn't right."

It's his Bat-Signal.

The key to this "hook" is NOT that something explosive has happened. It hasn't. Not a shot was fired. It's that this is something explosive enough TO Bruce Wayne, IN HIS LIFE, RIGHT NOW, relative to his current status.

Which is... balance.

Sure, the Caped Crusader seemed unhappy and discontent when we first saw him in the opening minutes of the film, but truth is: for Bruce Wayne, the retirement we see him in at the beginning of the film is as peaceful as it gets. His life, at the beginning of the movie, is in perfect harmony. There are, after all, no masked psychopaths menacing Gotham—not yet at least.

To write a story then, you have to find a character who is relatively, more or less, in some sort of balance. If someone asked him how he was doing, he'd say, "comme ci comme ça"—meaning, more or less, he's just kind of in the middle of things. Not to be confused with, "in the midst of things." But rather, he's just kind of existing. He's John McClane lugging the giant teddy bear around.

Then, that balance has to be smashed.

Now, if you've seen THE DARK KNIGHT RISES, or if you've watched it after reading this, you may find yourself feeling that what I just described wasn't much of a "hook." At least, the moment didn't really "hook" you.

And you'd be right.

There is a far more dramatic moment that happens even earlier in the film. From frame one, THE DARK KNIGHT RISES opens with its masked villain, Bane, hijacking an airplane and kidnapping one of its passengers, evidently "someone" important. You could say that this would be surely enough to hook the audience.

And that's why I chose the example.

It illustrates the elusiveness of "the hook," the concept of the catalyst, the inciting incident, the whatever you'd like to call it. Yes, the scene at the opening of THE DARK KNIGHT RISES hooks the audience—how could it not? The bad guys hijack a plane—via a second plane from above! Genius. But it's not a "hook" or a "catalyst" that's going to do you or I as writers any good.

What's the difference between this and the real hook of the movie?

The first hook the movie presents us with is an exciting spectacle full of "sound and fury," as Shakespeare would say. Writers Jonathan Nolan, Christopher Nolan, and David S. Goyer were faced with a story where the main hero—the main protagonist, the main guy, the person we're going to be "rooting for,"—doesn't really hop into the action until about the 45 minute mark. And so, the writers needed something to "wow" the audience up front.

They needed a "James Bond" opener, in other words. A scene, where, right off the bat, something is happening.

But it's not a <u>real hook</u>. It's not the film's inciting incident.

The business with Bane hijacking the plane leaves the Nolan brothers and David S. Goyer with nowhere to go but the completion of Bane's plan—which is to destroy Gotham City.

As a writer, as a writer searching for the true "beginning" of your story, you must look past spectacle, sound, and fury, to find what's truly going to pull you through the entire endeavor of writing a story.

And that true "beginning" lies in the exact moment when your character, the person we're going to root for, is forced off their butt, and into the game.

For Bruce Wayne in THE DARK KNIGHT RISES, it's when he discovers the theft of his fingerprints. Because in truth, THE DARK KNIGHT RISES is not an action film. It's a crime film that slowly morphs into a disaster/war story. And it starting out as a crime story, the writers needed to have the hero—the detective, really—<u>discover a crime</u>. Because it's the discovery of that crime that ultimately leads Bruce Wayne, at the climax of the movie, at the "ending" of the story, to flying off with the bomb that was always meant to blow up Gotham.

But without that moment of Bruce Wayne discovering that his fingerprints have been stolen, the character just languishes in his mansion until Bane destroys Gotham.

In other words, a true hook is something that will not only answer the most difficult question of writing a story, it will lead you to the answer of the SECOND most difficult question of writing:

"How will it all turn out?"

This example is why I do my best to shy away from "result" oriented language. Because it may lead you, the writer, to thinking that the "beginning" of your story is wherever the biggest bang happens. It's not. The beginning of your story lies with your hero, whoever he or she may be.

A story's true beginning will give you, however obliquely, its ending.

Here's a test to know whether or not you've got a catalyst, a beginning, an inciting incident, a true "hook,"—ask yourself, "Will this event lead my hero to the natural conclusion of this story?"

And 'natural conclusion' is… the story ends in a satisfying way.

Let's look at another example. In the 1996 movie SCREAM, the film opens on a teenage Drew Barrymore, alone in her house, readying to watch a scary movie. She receives a phone call, whereupon the stranger on the other line baits her into a game, taunts her, ultimately appears out of nowhere, chases her down, and kills her.

Is this a "hook?" To the audience, sure. And it's necessary. Because the real "hook" of the story, the "real" beginning, the thing that you, as the writer, are going to be most interested in, doesn't happen until a few scenes later when...

...The Sidney Prescott character (played by Neve Campbell), a sweet, insecure, and reclusive teenager, arrives at school the next day to discover that her classmate, the Drew Barrymore character, was brutally murdered. While unsettling, what really awakens her, what really grabs her attention (and ours), is the swarm of reporters clobbering her campus, alluding that the night's previous murder may have been related to a murder that happened last year—the murder of Sidney's mother.

This is exactly what an inciting incident needs to supply—it gives the hero SOMETHING TO DO.

In other words, this event gives her exactly what EVERY CHARACTER NEEDS: A goal. A want. A need. A desire.

In Sidney's case, it's safety from the killer who has obviously returned.

Does this mean that she heads for the nearest sporting good store, buys a 357 magnum and all the ammunition it can handle, then tracks down the real killer so she can set him straight? No. It means that she can now do what her character attributes (sweet, insecure, reclusive) will allow her to do: pray that nothing else happens.

Sadly, this strategy does not work. Within minutes, the masked killer finds her and comes within inches of hacking her to death. Happily, she's able to escape.

Which gives her a new goal: to hide from the killer.

But this only causes events—future "meaningful changes"—to escalate and escalate, requiring her to do one thing, and then another, all the while leading her up to the inevitable goal: to kill the killer.

The film "ends," or, rather, "climaxes," when Sidney finally puts a bullet between the killer's eyes, an act that arcs her from a naive, vulnerable, reclusive teen, to a worldly, ruthless woman who has found exactly what she wanted from the very beginning: safety, peace, and the knowledge that her mother's death has been avenged.

The ending, of course, comes directly from the beginning.

That's a true inciting incident, a true "hook."

Yes, SCREAM starts off with the killer knocking off a teenager. Why not? The spectacle, the "sound and fury," of the killer chasing around the Drew Barrymore character will hold more initial interest than the shy, reclusive Sidney Prescott character merely discovering the murder.

But the Barrymore scene won't sustain an entire motion picture.

It's not a true "beginning" until it gets SOMEONE ELSE INTO

THE GAME!

WRITING THE SCRIPT....

Truth be told, story writing is a skill completely unto itself that takes years to master. But, for our purposes here, without this book exploding into a thousand pages, it's best to take the above instruction as a general, overall look at story writing. We're almost to the stage of writing a script. But there is one final step—before we get to the script—that I suggest:

Write the <u>story</u> before you script it. That is to say, sit down and write the story as if you were writing a kind of novel, with full paragraphs, with the thoughts of the characters, and what's motivating them. It doesn't have to be literary. In fact, I urge it not to be literary. But instead I urge for you to write, write, write—and then—if you suddenly have another idea—just write out, "OK, that's not what happens"—or erase it, if you want—and then go with a different action. Write: "He wants this, but does that." Or, "he wants 'x' to happen, but instead, so-and-so wants the complete opposite to happen." The key here is to really penetrate the inner world of the characters, "fleshing them out," as it were, giving you a far deeper understanding of your story than if you were to just give it the lip service of a 10,000 word screenplay.

Because once you write it out like this, the screenplay will pretty much write itself.

Once you write the story, then you write the screenplay.

FORMATTING

First, don't worry.

Fret not if you don't at first understand the formatting of a professional screenplay—and how to write in it.

The truth is, it really doesn't matter.

Truth is, no one but you, and a few other non-filmmakers will be reading "the script."

Truth is, no one but YOU will be reading the script.

Truth is, it takes training to even read a script. A true screenplay is filled with odd acronyms, character names, and sparse description—all stuff other people won't understand. Think of it like this: if you don't

WRITING PT. 2

understand a professional screenplay, none of your friends or family will either.

Personally, I don't even think the vast majority of the Hollywood-powers really know how to read a script—let alone, read.

First, this is what a real script looks like:

46.

          NIKKI (CONT'D)
      (to no one in
       particular)
It just shut off the power... complete black... it turned on the fire alarm to make sure we'd all be scared and that we would want to be together...
      (crying now)

          AUSTIN
      (frantic, egged on by
       the story)
April, help me find the keys!

He tears drawers out, pens and junk spilling on the floor. He rips head-long through the whole office, riffling through papers.

          NIKKI
It knew we wouldn't want to be alone.
      (coughing, choking)
And then the screaming... Oh my god- it just kept coming... it just kept coming back again and again- the screaming...
      (breaking out of her
       trance)
You do understand you're all going to die, right?

Austin discovers the keys, holds them up.

          AUSTIN
Not if I don't run him down first.

EXT. CAMPUS DRIVE - NIGHT - MOVING

The roar of the POLICE S.U.V., the tires crunching through snow, the engine cutting through the wind- a surge of POWER.

INT. POLICE S.U.V. - SAME

Wipers BLEATING, Austin driving, keying the mic- STATIC BLASTING BACK.

          AUSTIN
Copy all channels! Anyone read me!?

JUST STATIC. He cranks the CB's SEEK button, the LED numbers dial up. All of it, STATIC.

          AUSTIN (CONT'D)
Every channels' out.

A formatted screenplay. From my script THE INVADING.

But let's talk a little about how to best format a screenplay that your friends and family will understand.

A normal script will begin with something like:

```
INT. HOUSE—NIGHT
```

What's an 'int'? Does it mean 'international?' Ugh, I struggled with this one when I first started out at 13.

"INT" actually means "interior."

If we made a list of stupid jargon in Hollywood, we could start with the choice of this word to describe something that's happening *inside*. For your sake, for your friends sake, for the people you will be sharing your script with, just write out the actual meaning:

```
INSIDE — HOUSE — NIGHT TIME
```

No one knows what an 'INT' is!

Or, how about the ever elusive "EXT?" Does it mean 'exit?" Is the script saying that we're "exiting" out of the last scene into a new one? Don't sweat it. It's just more jargon. It's short hand for the word: EXTERIOR.

Just write "OUTSIDE."

Please keep in mind, you're writing this script for the people who will be working on *your* film. And the people who will be reading it are not 'industry' people. Of course, if you're writing a script for someone on the "inside"—wink, wink—you should use the jargon.

Next in script formatting, there's some description:

```
Birds outside are chirping. Johnny is twiddling his thumbs, sitting, looking around. He looks really worried. He gets up and goes for the phone. He picks it up, dialing numbers, he clutches the phone to his ear, he waits as the phone connects.
```

This describes what we're actually looking at. Frankly, I'd like to polish the description up a bit just because I really enjoy writing.

```
BIRDS CHIRP OUTSIDE. Johnny, braced on the edge of his armchair, twiddles his thumbs, gazing at the carpet. Sweat beads his skin.
```

```
His knee bounces.

Suddenly, he leaps up and charges for the
phone. Clutches the receiver, pecks the key-
pad. He braces as the PHONE TRIES TO CONNECT.
```

Does it make a difference? Sure. It's "punchier" and more vivid, and reads like someone who has been writing for many years. "Punchier" and "more vivid" because I used specific verbs.

We're seeing something happen. Johnny isn't just sitting when the scene starts, as the initial description attempts to describe; he's braced on the edge of his armchair—something that's providing you and the reader with a very apt visual, and one that betrays poor Johnny's mental state. The first general description hints at someone somewhat relaxed. Because, after all, what is "HE LOOKS REALLY WORRIED?" How does someone "look" worried? You might have an idea of that. Your friend might have a different one. I personally had to think for a few seconds about how someone "looks worried." It forced me to think—**and that's never a good thing for a reader.**

Thinking about it now, writing it well and specifically at the computer, saves you time later. Especially when it comes time to direct the actor. Instead of saying, "OK, John, it says here you gotta' look worried." Just write down now the word "braced" and everyone later will be "on the same page."

Great writing is about controlling the reader's thoughts.

Further, you have the guy braced on the edge of his armchair. Not a couch. An armchair. And, now that I think about it, now that we're talking about it, I'd like to suggest that the guy be braced on <u>the edge of a coffee table</u>. You see how that changes things? That's someone who doesn't even want to begin to get comfy.

So, of course, the language matters. The choice of language matters even more. I suggest making a study out of it. It will improve how you think.

One other thing. Did you wonder why I capitalized "BIRDS CHIRP OUTSIDE?" I'm afraid this is a habit that I picked up from my earlier education in writing screenplays. If you read professional scripts, you'll see that certain words are CAPITALIZED. The practice got started so that the sound engineer, in post production, would have an easier time finding what sounds were necessary to be placed in. Capitalized words are used to describe SOUND. A sound effect.

Then, you have a line space, and then, centered, in caps, is the CHAR-

ACTER'S name who is about to speak.

>   JOHNNY
>   Pick up!

Yes, capitalize the character's name. It'll help separate WHO is speaking from WHAT he is actually saying. When I first started writing screenplays, I just naturally wrote the characters name, added a colon, and then wrote in what he or she said. I prefer how the pros do it by just isolating the whole chunk, rather than having a long, intimidating list of character names, and colons, and dialogue that just goes on and on.

Ease of reading is what we're looking for.

Sometimes you'll want to include who the person is saying the line to.

>   JOHNNY
>   (to the phone)
>   Pick up!

Very helpful.

How about when we change scenes? Reading the screenplay, the old "cut to," seems to be obvious. And it is. It simply means the scene moves to the next scene. CUT TO.

But it's superfluous jargon and will only confuse your reader. Better to just go from the description, or whatever was the last act of description, and go down a line—maybe even two (!)—and say, "INSIDE—HOUSE—NIGHT TIME."

It might not seem like a lot, of whether to keep "cut to" or to eliminate it. But it'll have a huge impact on whoever you convince to read the script.

>   JOHNNY
>   (to the phone)
>   Pick up!

    The phone CONTINUES to ring, mocking him. He
    slams the receiver.

    INSIDE — HOUSE — NIGHT TIME

Does that look like a scene change? Hm. Tough call. Would your Dad realize that the story has moved from one location to another?

WRITING PT. 2

The answer seems obvious, but, often, it's these little things that create the biggest of problems. Arguably, whole stories could be totally confused and convoluted because the reader of your script doesn't understand that a location change has occurred.

What then would signify that we're moving somewhere else?

For our purposes, two things might be a good start. First, switch "HOUSE" with "INSIDE." The reader sees a house, and then is told that we're on the inside of the house. Professional scripts will start off with whether or not we're on the inside or the outside, and that's fine, and maybe you want to do that, but, if you ask me, this reversed order is what an average reader would expect to see.

Remember, Hollywood professionals, do things for totally different reasons. Reasons we may not even have.

Another change would help. Putting the LOCATION in BOLD FONT. It should look something like this...

>   JOHNNY
>   (to the phone)
>   Pick up!
>
> The phone CONTINUES to ring, mocking him. He slams the receiver.
>
> **HOUSE — INSIDE — NIGHT TIME**

This would really hammer home the point to our proverbial average reader:

>   JOHNNY
>   (to the phone)
>   Pick up!
>
> The phone CONTINUES to ring, mocking him. He slams the receiver.
>
> **NEXT SCENE: HOUSE — INSIDE — NIGHT TIME**

Now there would be NO confusion as to what has happened. This requires no training or comprehension from your reader on how to interpret a screenplay.

And, because our goal is always, always CLARITY, let's take it a step further:

NEXT SCENE: <u>**HOUSE — INSIDE — NIGHT TIME**</u>

Underline it!

Of course, writing this way will not be amenable to most screenwriting software, such as FINAL DRAFT. Excellent software, of course. And perfect for the professional screenwriter. As it lets you just hit the 'return' key, and it knows what you're going to do next. You don't have to waste any time hitting the tab key to properly center the character's name, and it will automatically center the character's dialogue, and justify it within a certain margin.

Maybe you want to purchase the software, maybe you don't. Either way is fine.

But beware, beware, beware the dreaded, "INT. HOUSE — DAY." New readers will never know what "INT" means!

PART 2
EQUIPMENT

5
CAMERAS

I'm not going to give you the standard, "What camera works for me, won't work for you" line. Because what did work for me will work for you. But since what worked yesterday might not work tomorrow, and what's supposed to work tomorrow more than likely won't work today, we're going to inspect the topic of filmmaking equipment, camera selection, all of that, a little more deeply, and look past just brand acquisition.

First, no filmmaker actually cares about the difference between brands of cameras, of mics, of lights, of editing software. When an aspiring filmmaker asks a professional, "What kind of camera/mic/editing software did you use?" He or she is actually asking, "How can I get similar results?"

More specifically, "How can I make MY movie look like a real movie?"

The soul searching about brands, price, and type should always center on the ideal of making your movie look like a real movie—a professional movie.

But if it were just a matter of blindly chasing the ideal of making your movie look like a real movie—or, a good movie—or, a GREAT movie, for that matter—then I would suggest you buy a RED or an Alexa camera, a set of Anamorphic prime lenses (I'll explain what those are later), a fleet of steadicams, an army of ARRI lights, and a vault of hard drive space that would make even the NSA envious.

There are, however, other considerations.

For one, a filmmaker's level of expertise; for another, budget; time; amount of people involved; all factor wildly into what kind of equipment you need to get your hands on.

But the greatest determinant of your equipment choice will be, of course, price.

Whether you buy, or whether you rent, or whether you beg, borrow, or steal (not recommended), you must, and I stress must, get your hands on the equipment. By that I mean being able to sit with it undisturbed, and study it. Being able to take it for a walk, being able to study it without anyone else leaning over your shoulder, being able to experiment with it, to drop it (on accident, that is), and put it through its paces.

If you were a baseball player, you wouldn't go out on game day and use whatever bat was provided in the dugout. A serious ball player, a pro, anyone really into playing the game, would want his instrument long before game day—even long before practice. This is important for a number of reasons. With any tool of the trade, a master needs to get a real, intuitive, hands-on feel for whatever it is he will ultimately use to get the job done.

He wants this because he knows one thing: a bat is not just bat.

There are wooden bats, aluminum bats, one-piece versus two-piece, alloy, composite, hybrid, Turn Models, BESR, BBCOR, BESR-ABI; then there are the brands—Marucci: JR7, Louisville Slugger: I13, Old Hickory: J14, and on and on. What's the competition using? What's in? What's out? What's tried and true?

So, he goes out and buys all kinds. He submits it—and himself—to all kinds of grueling tests and conditions. He takes a number of swings with it, in all kinds of weather, in all kinds of wind conditions; he then repeats these tests against other bats, other kinds of brands and makes. All so he can test the limits, and to find out what, indeed, works best for him. He does this because he wants to maximize every potential resource.

Sadly, we're not ballplayers. And film equipment costs a lot—a lot—more than the average baseball bat. Just take the issue of buying a camera. Say you want to go top-of-the-line, state-of-the-art. You've heard about the RED camera, and decide that's the one you want. Their website advertises the "cheapest" RED camera model for $12,000 dollars. Not bad. While that's almost breaking the bank, it's "do-able." But this before you discover that $12,000 is only for the "brain" itself. Meaning, no lens, no battery pack, no viewfinder! Just… the brain. And a camera without out all those things… is not a camera.

Then, you need a lens. And if you've got the RED, you want to get a GREAT lens. So you discover that's at least another 5 grand. But that's just for one "fixed length" lens (meaning, you can't zoom in or anything; you're just stuck with what you see); and if you've bought the RED camera, you'll probably want to shoot in 4K, and well, you gotta' store

CAMERAS

that footage while you shoot, and then, back it up—

When you add in all of those items, then factor in all of the other supporting infrastructure (computers, hard drive space), the costs escalate into the tens of thousands—$20,000, $30,000, $40,000. Not cheap.

So, unsure, you move down a wrung. You look at the "prosumer" models. Panasonic, Sony, Canon, JVC, all make excellent cameras that enable the user to achieve pro level results. You can get everything you need—lenses, storage, viewfinder, etc—all in one compact model for around $7,000. But even here, if you can swing that big of a cost, the costs after purchase begin to spiral up. You discover you can change the lens, so you're tempted. Then, you discover that lenses cost almost as MUCH as the camera itself. And then you discover that the new lens only really gives you one "view." So, a "zoom lens" might be the answer. But then you discover, in order to combine quality of the fixed lenses and the zoom lenses, you have to pay triple! So, you start to question the legitimacy of actually buying a $15,000 zoom lens—especially when the camera evidently came with one for free (or so you think). So then, you have a camera with the capability to shoot 4K, and therefore you naturally want to utilize that resource too. So, the need for more storage. More storage means the need for more backups. And more storage necessitates a faster computer to handle it all. Then, add at least another $4,000 in change, depending on how crafty you are at selecting the "correct" computer. And THEN, since you've purchased such a nice camera, you're going to discover ways of improving the picture quality still more: lights and all their little trinkets, diffusers, etc. Buying a prosumer camera will tempt you into desiring prosumer results.

And prosumer results cost.

Then, there's another wrung down. The consumer models. The "user-friendly" models. Even here, the prices only begin to bottom out at around $200 dollars. Which, depending on your age, may or may not be a lot. If you're 13 or under, then $200 might very well be a fortune. It would take a lot of chores and a lot of driveways shoveled before you could confidently get your hands on that kind of money. But with all the time spent shoveling the snow and washing dishes, when will you make your films? If you're in your 20s, $200 might seem like a pittance. And yet, there are those car payments to take care of…

If you're in your 30s, 40s—$200 dollars is always a fortune, and it could always be better spent then buying a film camera. Diapers anyone?

At every level of the spectrum of equipment purchase, the money problem haunts.

Further compounding this problem is the fact that filmmakers, by and large, are generally broke. While due to many factors, this is mostly because it takes a long time to start making a living with film. And whatever investments made in filmmaking are not immediately rewarded. Filmmaking takes time. It takes a lot of time. And it's an extremely price-centric affair.

However, the downtown truth when concerning ourselves with price, fretting over it, is that the whole subject betrays an even bigger problem.

In essence, values.

When push comes to shove with education budgets, the first areas to get slashed are the arts. Then the humanities. Then the sciences.

Then, sports.

If the American public education system is any indicator of what's worth teaching and what's not, it's that "the arts," "the humanities" in general, are of questionable value. Always have been. And more than likely, always will be.

When was the last time you heard of a high school recently refurbishing their multi-million dollar arts facility?

It's been a while. If ever.

However, not a year goes by where millions aren't funneled into high school and college sports. Often at a deficit to the schools themselves! The sports tickets alone don't pay for it. It's on the student and taxpayer to foot the bill. Who else is going to pay for the training, housing, the "educating" and prepping of all those future athletes? Who other than the students plummeting into lifelong debt and the American taxpayer will willingly—whether they know it or not—fund a vast recruiting pool for professional sports?

But this is not a book about education values.

This is a book about filmmaking—and our relation to it.

Therefore, we have to understand society's relation to it.

If the arts are at the bottom of the scale, then filmmaking—the learning of it—is somewhere just beyond the abyss.

Just watch how a normal person reacts when you confess your filmmaking dreams. Watch their pinched smile, their doughy, softening eyes, their head tilting:

"Oh, good for you!"

Then the Epidural block suddenly kicking in:

"You're following your dreeeeeams!"

Blegh.

Or you get the, "Well, I think my cousin's one friend does something with movies. I know he went to high school with this one guy who now works for someone who last year or something saw a *real* good picture of George Lucas."

In fairness, these people are well-intentioned, and well meaning.

They're just trying to hide their despair for you.

No one cares about learning how to make art. Because while society will cheerfully toss billions of dollars at the sports-educational-industrial complex, people believe movie professionals just "come out of thin air."

Learning the craft of filmmaking holds very little value in our society.

What's worse, the majority of filmmakers don't even value it! When I was a kid, I always heard the same thing from other aspiring filmmakers: "Would love to do it, but just can't afford the camera." I'd then see these same people spend untold amounts of money on booze, drugs, cars, and a myriad of mindless entertainments—including but not limited to happily splurging six grand on a trip to Disney World. Not to mention also paying upwards of $20,000 dollars for a semester of college! Almost always on borrowed money. Think about that for a minute: People will pay upwards of $80,000, $100,000, even $200,000, for the privilege of attending classes (that go unattended), to use a library (that is often never used), to obtain a degree (that is, according to the stats, rarely needed). Arguably this is done for the ol' resume in the implicit, unspoken assumption that a degree will secure a high paying job (or at least one that will repay the debts it took to procure the job!). People will blindly mortgage their future on this leap of faith.

Then they will turn around and fret—and surrender—at the thought of obtaining and spending a few hundred bucks for some equipment that may provide them with an actual skill.

The point is... people's values, in general, are very confused.

And people's values aren't only confused about money.

But also about time.

People will gladly spend four hours watching a game of football—for free, mind you (meaning, they aren't being compensated for this time)—but will balk at investing just 30 minutes to read a book that may very well improve their lives.

"I don't have time to read," they'll say. But not a peep about idling away half a decade at college.

Of course, I'm guilty of this same confusion about how much—or how little—I actually valued my own filmmaking prospects. In 2001, I gasped at the discovery that a proper DV (digital video) camera would cost me $900 dollars. Gasped! And yet. I thought nothing of paying a similar fee every year to play hockey for my school.

Therefore, those confused values—even the ones about time—must be dealt with. At some level. And they will be dealt with, mostly, in the selection and procurement of the filmmaking equipment.

When you consider how you're going to obtain the equipment listed in the following pages, keep this in mind: lots of people waste lots of money on things that never bring them any pleasure, joy, or for that matter, value. Everyday people spend billions on illegal drugs that bring them only ruin. Alcohol that only winds them up (if they're lucky) in a rehab—or worse, in a coffin. Everyday, people spend billions on family vacations that only leave them with the terrible ache for another vacation. Further more, the United States spends, every year, over half a trillion—that's trillion with a "t"—on educating a populace that, if the rankings are any indicator, is continually falling further and further behind the rest of the world. And the government is currently looking to spend more! What, really, is a few hundred bucks—if you indeed have to fork it over—for equipment that might lead you to a fulfilling career?

Perhaps cameras would only be worth buying if they were the price of the average baseball bat. Perhaps these confused values could all be put to rest if all of the equipment cost the price of a bottle of aspirin.

But ask yourself—is that the value you put on this thing? On your dream?

Know this: if no one else values it, you must. Or see it perish.

When you look at equipment to buy, rent, borrow, whatever—you're actually contemplating the value you place on your own dream, your own aspirations, your own ambition… your own self.

And if you're reading this book, I would submit that you're already fairly serious about the endeavor. In buying and reading this book, you've already placed a value not only on your dream, but on yourself.

If I have one regret in my filmmaking, it's that I wasn't more relentless about securing funds for things I knew I needed: that I hesitated for many years in buying a graphics program, that I slummed it for so many years with subpar editing software, that I galled at spending upwards of a grand on Photoshop, that I just couldn't get past the fact that it cost $5,000 for a really nice camera, that I just couldn't even THINK about using a lens because doing so would mean having to think about buying one that cost a meager $100. And yes—I say, MEAGER! A hundred bucks for a lens is a steal.

Remember: this dream, this dream of seeing your film on a screen, is yours and yours alone—and therefore, it's yours to fight for.

With that, let's look at the equipment.

FINDING THE RIGHT CAMERA...

If there's any worry among filmmakers about what kind of camera to buy, it's traced to this single anxiety: what if I choose poorly? You know about "choosing poorly."

The truth is that camera selection is bewildering. And it's bewildering because, with a camera, so much can go wrong. The picture quality, the recording medium, the ergonomics, the audio recording, the frame rates, the codecs, the ISO, the this, the that. There are so many facets that go into a device that just simply captures video. Buying one requires not only a complete understanding of a camera, but a complete auditing of what even makes a good camera.

But there is a bigger reason why camera selection is such a bewildering affair: marketing. The selling and distributing of cameras, of RED, Canon, Kodak (yea, they still sell em'!), Panasonic, Sony, JVC, marketing them to the general public, is so matrixed in price points and jargon, that it's all but impossible for an author of a "how-to" book to recommend a single one—or, for that matter, for the uninitiated to make a sound, peace-of-mind, confident purchase.

Open any catalog selling film equipment—the B&H catalog is one I highly recommend—turn to the "camera" section (it's spread out over many sections, as you'll see), and you are assaulted by a labyrinthine, Gordian, enigmatic intermixing blitz of camera capabilities, terms, specs, this, and that, and the other thing.

Right off the bat, you see '1080p,' then '4K,' sometimes '5K,' maybe '2K;' other times you won't see these numbers anywhere. Do they mean anything? What's important? Why does '4K' seem to sometimes cost more than '1080p'—and, sometimes, less. If you have one quality, it seems, another is totally absent. You'll have the words "UHD," and you wonder, "Does that mean HD?" Sometimes you'll see "Super 35 Camera System," sometimes, it's conspicuously absent; in its place, some other, seemingly comparable gadget. One of the companies, for instance, offers something called a "BIONZ X Image Processor."

Then there are the names: Alpha a7s, PWX-FS7, HXR, Weapon, Dragon, Scarlet, Raven, a7RII.

Mind you, these are just the models. These don't even account for the various "brands" of camera manufactures—RED, Arri, Blackmagic, Nikon, Panasonic, Sony. Canon alone has a bewildering array of cameras at varying (always moving) price points—the C100, C300 (for a while, there was no C200, as if the C100 alone didn't merit any kind of sequel—at least, until recently), the C500; all of them differentiated by incremental capabilities—none of which, I guarantee, will make any sense to you whatsoever.

Frankly, it takes a lot—and I mean, A LOT—of film experience and film knowledge (deep knowledge) to make a sensible choice between something as inexpensive as a GOPRO and something all the way up to a RED Weapon 8K. From the consumer to the industrial, the road is lined with many cameras. And it's paved with even more suckers.

Thankfully, for us, most of the differences listed above—are, in essence, jargon.

Important jargon, to be sure. But jargon, none the less.

What's needed is clarity. What's needed is understanding of where we—that is you, me, and anyone who wants to make a real film—stands in the world of camera usage.

THE POLITICS OF MOVIE CAMERAS

In the world of cameras, as in the world of any item that's made, marketed, and sold, there exists three classes: industrial, prosumer, and consumer.

As with anything, the price only ever spirals up.

THE INDUSTRIAL CLASS

Industrial models are inevitably where your eyes will roam first. Some initial poking around has led you to some names: RED, Arri, Panasonic. These are the names you'll see on a Hollywood movie set. That's what industrial means—Hollywood. Big budget. These are the top-of-the-line, state-of-the-art, good stuff. These are the cameras you want. And, for the first time in history, they are being dangled from the heavens above to the masses outside of the industry. Through a finagling of price, many of the camera companies have created the illusion that these kinds of cameras can be had for a small amount of money. Which isn't a bad thing. It just means for you a long blind alley.

You've heard of the RED camera. Somewhere in your travels you've heard someone say, "I use the RED." Or, "You gotta' get the RED." And for good reason. Arguably no camera company makes a more radical, more advanced camera than RED. And, arguably, no camera company

CAMERAS

has created better marketing for their product; through their efforts in the past decade, the Red Digital Cinema Camera Company has created a rabid base of followers that is just barely rivaled by the Apple crowd. Seriously. Any talk about the RED camera being anything less than grateful, anything less than evangelical, is circumspect and prohibited.

So, you take a look at their models. You see many models, like the (as of 2017) Weapon 8K and Weapon 6K. Your eyes go immediately to them because they possess the most radical specs. They also start at the most radical of prices—$49,500. So, you drop down to the medium model, and that's $29,500. Read: that's $30,000 dollars. Of course, you've heard that RED makes their cameras affordable—and they do—so you go to the model you've likely been instructed to look at: the Scarlet. Happily you see that this model goes for only $12,000. Considering the specs, considering its possibilities, considering the results you've seen it achieve in other blockbuster movies, you tell yourself that $12,000 is actually fairly reasonable. Sure, it's pushing the bank. But it's do-able. After all, this is—kind of—what the pros use.

But then you discover $12,000 is only for the "brain" itself. Meaning no lens, no battery-pack, no viewfinder, not even a handle to hold the thing, no supports, no battery. Just the "brain" of a camera. Sadly, a "brain" alone is not a camera.

So, you add in the materials that will enable you to actually "hold" the camera and actually view what it is you're shooting—and you're blown away to discover that it is going to run you another $10,000. Think about that—$10,000 just to hold the camera and see what it is that you're shooting.

We're not finished. You'll need media cards, batteries, a special adapter for the batteries, a special charger for the batteries, power cable, lens mount—all of this even before you buy a lens! Because, yes, you still need to buy a lens. If you're like I was, your assumptions about buying the camera are based on going to Best Buy, and therefore you think that every camera you buy automatically comes with a lens. Not so. At least, not in the industrial bracket of camera sales.

You have to buy the lens separate.

This alone, you'll discover, holds about as wide of a price range as a camera does. You're relieved to find that you can pick up a lens for $100, but then you're confused, and flummoxed, as to why there are lenses available for upwards of $70,000 dollars. You can't believe anyone would pay that much for a piece of glass! But, believe it or not, that's how it is. So, you feel you can get by with that $100 lens. But then you discover there is a remarkable difference between that cheapie thing and a lens that goes for $5,000. These $5,000 dollar lenses are called "compact primes." The 'prime,' however, is not in the cost. It's in the fact that you get one view out of it. What you see is what you get. Which is a shock if you're used to having the ability to "zoom in" and "zoom out." In the industrial world, if you want to zoom, it's going to cost triple that of a normal lens. $30,000 dollars isn't unheard of for a run-of-the-mill zoom. That one is especially shocking when you remember that all camcorders and prosumer cameras come with a lens—ostensibly one that's for free.

Then there are the master primes, which go for master prices.

And if you've bought the RED camera, you'll probably want to shoot '4K—perhaps even higher—and well, you gotta' store the footage, and then, back it up—then you add in all of those items, then factor in all of the other supporting infracture (computers, hard drives), the lenses, all the doo-dads, the costs escalate into the tens of thousands—

—$30,000

—$40,000

—$60,000 dollars…

This for the "starter" model.

None of this is in no way meant to knock the RED camera. It really does produce excellent results. But so did the 35 MM Panavision cameras of yesteryear, so do the Alexas, so does the Panasonic Genesis. Indeed, all of the industrial level cameras produce industrial level results.

But, as you might be starting to understand, industrial level results call for industrial level budgets.

Something tells me you're not working with an industrial level budget.

THE PROSUMER CLASS

So, unsure, you move down another rung to what's called the "prosumer" market. These are the cameras listed under the "Professional Video" heading in the B&H catalog. Some of the models include Panasonic, Sony, Canon, JVC, BlackMagic. All make excellent cameras that enable the user to achieve pro level results. Unlike in the industrial level, you can find a camera here that includes everything you need all in one package. Whether you buy an "all-in-one" model, or piece it together via the DSLR route (we'll get into that later), you can get everything you need—lenses, storage, viewfinder, etc—for around $7,000 dollars.

A pinch, to be sure. But, again, do-able.

Maybe.

Because while time is very relative, money is doubly so. I remember when I was 14, I would have looked at the number $7,000, and blanched.

Stay with me though.

Because even if you can swing $7,000, even if you can get your hands on that kind of money—however small or big it may be to you—the costs, after purchase, continue to spiral up.

You have a camera with the capability to shoot 4K, so you naturally want to utilize that resource. So, the need for more storage. More storage means the need for more backups. And more storage necessitates a faster computer to handle it all—lenses, handles, viewfinders—add at least another $6,000 dollars. And since you've purchased such a nice camera, you're going to discover ways of improving the picture quality still more: the purchase of lights, of boxes, diffusers, microphones, light meters, tripods, jibs, gimbals. Buying a prosumer camera will tempt you into desiring prosumer results.

…and prosumer results cost.

THE CONSUMER CLASS

Knowing this, you drop down yet another wrung into the wide, wonderful world of the consumer.

Here, the "filmmakers," the more aptly called "consumers," are recording the dance recital, the soccer game, the football game, the baby's first steps, the graduation ceremony, the Amazon review, the proverbial "home movie."

The cameras at this level are available at Best Buy, at Wal-Mart, at stores where your family shops. These are the brands your parents feel comfortable with; brands like Sony, Panasonic, and JVC. Your parents are comfortable with them because these are the names on the television sets. Purportedly, these cameras all shoot picture in a wide range of resolutions, and they all record sound.

This is the camera most likely already in your home. This is the camera that most likely defined, for you, what a camera actually is. For me, it was a 90s-era Panasonic camera that had the bulging, bulbous, sloped shape of a mini-van. It had an internal mic, a viewfinder, a flip-out screen, and a cute little light that would drain the camera's battery in 10 minutes flat. It shot on tapes that weren't big enough to fit in the VCR (argh!) and so required a special videocassette adapter. I can't recall the name or model or make, but I can tell you it was a 'camcorder.' The picture quality was garish, and grainy, and uneven, and spotty, and went in and out of focus at will. Because I believed this was the camera they shot GHOSTBUSTERS on, I attributed its poor quality to the main operator of the camera: my Father.

I was too ignorant to know the truth: My Dad was using a camera designed for his interests. Nothing more, nothing less. He wasn't filming GOODFELLAS or LAWRENCE OF ARABIA, or even GHOSTBUSTERS. He wanted pictures of his boy playing ice hockey.

To do that, he only needed something that would turn on, zoom in, zoom out, and actually RECORD! Nothing else.

That's all he knew how to do.

That's all he wanted to know how to do.

This is the consumer market. It is a market limited <u>not by price</u>, but ultimately... <u>by level of interest</u>.

That's how the camera market is actually constructed.

What, ultimately, is the buyer's interest? Notice, I didn't say "needs." A person seldom knows what he or she needs, nor does he or she care to know. They have an objective, and that's that. The usual advice in buying a camera other filmmakers hand out is to "buy according to your needs." But you don't yet know what you need—in spite of knowing what you want:

You want your film to look like GHOSTBUSTERS, like THE DARK KNIGHT, like FORREST GUMP, like any number of the blockbusters playing at the cinema; and you want those results for rock bottom prices, and you want em' yesterday.

However, we share a lot in common with my Father.

While his and your objectives are crystal clear, what remains lacking is knowledge:

You don't know what you don't know.

That's really what creates such a terrible conflict between us—the buyers—and the camera companies. They're more than aware of this matrix of interest, demand, and lack of knowledge. And they're in the business of maximizing a bottom line. Which means catering to the bigger crowd:

My Dad.

Your Dad. Your Mom. Your sister. Your friends flinging the GoPro around at the beach.

There are more of them... *then there are of us.*

Get it?

If you were the camera companies, who would you cater to?

This is why it's hard for you to decide on a camera: none of them are made with you in mind!

So, you need to flip the whole script around.

CAMERAS

When buying a camera, you have to look beyond price, **and instead look at process**.

By process, I mean looking at what you'll end up doing with the camera. As with price, there are three types of processes: industrial, prosumer, consumer. But unlike with price, these three categories, here, are defined around what actually ends up happening.

THE INDUSTRIAL PROCESS

To begin, let's start with the industrial, Hollywood level process. Here is where you'll see professional level cameras like the RED and the Alexa being used. But unlike on an indie shoot, the cameras are perched up on a massive dolly, or jib, or crane, clobbered by a team of people pinching the lens, adjusting dials, squinting down the barrel, hooking up all kinds of wires that lead in an array of directions. Some of these wires lead to the director, who is sitting there at a pyramid of monitors; some of these wires lead to the cinematographer, who is at another pyramid of monitors; some of these wires lead to the actors, who are comfortably perched in the proverbial fold-up chairs in front of yet another pyramid of monitors. To be sure, there's a lot of interested parties involved with what the camera is seeing.

These assembled experts, when filming begins, will produce cinematic results on par with the best our planet has to offer. Here works a master cinematographer like Roger Deakins, who has produced some of the 20th and 21st century's greatest masterpieces of photography—THE SHAWSHANK REDEMPTION, NO COUNTRY FOR OLD MEN, SKYFALL, A BEAUTIFUL MIND, THE VILLAGE, and too many more to list. Here works masters like Tak Fujimoto (SIGNS, THE SILENCE OF THE LAMBS), Michael Chapman (GOODFELLAS, GANGS OF NEW YORK), Robert Richardson (SHUTTER ISLAND, KILL BILL), Haskell Wexler, and so many more. This isn't even to include the list of directors who, film after film, manage to illicit out of their crew the most beautiful of film visuals—Christopher Nolan, Martin Scorsese, Steven Spielberg, etc.

When you see the work of these experts, it's the result of a very arduous and costly process.

It's a process that is a long, long way off for you.

In filmmaking, there exists—or has existed, as of this writing—a deep and "profound" debate about film acquisition versus video/digital acquisition. On one hand, purists rage that film—the actual, tangible act of feeding a camera those brown reels of celluloid—will forever rival video. Most have come over to the side of video—William Friedkin, Martin Scorsese. Roger Deakins said in 2016, "it's over," in regards to film. Without adding to the debate, I would like to submit that the conflict betrays a deeper truth:

The process found on industrial level films, with everyone grappling at the camera, with the artists squinting down the viewfinder barrel, with the wires, the cables, the video village, the pyramid of video monitors, is really just a huge hangover from the days when the masters—and their masters—shot on 35mm film. Which was an ungainly, nasty affair.

One that required many, many, many departments.

And one, more importantly, that necessitated a certain design to the camera.

Namely, it necessitated a tuba case-sized device that had to be placed on the shoulder, with a barrel so one could peer into a labyrinth of mirrors designed to reflect what the camera was seeing; it was a device that needed massive gulps of power and had to be loaded and unloaded with great care (the handling of 35mm footage is touchy stuff).

It, in other words, necessitated a certain kind of process.

If there's any important element in the debate of film versus video, it's in looking at the process underlying each medium.

If I make any real, strong suggestion in this book, any kind of radical claim, it is that you adopt a steadfast resolution to NOT emulate how Hollywood films are currently "shot." If only for one reason: you are going to be used to a completely different process than the master cinematographers and master directors are.

You have to consider: the masters you admire today didn't begin their craft by using a consumer grade camcorder. They learned on something that was similar to what they would ultimately use: film. Whether 8mm, or 16mm, or 35mm, it was always done via a big, hulking machine that required looking down a tight barrel which disabled the operator from any movement requiring peripheral vision.

If you were born sometime in the 1980s however, if you grew up in the 90s or afterwards, you are used to an entirely different way of shooting. You know the stance: pinching a tiny screen in one hand, and palming the camera in the other.

A screen already attached to the camera, a live video monitor, one that simply flips out, really changed a lot. It liberated filmmakers from actually having to squint down a dark barrel, allowed them to see out of their peripheral vision and move unaided; to run forwards, backwards,

CAMERAS

sideways, jump, and more efficiently scale any kind of terrain that would have been risky for a camera operator who was forced to constantly stare down a barrel, hoping for the best.

If anything changed filmmaking, it wasn't so much the ability to "film" on video. Rather, it was the ability to immediately view what you're actually "filming," what you're "taping," what you're actually "recording."

Whether you agree with this or not is moot. The fact remains: if you were born after the 1980s, you began your craft on a camera that was radically different than the so-called "standard."

That is to say, your process of filmmaking, the one that circles around the expectation of right then and there seeing what's being filmed, is the one you and your generation must be concerned with. Everything else is just someone who is confused, mislead, or nostalgic. Most likely all three.

I illustrate all of this for one reason: the cameras that you may really covet, the industrial level cameras you might really admire, the ones you REALLY, REALLY want, were NOT—and I repeat NOT designed with YOU in mind. The RED camera, the Alexa—anything made for the industrial level—was not made with you in mind.

Let me repeat that again.

YOU WERE NOT FACTORED IN WHEN IT CAME TIME TO DESIGN THE NEWER, DIGITAL CAMERAS. You were, at best, at best, a brief afterthought. Truth be told, the RED camera, the Alexa, all the really good, top-dog cameras, were designed and made to emulate the process of shooting film. Or, in other words: knowing that the current masters (re: the men and women who can actually produce the money needed for such a camera) wouldn't like switching to film, the camera companies designed the digital cameras to reflect and emulate the feel of a 35mm camera.

Camera companies don't make cameras for people like you. They make them for people who **don't** use cameras—the master cinematographers and directors who haven't touched a camera in decades.

Let's put it another way. If you're coming from the background I suspect you're coming from, an experience with the RED camera will only serve to bewilder you. Where's the viewfinder? The internal mic? Where's the hand-grip? Where's the focus ring? Where's the lens? Of course, to a professional in the business, my words will illicit a groan, and brand me very ignorant to the ways in which a professional movie is shot.

They would be very right.

But this isn't a book about how professionals think movies should be filmed.

This is a book on how movies are actually made, in the real world.

And should a professional laugh at you for following my methods—they are a professional <u>in occupation only</u>. Meaning, they operate in a secure environment where the work is presented to them in a very organized manner—and—at the end of the week, they are awarded by the accounting department a very sizable paycheck for going through the motions.

You'd be shocked. If most of the masters actually had to make a real movie, if they had to operate <u>without</u> the budgets they've grown to rely on, they'd—well. They'd significantly curtail their output.

You however, must be a professional in practice and spirit. This starts with knowing how bad it can get. You have to know how inhospitable the world is to the process of actually, physically, actually, actually PRODUCING A MOTION PICTURE:

In the trenches, the bullets flying, the mortars crashing, your buddy whining that he's gonna' be late for soccer practice, the mom walking through the shot—and snickering—the surrounding pedestrians (that you can't control) uncertain of whether or not they should continue walking through the shot, the dog barking and ruining your take, the tripod falling over, the winds howling, roaring, the darkness ever encroaching, the sunlight ever hanging high in the noon sky, the neighbor screaming and yelling for trespassing on his property, the police showing up just as you're about to film a scene with the gun, the gawkers, the headaches, the fights with friends, the heat turning up, the light falling over and exploding, the electric socket blowing out, your dad hollering and yelling to pack it in, your brother turning on the TV just as you're about to get The Shot, the animals wandering through, of time running out, of your dreams literally dying before your eyes.

At the end of the day: <u>this process is what's king</u>.

It's a mean, nasty, process. No matter how much money, or time, or talent you throw at it, it only grows uglier.

When you're out there, and the winds blowing over all that stuff you've set up in attempt to control the direction of the sun, when your buddy "recording the audio" starts whining that he can't hear anything, when your "actor" confesses—on camera—that he, or she, didn't even read the script—when everything is conspiring against you—and it will—you will know who is actually boss:

THE PROCESS.

It demands respect.

Approaching it with the gizmos and gadgets designed for a professional operating in a totally different process will end not only in complete and utter failure, but in total disillusionment of the entire field itself.

To repeat—there is no camera made for the kind of process you're going to end up engaging with.

STRICT GUIDELINES

So, if there is no camera, what then do you do?
How DO YOU successfully select a camera?
You follow some strict guidelines.

When looking to purchase a camera, you must search for—and consider only—a camera that has all of the following functions I'm about to talk about. Forewarning—a lot of these functions may seem terribly obvious. But if the available cameras and their sporadic lack of such key features are any indicator, then the following bears repeating.

First and foremost. And I mean, this is a biggie. A huge one. The camera has to… HAS TO… have a visible, USABLE, "on/off" switch. It has to say "On/Off" in plain white letters. Because, sure, maybe you can figure out where the switch is, given enough fumbling in the dark. But when you pass it off to a friend, they're going to look at it with all the wonder of the apes discovering the monolith in 2001: A SPACE ODYSSEY. Precious time, I promise you, will be wasted on explaining how to simply turn the camera on and off.

It sounds like a very, very obvious thing. But take a look around you. At the electronics that have embedded themselves in your life. The iPhone? No switch. There's an unmarked and camouflaged button on the side, to be sure. But have you ever tried explaining that to someone who isn't a "Mac person?" Hand someone your phone and ask them to take a picture. Anyone. Doesn't even have to be a non-"Mac person." Just watch the hassle unfold. TV's don't have on/off switches anymore. Computers most certainly don't. They have that little circle with the line through its peak—but that's not an "ON/OFF" switch.

I stress this so hard because of how much time—very, very valuable time—can be wasted on something so simple. One day, somewhere in the mid 2000s, my father came home agitated. The state of Pennsylvania had mandated all employees receive "computer training." He was complaining bitterly of how ineffective it was, and how he was left even more bewildered than when he began. Keep in mind, my pops isn't a dummy. College educated, Duquesne law school graduate, many years in the Navy—many years driving these huge, hulking aircraft carriers, using the stars to navigate. This is a smart, intelligent man.

He said something about the computer training that's always stuck with me:

"I wanted to turn the computer 'off,' and the instructor said I had to first hit 'start.' He was using Windows 98, and in those days, you did in fact have to first click the 'Start' button <u>to begin</u> the process of <u>shutting down</u> the computer. Have you ever thought how silly that was? Click 'Start' to 'end.'

This is a dissonance that derails most logical people.

And by logical, I mean NON-geeky people who actually have better things to do than play around with computers.

Again, you might find this is a completely silly issue. But do you know what camera DOESN'T have an "on/off" switch? The RED camera. A $100,000 camera—no "on/off" switch. Sure, it has a button marked "PWR"—but what does that mean? You might know, but I can promise the people helping you won't. "PWR." PWR? Would it have killed them to write out the word "power?" And even at that—what about "power?" Power to what? Me? The camera? The monitor? Push where? Here? There? The red button? Well, you wouldn't dare push that because right below it is the word "REC." Which—maybe—probably—means "record." And if it does mean record, why is it sharing the same button with the "power" function? There's a world of difference between 'recording' and the machine not even being on.

And I stress the word 'SWITCH!' A switch! A switch! That means something that goes from "ON" and flicks up, or down, or sideways, or whatever, to "OFF." On...Off. They are two totally different positions, two radically different propositions that demand and deserve, at the very least, some tangible sense of signifying that you are in one position or another. And by switch...I don't mean a button that you push in, and have to hold, and have to pray has been engaged. I don't mean some cleverly hidden button, I don't mean something you have to shake, something you have to breathe into, something you have to wish for, something you have to blink at, something you have to spin, shake, drown, or whatever clever way a company comes up in turning on their product. I'm talking a good ol' fashioned toggling between 'ON' and 'OFF.' Two different states.

Further more, this "ON/OFF" switch, when triggered, must either lead to the camera actually "turning on," or, it actually "turning off." If you flip the switch and a series of noises must first play, if a couple of little servos must whine and chirp, if first a fan must "boot up," if anything more than 5 seconds has to pass—and 5 seconds is pushing it—then you've got yourself a bonafide piece of junk!

Harsh, yes.

But when you're standing there, desperately trying to get the camera on because—"this is it"—because the actor is finally ready, because the sun is peaking, because the stars and moons are finally aligning, because—"c'mon, c'mon, hurry up, man!!!!"—then you want that thing to TURN ON! There is no waiting on a movie set. At least, not at our level. Perhaps on a Hollywood movie set, where the actor is being paid 20 million dollars, where everyone is making thousands of dollars to patiently stand around and wait for the beautiful, special camera to "boot up." But not here. Not with your friends. Not with the people helping you.

Their time is super, super valuable. Made all the more valuable by the fact that you aren't paying them. The last thing they want to see is you gazing down, chin at your chest, absorbed in waiting by this little device.

Frankly, it's been my experience that, as a general rule, the more expensive the camera, the longer it takes to turn on! No stuff. Perhaps this is because there are more gizmos and gadgets to fire up. I agree—a 747 would naturally need far, far longer to "boot up" than a little Volkswagen. Perhaps that's as it should be.

But not here. Not with the process you're going to be faced with.

You need that thing to turn on—and you need it to turn on FAST.

Remember: ON… OFF. And fast, too.

The camera must have a flip-out monitor. Never buy a camera that doesn't already come with a monitor, a screen (to be more specific). Never. And never listen to anyone who suggests you buy a camera that doesn't already come with one built in. And I mean that even with the knowledge that some cameras require you buy an "external monitor," an "external screen." Frankly, I think that's asking for trouble. It means you are going to have to attach something extra. And then that means you have to attach something to that. First, the "mount." Second, the monitor. And something extra attached, is something that will eventually come unattached. Usually when you're about ten feet over concrete.

More importantly, this flip-out monitor, this flip-out screen must actually FLIP OUT, must be adjustable, in one fashion or another. You're going to be in a lot of different positions when you're filming a movie, and there will come a moment—and you'll remember me saying it when it does come—when you'll be so happy, yes, thank you, that you can reach out and just—*ee*—turn the screen just a smidgen. It's the difference between being able to actually see what you're doing and the sun-glare washing out the picture. I find it totally bewildering that

Canon would make such an excellent video camera with with their 5D Mark III, and yet trap the monitor right into the back of the camera. This is even more bewildering when you consider that the cheaper Canon model, the Rebel, comes with a screen that—yes—pops out, can be swiveled up, down, and all around.

Of course, I can hear the reasoning: "The people using our cameras wouldn't have need for such a viewfinder because they'll be using a separate monitor." Then why even include the screen in the first place?

Because: marketing.

Canon, in fairness to them, isn't totally sure who exactly is going to be buying their cameras. In fairness, DSLR cameras used to be strictly for photographers taking pictures. They only needed that fixed screen. Now? Well, it's kind of an expectation that the camera also shoot video. And, after all, a screen that pops out, that swivels and does all the things a video screen should do, might offend—somehow—the sensibilities of the stalwart photographer.

Alas, there are things we'll never have an answer to.

What's more, not only must this monitor flip OUT, it must actually FLIP. That is to say, you could be in front of the camera, reach around, and flip the monitor toward yourself.

Sure. Again, sounds painfully simple.

And yet…

Just today, I'm looking at the most recent BlackMagic camera, the URSA, or the whatcha-ever-ya'-call-it model. It looks fabulous. It's got all the right specs, all the right ergonomics (more on that later), all of the right stuff. And then, the viewfinder. It pops out, to be sure. It flips, to be sure.

But only half way.

Alas, close—but no cigar.

Further, this monitor, ideally, should ONLY BE A MONITOR, should ONLY BE A SCREEN through which you view things. Please, no 'touch' screens! Ugh. We can't be too picky on this one, sadly. Because it seems, like every electronic in our world, companies have eliminated actual, tactile buttons in lieu of holding valuable camera functions hostage to a screen that doubles as some kind of control surface. Everywhere you look—touch-screens. None of them working without a huge degree of uncertainty from the user, none working without the old "tap-and-pray."

That means waiting.

When the bullets are flying, you want to feel the button "click." No uncertainty. One shot. Like they say in THE DEER HUNTER. One shot!

CAMERAS

Think of it like this: you wouldn't give a soldier a touch-screen trigger for his weapon.

If the camera doesn't have a screen like the one I've described, then let's just say it's a camera you can't afford to be wasting your time on. Just remember: you gotta' be seeing what you're filming—and you need to be seeing it in a reliable, convenient manner.

This camera, meeting all the above conditions, then has to be assembled in such a way. I can only describe that way as "ergonomic." A dressed up word for something that is very agreeable to being held by the average person, in the average environment, in average circumstances. Meaning, you can hold the camera comfortably in your hand for long periods of time; meaning, the entire package, the camera itself, won't end up demanding a host of attachments that will make operating it a feat of acrobatics.

I want you to be able to hold this camera, to move it around fast, to pack it up fast, to unpack it fast, and to move it with speed and agility.

Because you're going to need that. Agility.

The camera should come with some way of being able to <u>actually hold it</u>. A harness, a strap, a, a, a, SOMETHING! Again, if there is no way to hold it, that means this camera isn't really a camera. It's a brain demanding more attachments.

And when you go to put these attachments on—boy, oh boy. Have you ever seen a typical "camera rig?" Forget about the ones you see on a Hollywood set—those are complicated and graceless enough. I'm talking about the one you see on an "indie" set. Where the camera, sitting on the tripod, seems to have vanished beneath a delicate exoskeleton of arachnid-like arms, all precariously balancing very expensive looking toys; monitors, cranks, dials, pins, clamps, cables snaking all about. You marvel that this "camera" at one point only weighed maybe a pound.

Holding this thing? Forget about it.

No. For our kind of filming, you want durable, integral. This camera, this "rig," if you want to call it that, doesn't look like a shambling corpse with its insides and intestines hanging out just waiting to cinch the door handle and gut the entire inside. Integrity. Compact, without being too small. Too small and it just becomes too delicate. Too big, and you can't hold it for very long. You want something in the middle, something with some heft. The Panasonic HVX-200a is a good example of this. It's got a nice, fat heft to it, and when you move it, the whole piece moves as one—no wires and doodads just waiting to snag whatever passes it by. It seems camera companies are aiming toward making cameras smaller.

GoPro, BlackMagic, the iPhone aim to make their cameras very tiny, almost, dainty in size. And perhaps that's nice. But tiny and dainty can easily end up being flimsy.

A camera is a delicate device, and you're going to be putting it through some serious action. Remember—you wouldn't drive a Beamer through a war zone. You'd want, at least, a Humvee. A tank would be better, of course. But for now, think "Hummer."

Then, there is the issue of the battery, of how the camera is powered. I include this in the ergonomic section, because how the camera is powered ends up greatly affecting how the camera "feels." Case in point, the RED camera. The battery that goes on it is less like the consumer blocks your familiar with, and more like the battery that powers your Dad's power drill. Big. A brick.

And sometimes, you can't even attach it straight to the camera.

I was shocked the first time I used a RED camera. Not because of the size of the battery—I expected that—but because, get this, I had to run a cable from the camera down past my body to a clip on my belt that was designed to holster the brick-sized battery. Have you ever holstered a brick on your belt? Uncomfortable. Worse still that you're then essentially—body and soul—tethered to this $30,000 dollar contraption.

I understand, I understand. This is how it was in the 80s, how it was when they first introduced videocameras to the public. Big, hulking affairs that required a battery clipped to the belt.

But that was the 80s! I couldn't believe it. 21st century, and I'm dragging around a battery belt like Garth Algar in WAYNE'S WORLD.

Understand—people will try to persuade you that this is progress. I submit that if your camera requires you to carry around a battery belt, brick in toe, then you've made one step forward, two steps back.

Others will definitely disagree with this—and vehemently so, citing that it's completely worth the tradeoff. But I suspect someone who is willing to make that trade-off has yet to experience—or has forgotten—what it's like in the 11th hour on the set of a no-budget movie. Trust me—when the hours pass, and the novelty of having a big-boy camera has long since waned, and you're just trying—just absolutely desperately <u>trying</u>—to get those last few set ups—you'll be happy you have a camera that isn't so high maintenance.

Remember, moviemaking is a game favored most of all by Murphy's Law. Murphy's Law being the adage that "if something can go wrong, it will go wrong." And that's always in full swing on a movie set. Especially when the tension mounts. <u>Especially</u> when the tension mounts! It's as if Murphy himself is drawn by conflict and anguish, and approaching stop-times (re: the time your friend has to go to soccer practice). The more variables you introduce to the whole equation, the more bear traps there will be waiting to slam shut just as you're about to get that perfect shot.

Therefore, picking a camera is all about eliminating variables.

If you're serious about this, then you have to cut right to the truth of the matter: in the end, do you want to actually make a movie, or do you want to feel like you're making a movie? A lot of filmmakers, with all the gear, gadgets, gizmos, huge lenses, clapboards, rigs, lights, the jargon, the camera tracks, are putting on a big show. Because, truth be told, most filmmakers, most people interested in making a movie, are really, really in love with the entire romance of filming a movie. I know I am. There's nothing headier than a bunch of people, armed with cameras and lights and lenses and dollies and monitors, all surrounding some important event, all trying to capture some kind of magic. It's why "behind-the-scenes" are so much fun to watch. All of that, "SPEED! ROLLING! CAMERA MARKER! AND ACTION!" It's totally thrilling.

Again, some people would rather just feel like they're making a movie.

So, know your interest, and use that to guide whatever camera you buy. You may want to use the RED camera, or, like me when I was 14, whichever one I saw Steven Spielberg poised behind, but you will be far better suited by the one that FITS YOUR PROCESS.

And the one that fits your process is usually the one you can afford. If you can only buy a $200 camcorder, then you should only buy a $200 camcorder—and be happy you can get that! Take it as a message from the world: This is what we think you are ready for, at this point. Be thankful for this. It'll save you from getting in way over your head. Personally, if I had gotten the camera I'd really wanted, I would have had no idea what to do with it.

THE ULTIMATE TEST

All of that said, and with all of that in mind, apply this rigorous test to your camera selection:

"Can I teach my friend, my Dad, my Mom, my helpers, how to use this thing?" In filmmaking, not only do YOU have to completely understand this camera, but you have to understand it in a way that enables you to teach its workings, in minutes, to someone else, including the actors. If anything will surprise you with moviemaking, it's how seldom you'll get to actually operate the camera. For whatever the reasons, you'll find yourself busied with some other important task, and you'll have to—gah—"delegate" the business of operating a camera to someone else. At some point, you're going to be on your mark, in the scene, and you'll find yourself trying to explain to someone else how to turn the camera back on (because you won't want to have the camera on all the time, draining power), how to focus, how to lock on to you, and how to record. The more variables you introduce, the more concepts you'll have to explain. And you will find yourself engaged in many exchanges with bewildered dads and moms, totally confused friends, all terrified that they're going to break this mysterious, obviously expensive, device; all of them just doing their absolute, good-hearted best, to please you.

Don't make it any harder on them.

6
IMPORTANT NUMBERS

When a camera records anything, it records at a certain frame rate. Each "picture" the camera takes is a frame. So, if you have one second of a typical piece of footage, you would have 24 still pictures. And so, when film runs, when professional video runs, it's running at "24 frames per second."

This is described as '24p,' '24fps,' sometimes even '23.976,' or whatever wonky concoction of the number '24.'

I'll never forget when I really learned about frame rates—and how important they are. It was 2004. As a budding filmmaker, I had always used ignorance to shield me from feeling too bad about being unable to obtain the latest and greatest camera. Couldn't afford to know about it! So when my friend was telling me about the new Panasonic DVX-100, I turned a deaf ear.

And so, he's telling me about this new camera, and how it's a game changer. And I'm really jaded, because a camera is a camera is a camera. Or, at least, I wanted to believe that a camera is a camera is a camera.

"No, you don't understand," my friend continued. "It shoots at 24 frames per second." Seeing I was unimpressed, he added, "24 frames per second is what film records at."

Bingo! That caught my interest. You see—to me, as a boy, even now—film was—is—will forever be—EXPENSIVE. And frankly, in Johnstown, PA (where I'm from), there was NO FILM. Read: no film. No 16mm, no 8mm, no 35mm, no 65mm. Nothing, kakka. Or, at least, I didn't know how to get a hold of it.

He pulled out this grey and black camera. He filmed me for a few seconds. Then he hooked it up to the TV, and pushed play.

I was wearing a green t-shirt that day. That's how much I remember this moment. The holy moment! There I was, on screen, in my green tee, just seconds ago, looking like I was actually being filmed with FILM!

I still get excited when I think of this memory.

For me—I don't know about others—it was a revolutionary, exciting moment. That was the moment I knew "it was possible." That is: possible to make a "real film."

Now, maybe it wasn't revolutionary. You could, if you're a super expert, argue that the '24p' could have been achieved "in post." That is to say, I could have taken whatever 30-frames-per-second footage I shot with the consumer DV cam, uploaded it to the computer, then, pushed it through a special effects program like After Effects, or very well just changed the settings of the timeline to '23.976' (that's what the frame rate actually was in the DVX), and voila. Probably.

But you're also reading about a time in my life, a moment in my life, when I didn't know very much in the way of video cameras, and how they operated, and how they could be hijacked, and so on and so on. So, '24p' was a huge deal to me!

I suspect it was to most of my generation.

In fact, I suspect that most of my generation owned, or operated, the DVX100. And used it as their main camera for most of the mid to late 2000s. I suspect.

But that's neither here nor there.

What is here is me saying that you must—must—shoot in 24 frames per second. Whether that ends up being 23.976, or 24p, or 24f, or whatever way the camera companies sell it to you, you gotta' shoot in 24 frames per second. That is, if you want the "film look."

I stress the point because, when I was growing up, cameras only ever—ONLY EVER—shot at 30 frames per second. And 30 frames per second?

A dreadful look, if you ask me.

It's the look of home videos, industrial tapes, promotional materials, news shows, and—worst of all—SOAP OPERAS.

If you want to get a pro-level look, stay away from 30 frames per second, and stick with 24. Just six little frames make all the difference in the world.

And what about the other number-of-frame-rates you might see? In the ads, you'll see, again and again, 60p. And, 120p. And multiples of that number. Since this is a paradoxical topic, I'll be brief: these numbers are indicating that you can shoot in slow motion. I know. A paradox. Why a higher number if you're going to shoot SLOW motion? Because the more pictures going through the camera per second, the slower it takes to play on TV—hence, slow motion. Don't worry if that's confusing.

If you want that big, slowish movement, that dream-like "slow motion" (not the jittery, hazy slow motion you might see in older films), then you need to shoot at a higher frame rate. This can be done while still retaining the "film look."

But that's straying from the important part of this topic.

What is that "p" in '24p' standing for? Progressive. Don't worry. It doesn't mean anything. At least, it doesn't mean anything now. If it ever meant anything, it was from when cameras shot in what was called "interlaced." The frame rate recorded pictures in a certain way, and it was demarcated by the dreaded "i." The DREADED "i." The "i," short for 'interlaced,' meant 'home movie.' Because when you shot, you got these terrible horizontal lines that went through the picture. I haven't seen that in a long time, actually. So, just stick with 'progressive!'

Always shoot at 24 frames per second. All consumer grade cameras have 24p, all prosumer cameras have it, and all pro cameras have it. If the camera doesn't have it—don't buy it!

WHAT TO RECORD "ON"

Recording media. You can have a camera, but the camera needs some kind of media to record onto. Put simply, you need something to record "ON TO." In the old days, the de facto "media," the "medium of recording,"—whatever you choose to call what you're recording your images onto—was film. Back then, the pros shot on 35mm. The "prosumers" tended toward 16mm. The beginners, consumers, shot on 8mm. What these were, what they did, isn't so important to us; rather, it's important to recognize that, even back then, the choice of "recording media" was almost as complicated as it is today. Once you considered the different "MM" variations, the film selection itself broke down into a myriad of "film stocks": all kinds of numbers and letters denoted varying "kinds" of film, all of these split among the varying brands—Kodak, Fugi, Agfa, etc. Then, in terms of film variations, in terms of "what kind of film to record on," it just totally exploded into a matrix of options: Academy vs.

widescreen vs. Super 35 versus 3-perf, VistaVision—and that's just with 35mm film. Then, BH perfs, KS perfs, DH perfs, black and white, color, cellulose dictate (which didn't burn up), nitrate (which did burn up), Kodachrome, Bleach bypass, SuperF negative, IMAX, 65mm, 70mm… and it just goes on and on.

While we can be thankful those days are gone, we now must cipher through an environment that is infinitely more complex than it was 15 years ago. Just a taste of some of the anagrams you'll run into: 720p, 1080p, 2K, 4K, 5K, 6K, 8K, NTSC, PAL, AVCHD, MPG-4, CF vs. SD, 4:4:2 versus 4:4:0, 10 bit versus 12 bit—then, there's the 8 bit—which is always a disappointment—sLog, Rec709, Mbps, Fat 32, SD, SDHC, SDXC, MFX, MB/s, stops, 2:1, 2:4:1, 16x9, 60fps, 30fps, 24p, LT, DNxHR, HQX…

On and on it goes.

By the time this book should find you, the above list will be not only pitifully old-fashioned and out of date, not only will everything on the list be old hat and embraced with nostalgic fervor, what's on the list will pale in comparison to everything that arrives in your time.

It will never get any easier.

Let's just start off with that. It's never going to get easy when it comes time to picking media.

Already your head is probably hurting, you're probably feeling confused and intimidated (I am, and I've been playing with video [and we're talking only video here] for close to 30 years). So, don't worry if this chapter is causing your brain to fog and your stomach to churn.

But it's important.

What you choose, ultimately, to "record" your video/audio on, the specific blend of formats and codecs (which is what's used to make the file size smaller and more manageable), will come to determine your entire process of shooting, and editing, and even more importantly, delivering the movie to your audience.

This topic isn't to be taken lightly.

For the truly tech sophisticated, for a true, expert analysis of this business on what to record your movie on (again, I am referring to media, not the camera), I highly suggest obtaining a copy of a book titled *Digital Moviemaking 3.0*. It's written by an extremely knowledgeable professional named Scott Billups, and it's the book I return to whenever I'm looking for advanced understanding on the subject.

Here, I want to approach the topic with some normalcy. Some sanity. Thankfully, I can promise you're in the hands of someone whose made it through a number of features and shorts, and who has always managed

IMPORTANT NUMBERS

to make media choices that I never regretted.

So, let's depart away from some of these technical terms—which, by the way, are largely due to the multitude of companies trying to monopolize the market. Well, maybe "monopolize" is a strong word—but, it's like the old song goes: Everyone wants to rule the world.

A simple story will bring us back to Earth:

As a kid, I was enamored with the show MACGYVER. It being the 90s, I could only ever catch re-runs that were broadcast on television. Because I wanted the ability to watch the show over and over again, I set out on the ambitious project of "taping" every single episode—stoping and starting the recording to eliminate commercials. I felt this to be a lofty, serious, worthy task. It had to be done right.

In those days, the way you recorded something was via a thing called a VCR (I'm actually hoping you know what a VCR is, but). You needed what were called VHS tapes (just in case you've never heard of those), which were the de facto home video media "back in the day." That is to say there was a "day," and that the day encompassed, roughly, 1980 to 2004. It was the "de facto media" because home video was set up around VHS tapes. Readily available. Cheap. Available at your local grocery store.

But because this was a really serious project, because I wanted my library of MACGYVER tapes to be uniform and complete, I began agonizing over WHAT kind of VHS tape I would use.

At the grocery store, it came down between Sony and Polaroid. The Sony ones sported better quality; meaning, they were more expensive. The Polaroid tapes were cheaper. The decision filled my gut with total apprehension. This was MACGYVER. And taping the entire series would take many months, many painstaking evenings of stopping and starting the recorder, much passion, a little luck, and a lot of love. It had to be done right.

But there's 7 seasons of MACGYVER, and so that's going to eat up a lot of tape. Sure, you could play games on the VCR with what was called "LP" (long play) and "SP" (short play). But I wasn't taking any chances. This had to be done in the highest quality.

At the lowest price point.

As it stands now, I am the proud owner of the complete series of MACGYVER, commercial free, all recorded on a set of 21 Polaroid VHS tapes.

20 years later, I'm still not sure if I made the right choice or not. The recordings just don't measure up to my DVD collection of the show.

In the end, I guess, it didn't really matter.

The key is: it mattered at the time.

And it mattered because of money, space, and expectations. Money—because Mom and Dad were picking up the tab for the tapes ("Maw, we need more MACGYVER tapes!). Space—because, well, 21 VHS tapes don't easily fit just anywhere. Expectations—because, well, capturing all the MacGyver goodness was literally one of the most important things in my life.

So, on one hand, what you record on will matter deeply—today. On another, what you record on will matter very little—in the future.

What options are you going to be confronted with, today, when you go to buy a camera, and ultimately go to shoot your film? As usual, there's a ton of factors.

There are differing "resolution" sizes. Which means how big of a picture you're going to have to shoot on. Currently, you'll see anything from 720p to 8K. When I started shooting on DV video, the standard resolution was 480i. To clarify the concept, picture a postage stamp; now affix it to a standard envelope. The postage stamp is "480" resolution, the envelope is the full '1080p' resolution.

Now, think of that postage stamp and the entirety of the envelope as the canvas you get to work on. If you were a painter, you could either draw on a postage stamp, or an envelope? Which would you prefer, in terms of space?

How about an entire sheet of paper? That would be better, right? Yes! A whole sheet of paper, in comparison to an envelope, would be, perhaps, 2K. Roughly. We're just trying to make rough comparisons.

How would you like two sheets of paper put together, side by side? That's 4K.

Of course, the bigger the paper, the bigger the canvas. And the bigger the canvas the more unwieldy the whole process becomes. Literally. Choosing 4K, or whatever is the "top recording" format may seem like a no-brainer. That is until you start shooting, and your card, or disc, or whatever it is you're filming on out there in 2030, starts overflowing, and you're constantly changing drives or whatever.

Except, these cards, these discs, whatever you're recording on to, will not likely be something you can buy at the grocery store. They're likely to only be available at a Best Buy, at B&H, far away, and very, very expensive.

This I can assure you: recording media will always be expensive.

And deliberately out of your reach.

In the mid 2000s, just as filmmakers conquered the '480' realm—and by 'conquer' I mean that we as filmmakers could get the little DV tapes for cheap. Just as we conquered that peak, just as we had more than

IMPORTANT NUMBERS

enough hard drive space, "the companies," "they," began with 720p, then 1080p. Then we started hearing whisperings of "2K" because that's what "film was," then within the blink of an eye, it was "3K," "4K," now, as of this writing, "they're" pushing 8K.

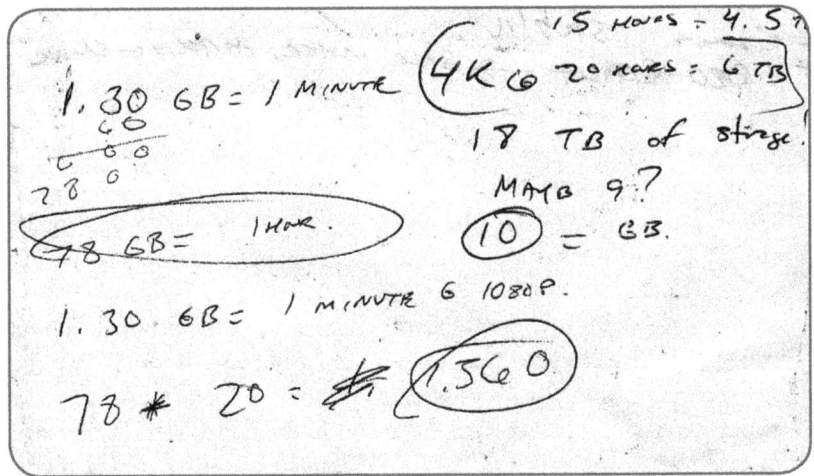

Pictured above are my calculations for how much space would be needed for 4K footage. Is my math OK?

And the bigger the video size gets, the bigger the resolution, the more space needed. Of course, space does get cheaper.

But it's the same old problem I had with recording MACGYVER on the Polaroid VHS tapes: you want the best possible quality for a project you care about, you're tempted to seek out the best possible quality; you can only afford so much, and there is only so much space that can be reasonably taken up by episodes of MACGYVER.

Like cameras, there will always be something better.

The key is in remembering REALITY.

And reality is: this is going to be a big project for you, recording a feature film (or recording episodes of MacGyver), and you're only going to have so much at your disposal. So much time, money, space.

Make it easy on yourself.

And making it easy on yourself means, in a sense, looking back. Whereas everyone, all camera people, electronics freaks, like to look forward at what's just over the horizon, I suggest looking to the past.

Figure at one point a certain resolution DID work, and worked well.

In other worlds: if all the advertisements are pushing 4K, then see about filming on 2K. 1080p, even better! When I shot EMULATION in 2008, when I was doing the math about how much footage I would be shooting versus how much it would cost, when the camera-world was really pushing 1080p—and by pushing, I mean people were doing everything in their power to obtain that holy grail—I opted to shoot the picture in '720p.'

And even that was pushing it.

Because, unlike my VHS tapes of MACGYVER, I wanted to have BACK-UPs of what I shot. In industry jargon, it's called "redundancy." That means that whatever you shoot, you're going to want a backup copy. Then, if you live in the real world, you're going to want <u>another</u> copy—one to be stored somewhere else.

This is really what determines your choice in resolution sizes. You've got to "maintain" the footage. That includes backing it up AND storing the backup.

Factor how long it takes to move the footage from the original camera to your hard drive, to your backup hard drive. Then—if you're like me and not super technically savy—factor in how long it will take to copy everything to yet ANOTHER hard drive. And then, factor in the physical location for that 3rd back-up. Because if your house burns down, if you get flooded, if you get robbed, you're gonna' want to have that 3rd back up in a "REMOTE LOCATION."

Time, money, space.

Make sure you're doing the math and taking all of these things into consideration.

7
WHAT TO RECORD 'ON'

When talking about "what recording media" to shoot on, we have to talk about a thing called a "codec." Without getting bogged down, let's just say this is like… umm… the digital "stuff" your footage is made up of. I initially say, "It's the digital stuff your footage is made up of" because it essentially becomes the soul of your video clips. Technically, it's about how the footage is "compressed." When thinking about "compression," think about how someone going on vacation packs their suitcase. It's literally how the footage is "packed." Simply put, it's either packed well, or it isn't.

To me, 'packed well' is… I can eject the card from the camera, pop it into the computer, open the card's "folder," and then start dragging and dropping clips—unfettered—into the software I'm going to ultimately edit on.

That's it.

And believe it or not, this is where everything usually gets screwed up. This is literally the bottle neck, the end, of all the marketing hype and the lies, and the nonsense, and the competing brands; where it all either culminates in your favor, or in utter catastrophe.

To simplify, if you're lucky, if you pick the right codec, you'll be able to take the footage from the camera to the computer and start watching or editing immediately. Ideally, this is how it should be.

If you're unlucky, and you've chosen poorly, you'll find yourself trying to decipher through a bunch of garbage you could care less about, find yourself downloading "firmware" updates, going on digital wild-goose chases, and changing editing softwares.

Before you make any final decision on what codec to shoot on (and this choice is usually determined by what camera you've purchased), you gotta—and I EMPHASIZE 'GOTTA'—gotta, gotta' make sure you can shoot, then easily—EASILY—move the recorded footage to the computer, then EASILY edit it.

There's no possible way I can prescribe which codec is best. They're constantly changing, constantly being upgraded, and constantly being implemented into a complicated network of editing systems and cameras.

Choice of a codec is like choice of beer. Codecs, largely, are a matter of brand—ProRess, MPG4, H.264, XF-AVC, etc. What's best is what gives you the happiest experience.

What is important, beyond a question of resolution and codecs, is a series of numbers. You'll keep seeing a three digit sequence like "4:2:2," or "4:1:1," or "4:4:4." The three digit sequence usually starts with a '4.' This sequence of numbers has to do with how much color the camera can record.

Let's cut right to the chase: 4:2:0, sucks. 4:1:1 (which I started out with), sucks even more. 4:2:2 (or as it's usually written, 422), good. And 4:4:4, the best.

These numbers are important for two reasons. When you go to "color correct" your footage (a process for making the footage look better), you'll find 4:2:0 gives you limited options. Because, get this, 4:2:0 is not recording the full spectrum of colors. When the camera records to your media, it's tossing out a few of the colors for the sake of brevity—for space.

You can get by with this number, and do so no worse for the wear, but just know that it's tossing out colors.

4:2:2 is better, and better because not only is it "grabbing" more color (more color, better), when you go to do a green screen shot, when you go to do a "visual effects" shot, you'll be able to cut out the green far better than you would with 4:2:0. When my generation filmed with the old DV cameras, which captured something like 4:1:1 or 4:2:0—something like that—we could seldom think about doing green screen work. Because it always sucked! The results were always laced in that fringy quality that smacks of bad special effects.

Now, 4:4:4? You're getting all the colors, ostensibly. For our purposes, this is good!

WHAT TO RECORD 'ON'

Then, there are three other numbers. There's 8 bit, 10 bit, 12 bit. Again, to streamline: 8 bit, the worst. 10bit, good. 12 bit, even better. Although, I imagine you surmised that by the order of the numbers. Bigger is better!

If this is your first rodeo, these numbers are literally going to mean very, very little.

If this isn't your first rodeo, and you want to 'up' your game a little bit, then I suggest seeking out a camera, a recording media, that will allow you at least: 4:2:2 10bit.

The key with all of this, of course, is to test, test, test. Whatever you use, make sure you test it and run it through the entire pipeline of filming, importing, editing, AND delivery to whichever place you're going to deliver your movie. Make sure it works, make sure it works well, and most of all, make sure it'll give you a pleasant ride.

This is important stuff.

8
AUDIO

Audio.
   It really deserves its own section.
   Perhaps you've already heard about how important audio is. Perhaps you've already heard the cliche that "you need good audio." Or that, "lots of movies are ruined by bad audio." Not only do these cliches bear repeating, not only do they bear being emphasized, highlighted, they require a great deal of clarification. Seldom are the cliches about "audio" and motion picture "sound" ever clarified, or placed in any kind of context that the beginner might be interested in taking note of.
   If I seem to agonize over this point, it's because I know how eager you are to just get to filming your movie. Because this field is called 'filmmaking,' 'moviemaking,' you may just believe that creating cinema is, largely, a matter of procuring the correct camera. Sure, movies are primarily "about the visual." At least, that's what one might have you believe. I would say that movies are about their sound—and not their visuals. Or, at the very least, the visual takes a distant second to the priority of sound.
   Yes, that's:
   1) sound.
   2) visual.
   Because our craft is called "moviemaking," it's easy to assume that visuals come first. But as you progress in your craft, you'll find it's the exact opposite.
   Doesn't it stand to reason? Ever sit around with family or friends, watching a great, Hollywood movie, one that's beautifully photographed,

AUDIO

one with all these lush vistas and aerial panoramas—and then, suddenly, right in the middle of everything a family member goes, "whad' he just say?"

"Whad' he just say?"

If you can't hear something, if someone can't understand what was just said, no amount of beautiful photography, no amount of money is going to stop that audience member from jumping up right there in the middle of something like Christopher Nolan's INCEPTION and go, "Wait—whad' that guy say? 'Reception?' What's that?"

And then it just goes down hill from there. Soon as someone can't hear something, soon as they get lost because of that, then—most people—just sit there with their arms crossed, silently, not wanting to sound totally stupid. They don't say, "Well, I got lost because I couldn't hear what they were saying." They just simply say, "That movie sucked!"

In movies, the audio—especially the audio of the actor's talking—has to be absolutely, 100%, crystal-freaking-clear.

No amount of cinematography, beautiful lighting, beautiful composition, can save a movie if your parents, or your audience, or your friends, are leaning forward at the TV the entire time, concentrating on trying to hear.

Further, when was the last time you watched a movie that didn't have sound? I'm talking, dead silence. And no, not even the "silent films" were all together silent. Even then they had someone play a piano along with the movie on screen.

If I hammer this point, it's because I don't want you to have the same troubles I did.

There really is no need for them.

If there's a reason why audio, sound, gets overlooked in beginning film production, it's because the subject is usually presented in terms that you're unlikely to have any frame of reference for; or it's presented with the onerous warning that your best course of action would be to go out and recruit someone to do the sound for you. I remember reading a book that suggested the beginner "find someone" who was a sound specialist. Good advice. But at 14, I found the prospect of finding a "sound man" or "sound woman" not only daunting—but unsettling. Daunting because I certainly didn't know any sound people, nor did I suspect there were any idling about Appalachia just wishing and hoping for an opportunity to provide sound for THE Tommy Getty! Unsettling because, even if I could find someone, I would have—rightly—had hangups about approaching people who are, ostensibly, already professionals at their trade. Professional, meaning... they're paid. Paid means... they don't want to deal with amateurs. Simply put, there are few professionals worth their salt who would want to hang around with amateurs. At least for as long as it would take to make an actual movie.

Furthermore, the equipment required for recording audio seemed… at best… esoteric. I'd never seen any of the suggested items at Circuit City, Wal-Mart, or Best Buy.

Further, the attempt at teaching sound necessitates a whole host of concepts. A 'shotgun mic?' A mics a mic, right? 'Omni-directional?' What's a 'Nagra?' Where do you get one of those polls, you know—that poll you see the one guy in the headphones dangling over the actors? Why do you need that? Why's the guy have to hold it over the actors? Why does the sound person have to move along with the actors? And why does the mic look different from time to time? Sometimes it's got a sock thing over it, sometimes it's got this big fuzzy thing over it, etc.

The teaching of sound is usually presented as such: "Great audio is a must. You gotta' get it."

And… that's that.

I submit this is for one reason. It's easy for an expert to forget their initial—incorrect—conceptions.

So, to begin the topic—and it's a lengthy one—let me tell you about my own initial (mis)conception about audio.

It was my first time actually venturing out with a group of people in trying to make a movie. My first rodeo. I'd stayed up the whole night before, writing the script (yes, the night of shooting!). Yet, I'd never been more alert as I lead my assembled recruits up to the woods, where we were going to shoot a sci-fi epic in the vein of PREDATOR.

And like PREDATOR, I needed a scene where the one character briefs the team leader on the very scary scenario ahead of them:

> "Sir, the craft went down at 0-200 hours; the locator has them making touchdown somewhere on the western face of the region—No SOS, No Mayday, just radio silence. Sir, this was a classified mission—and they have no idea of the creature they're up against!"

To capture this bit of exposition, I envisioned the kind of shot you see in every movie where exposition (that's information about the plot) is wielded out from one of the supporting characters to the hero. You know the shot: the actors are walking TOWARD the camera, but because they're really "big" looking, the effect makes it seem like they're almost walking in place. In my envisioning the scene, not only could I "see" in my mind this shot, I could also hear in my mind the actors talking out the dialogue.

I don't know why, but I just assumed that my envisioning of this would make it so.

Sadly, after I placed the actors really, really far away, I discovered, on screen, the actors were the size of dots. They were totally dwarfed by the forrest! It looked like this:

This, pictured below, is what I really wanted:

Through some trial and error, I figured I could achieve this "big" look by ZOOMING in. And there it was. I could see the actors (my friends) on the viewfinder, from far away. But instead of looking small, they loomed real big. Now, I'd never been more proud of a shot. I had it, right then and there. The trees were hanging above the actors, the road receded behind into infinity. It looked like a real movie.

So, being in the scene as well as directing it, I rushed back to the actors, I gave my camera operator—about 50, 60 feet away—a thumbs up; he flashed one back. Myself and the other actors proceeded to do the scene—and we did it perfectly. This banter going back and forth, all this, "What do you mean it was a classified project? Do you know what this thing is capable of!?!?" I was so elated.

After the take ended, I hustled back to the camera—Christmas morning—I flicked the camera into VCR mode (meaning, the mode you could review your shot in), and, in rewinding it, I could see we HAD actually gotten the shot, and that the actors did move on screen in the way I thought they would, and the whole effect was wonderful. DIE HARD. PREDATOR. **THE LOST WORLD**!

Only problem—I couldn't hear a single thing the actors on screen were saying. I knew the volume was up, because the camera seemed to have no problem in capturing the surrounding ambience of the forrest—lots of birds chirping! It seemed to have captured all the grunting and sighing of my camera operator—those sounds came through like bell! But no dialogue. No voice! Nothing!

For a second, I truly considered just moving on. Exposition be damned! The shot was that good! But I knew the rest of the movie would make no sense if you didn't hear the dialogue about how this creature was, like, really, really powerful and cunning, and—because of budget—invisible! So, I pressed on. I figured, "well, we can't hear because we're so far away." So, I moved the camera up a few feet, zoomed back in—But not as much as before. Did the whole scene over again, ran back, hit 'play,' and then…

Almost the same thing. This time, the voices of the actors were a little more "there." I noticed that the closer WE, as actors, got to the camera, the better the camera could pick up our voices. So, I placed the camera even closer. I lost a little bit of the "grandeur" of my original shot. But I made up for it—kinda—in being able to actually hear the actors. I discovered that the closer I moved the camera, the better the sound.

I did this trial and error again and again, through a process of elimination, until the camera was literally right on top of the actors.

And by this time I was sick, because the whole set-up looked like crap, and it required the camera man to move along with us—which always makes for painful work—and it made the final take look exactly how I DIDN'T want it to look: amateurish.

I truly, truly believe this is why most amateur movies end up with terrible camera work. The young filmmaker, in trying to get the scene, finds the camera isn't picking up the actor's talk, and so eventually, he finds he has to move in <u>right on top of the subject and point at everything he wants to "hear."</u>

This is exactly what I didn't want the shot to look like.

Camera work in amateur movies isn't bad because the filmmaker can't compose a shot—it's because he figures out, through trial and error, that he's gotta' be right in on top of the person if he's to hear any of the important dialogue.

Simply, bad camera work is more a matter of necessity than it is any lack of talent.

The filmmaker, in reality, becomes leashed to the microphone.

Because he or she has yet to figure out… has yet to learn… that a microphone—as obvious as it may seem—does not work in the same way a camera does. Intuitively, you can't just <u>point</u> a microphone at a subject and actually get what it is you think you're going to get. Because unlike a camera, you can't "ZOOM" with a microphone.

And, I know. That sounds horribly elementary, like pre-school. You might say that you're already well aware of this. If you're a professional reading this book, I imagine you're absolutely aghast that you're even reading that someone—at any level—might have that misconception about a microphone.

But, I did. In my 13 year old mind, microphones, ostensibly, worked exactly like a camera—just aim it, and voilà. But that's a trap. If the dismal sound quality of most filmmaker's initial work proves anything, it's that this confusion begins in having a microphone built right into the camera. It naturally makes the beginner assume a microphone works just like a camera.

If you're wondering why microphones are so long, why they're sometimes called "shotgun" mics, it's because, truth be told, microphones <u>have to be almost right on top of the subject</u> in order to obtain a clear, pleasing audio recording.

The trick in getting good audio... and brace yourself for it... is in finding a way to keep the microphone and the camera... separate. So that they can be moved and positioned independently of one another.

If you don't separate the audio, if you actually do rely on the microphone that is already built INTO the camera, then you will live to sorely, sorely regret it. Your production will forever be at the mercy of wherever sound is coming from. That internal mic will end up determining the entire look of your motion picture.

Now, this is a confusing topic. It's the simplicity of the whole thing that makes it so... complicated.

This is why you see the "sound man" standing there, hoisting that broom-stick looking thing up in the air, hanging the microphone over the actors. He's moving independent of the camera.

Before we just leave the topic at that and move on, we have to realize that there's more to this business of recording good audio. Because if you ask a professional, if you look at any reference material on the subject of recording audio for film, they will tell you it's a matter of not only being able to move the microphone and camera independently of one another, they will tell you it's also a matter of recording the audio separately as well.

Meaning, the sound man has his <u>own</u> recorder, the cameraman has his <u>own</u> recorder. Sound and Video are being recorded on two different recorders, with the purpose of later merging them in "editing," in "post production."

It's this part of the process, it's at this point of the whole deal, that I want to stop, and throw up a giant, flashing yellow light—one that says CAUTION, CAUTION, CAUTION.

In the industry, in Hollywood, indeed anywhere video is captured, it is standard operating procedure not only to separate the microphone of the camera (a good thing), but also to record these two media—audio and video—on separate devices. Again, with the purpose of merging them later.

AUDIO

Between you and me, I'm completely against this process. Or, at the very least, I'm extremely suspicious of it, extremely reticent about even considering the two being recorded on separate devices.

Sure, it's the way it's always been done. In Hollywood, everywhere. When they first started making movies, it was something of an innovation to couple picture with sound (movies weren't always "talkies," as they started referring to them in the 20s when sound was introduced). Since the camera really had no way of accepting sound, it then had to be recorded separately, on a separate device. So, they had to start with the "clapboard." You know the thing: It's like a "slate," but it has these zebra-like stripes at the top, where a person flips it up in front of a camera before a take, and then, SNAP! Action! They did this (still do) to create a definite moment on film that could then be identified and corresponded with the audio (you can make out peaks and spikes on an audio track; it's called a "WAVEFORM"). Confusing, I know. But stick with me.

If you're already imagining the difficulty of this process, of taking EVERYTHING you've shot, and then re-cataloging, and then re-joining it up with all of these other different things, then you should go straight to the head of the class! You're right! The process, by the way, is called "syncing." And it's a miserable, nasty affair. It truly is as bad as it sounds. In fact, read Robert Rodriguez's *Rebel Without a Crew*, and see what he had to go through in order to sync up all of his footage with his audio.

So why does the process continue to this day? Why do they—Hollywood and professionals—record the sound separately? I'm sure someone can give a reason. I'm sure someone could explain it. Because, in truth, someone can always, always, always, find an explanation, a rationalization, a story, as to why something HAS to be done a certain way.

Sure, the audio has to be captured by a sound pro, and then some other department has to clean up the audio, has to tweak it, or whatever, and then, later on down the line, in the editing bay, it can be synced up by an intern, or some post-production assistant. There probably is a good reason.

But what if you want to bypass this madness?

You must then rigorously assure that the microphone is somehow patched into the camera, and records onto the audio already being recorded in camera.

Whatever camera you have, it's already recording audio. Meaning, the camera is already syncing up a soundtrack to your video. Why not tap into it?

So, whatever camera you pick, make sure it has some way of physically plugging in a microphone. The key is to be able to move the microphone away from the camera. Even if it is only being able to attach the microphone on top of the camera. You, at the very least, want to get the audio recording away from the inner workings of the camera. My earlier films, shot on an internal mic, are plagued by this sound. This constant hiss, this constant whir of the camera threading and unspooling the tape. Now, that was in the days of recording on DV tape, and that sound has been eliminated. But why bother chancing it? When it's so easy to separate the mic from the camera.

You do it in one of two ways.

One, you ensure that the camera has an XLR input. Don't be intimidated by that collection of letters—'XLR.' I literally have no idea what it stands for, nor do I want to know, nor is it at all important to know—what's important is to ensure that the camera comes with an X-L-R input. This is so you can plug in an X-L-R cable. That's important because only an XLR cable will attach to an actual, good, bonafide quality microphone. Which is something you will buy, if you're serious about filmmaking. Don't play around with this. If you have to spend 200 dollars less on the camera in order to buy a good—decent—microphone, do it!

The XLR cable will allow you to take the microphone and move it almost wherever you please. You can then take the microphone off the camera, run it all across the room via however much cable you have (and these cables are really cheap).

Then, instead of going out and buying a "boom" pole (which, surprisingly, isn't so cheap; it's very expensive, actually), instead of hounding someone to do the very difficult job of holding their arms up in the air, trying to dangle the microphone over the action… you use whatever attachment came with the microphone and you attach it to a tripod.

And you treat the microphone, almost, like a camera itself.

Professionals in the industry will tell you that the microphone needs to be up in the air, tilted down and above the actors for the best possible recording. And perhaps they're right.

But we're not in the industry!

Doing it the way I've prescribed is far better than using the microphone that's built into the camera. Just hooking the microphone up to an XLR cable, just putting it across the room, closer to the action, on a tripod, will put you far ahead of 95% of filmmakers who never give audio a second thought. Trust me! Do this!

Even better would be to purchase what's called a "lavalier mic." A lavalier mic is the kind of microphone guests on talk shows, on the news, have clipped to their "lapel," or tie. You've seen them before. They're small and almost undetectable. And they can literally be placed right

AUDIO

by the source of all your actor's words.

Even better would be if you could procure a lavalier mic that's wireless. A wire is fine, sure. Better than nothing. But if you can eliminate the wire, if you could spend the money on such a system—a system because you need the lavalier mic, a transmitter, and a receiver (that can be placed on the camera)—you would really put yourself on the road to some good filmmaking. You could mic your actor—or actors (if you buy two)—and that would be the end of it. The sound would be beamed back to a receiver on the camera, which is then plugged into the camera via an XLR cable. No more mic set ups, no more playing around with clapboards, no more syncing sounds. Just you, filming your actors, and getting your material in the can.

And that's as it should be.

With all that being said, I have to point out one thing. Not every camera comes with an XLR input. Mostly, consumer cameras don't have them. If there's any distinction between the consumer market and the so-called "prosumer" market, it's the inclusion of an XLR input.

So you're saying, "C'mon, c'mon—I get it. Make sure the camera comes with an XLR input! It's real simple, Tom!"

Well, let me point to a camera that doesn't come with an XLR input: The RED camera.

First thing I do when I try out a camera is to try and attach a shotgun microphone to it. First thing. It just makes me feel good, knowing I can start shooting, picking up audio from far away (why shotgun mics are so long). Just makes me feel, feel… safe! Ready to go, ready for anything. I imagine it's akin to what a sniper feels when he receives a new rifle and he mounts a high-powered scope to the barrel.

Sure, a weapon can fire without a scope. But to what purpose?

Read: a shotgun mic to a camera is a scope to a rifle.

So, imagine my dismay, my surprise, when I was flicking around the RED camera and found nothing in the way of any XLR input. Before this, I believed that XLRs were specifically excluded to just the consumer class of cameras.

The mistake was mine. I was thinking in terms of "price," of something being "advanced."

"Oh, well, it has a 3.5mm jack," a friend informed me.

If you're new, a 3.5mm jack is what's on every single electronic in your house.

In other words, the RED camera is so advanced, so "up-there," that it doesn't even include a professional way of recording sound—yet it DOES come with an input that you can find on any household electronic. A $30,000 camera and it only accepts a consumer grade microphone. Sure, there are attachments. There are ALWAYS E-X-T-R-A attachments. And you can usually buy the extra attachment from the same company you bought the camera from. To be sure, these attachments are always expensive.

Determined to use the RED camera, and determined to record some kind of scratch audio to the camera, I suggested my friend and I obtain a 3.5mm adapter for one of my shotgun mics, if any such adapter should exist.

"Won't work," my friend countered.

And sure enough, after a brief search on the internet, I discovered there are many, many other filmmakers who tried using an adapter—and failed to get any joy. Adapters, when it comes to 3.5mm jacks and microphones, seldom work.

To repeat: the RED camera—along with the Alexa and all of the other industrial models—are made for professionals who don't think in terms of sound, who don't need to think in terms of sound.

Because someone else is handling that business.

But you, I promise, NEED to think about sound.

Perhaps as a note of amusement—the RED camera DOES come natively with a way of plugging in a set of headphones! Read that again. No XLR input, but you get a jack for a set of headphones; ostensibly to listen to the audio that allegedly doesn't need recorded.

The point is that if your camera doesn't come with an XLR input, you're going to have to deal with the 3.5mm jack.

And sadly, dealing with a 3.5mm jack isn't just a matter of buying accordingly. When dealing with a 3.5mm input jack, you've gotta' tread very carefully.

3.5mm input jacks are a murky deal.

If you've ever tried plugging in a microphone (one with a 3.5mm tip), you've probably discovered that it doesn't always work. Some microphones work, some microphones don't. You discover on Amazon.com that you can buy a lavalier mic for $20 dollars. Excited, you buy it, open the package, plug it into that little 3.5mm input jack marked "mic" and you wait to revel in having glorious sound.

And when you play back the footage, you discover there's no sound.

You try the microphone on a little handled recorder—perhaps the kind your Dad or sister uses to take notes. Doesn't work there either.

You must have bought a bum microphone, right?

It's at this point in our discussion about audio that we're about to

AUDIO

open up a whole can-of-worms.

Electronics companies, when it comes to recording audio, will try and play all kinds of games with you. Now, I say that tongue-in-cheek. Kind of. But, in effect, the companies are playing games with you.

Simply put, electronics companies are certain that their general constituency know absolutely nothing about recording audio. So, it doesn't really pay them to make a big deal out of its inclusion. It doesn't really pay them to fuss around and clarify the usage of that 3.5mm jack that they've just included as a, "well, it's there, if ya' need it." It wouldn't pay for them to explain that a microphone, unlike a pair of headphones you might have, requires power—or, at least, that the device you have doesn't power the mic like it powers headphones.

Just a complicated issue. Suffice to say, we take it for granted that the headphones we're used to using—say on our iPhone, or our old CD players—are truly plug-and-play devices. We don't realize that the headphones are pulling a little power from the device.

This is just something I always took for granted.

And yet, whatever accessory you plug into an electronic—it's going to require power.

The same holds true for microphones.

If you find that some microphones work, and some don't, It's usually because of this "power supply" problem.

This holds true for 3.5mm jack-type inputs AND XLR inputs.

Simply put, there needs to be some way of powering the microphone. And most cameras won't supply power to whichever microphone you plug into it. Beware. The whole business is obfuscated beneath a concept called "phantom power." And while it's an important topic, it's going to require some trial-and-error on your end.

Amazon.com has a wide array of microphones that can plug into a 3.5mm jack—and some of them might even work. RODE has a nice line of shotgun mics that connect via a 3.5mm jack, for about $100 dollars. There are other companies too.

Frankly, I trust 3.5mm audio jacks about as much as I trust a trench-coat-clad man lurking the depths of a dark alley. But, it may just be your only hope.

It sure beats using the internal microphone.

Which, incidentally, you won't even find on a RED camera. Not to go back to that. But. Can you believe it? $30,000 dollars and it doesn't have an internal mic! Which, if you've got a team of people, perhaps that's not a bad thing. Again, the camera is made for a different market (ostensibly) (I would argue that they're trying to market to anyone with at least $10,000 bucks). But when I pull footage out of a camera, I at the very least like to have some kind—SOME KIND—of rough audio (professionally called "scratch audio") just to provide me with some kind of aural context outside of what the camera is seeing. Scratch audio can provide some very important "clues" when reviewing footage, and can provide some much needed context—like, "oh, the scene's about to begin."

Whatever you end up doing, however you end up handling this issue, I strongly urge you to avoid the most common method: RECORDING THE SOUND ON A SEPARATE DEVICE.

This, of course, is how they do it in Hollywood. And it's, of course, the most complicated, time inefficient, archaic, uncreative method out there for accomplishing the task of separating the camera from the microphone. More steps, more variables, more trouble. With their process, you need someone to stand in front of the camera with the clapboard, have them clap it down—and doing that gets old real fast. Then, you need someone not only pushing RECORD on the camera, you need an additional person, somewhere else, hovering over yet another complicated, expensive recording device pushing a button marked "RECORD." Read—that's needing two people to do essentially the same thing at essentially the same time—and in the same way. By "in the same way" I mean they both actually have to remember to HIT "RECORD." And if you live in the real world, you know how easily people—especially me—forget to do repetitive tasks.

"Oh, wait, we were recording?"

Then, you've gotta' log all of this stuff—and log it really well.

Because, after you're done shooting, when you're eager to sit down and edit, when you're already dead tired form having written and produced and directed the movie, you'll have to first sit down and sync up every single piece of audio with every single piece of video you shot.

I promise you: it is every bit as grim as it sounds.

If you must use this method—and heaven help your sanity if you do—I suggest one action: Look into a program called "Plural Eyes." Installed in your editing system, it will examine the waveform of the audio recorded with the video, then compare it with the waveform of the audio recorded separately, and it will automatically sync the two up based on the corresponding tracks. Truly a magical program.

But it requires you at least have audio already attached to the video!

Which is why I stress, why I emphasize, MAKE SURE YOU RECORD AUDIO RIGHT INTO THE CAMERA. There's no reason not to. The camera's already recording audio, already doing the painful

AUDIO

task of syncing the audio up. Take advantage of it.

As an aside, here's my vision for the perfect, perfect audio/camera set up: multiple cameras with audio receivers jacked into the XLR inputs. To go further, have the audio receivers just built into the camera. Then, have all the actors wearing lavs, have the the shotgun mics operated by the boom operators—the sound man, the sound woman, the "mixer," whoever has to play with the audio—anyone!—and have it all beam the audio back to these wireless receivers, the audio recording right onto the video's audio track, the whole affair in one, single device.

I'm sure someone would find problems with this. But it's a set up I'm always moving toward. One I'd like to someday see come to fruition.

Whatever you choose, remember this: a Hollywood movie set might have an entire department devoted to the recording, mixing, and storing of sound—but I can promise: It's all going to be on YOU!

It is on you, you, you!

9
TO LENS...OR NOT TO LENS...

As if it's a choice, right? I'm not really sure how to approach this topic. On one hand, I want to report to you all of the wonderful benefits of lenses—and on another, I don't want to lose you as a reader. It's a complicated topic. And made that way by people like me.

First off, let's get it on the table. If you're like I was at 13, you would probably be shocked to learn that some cameras—SOME cameras—do not come with a lens. In fact, not only do they not come with a lens—but you can attach many, many, many types of lenses (and their respective gadgets).

The camera companies call this feature an "interchangeable lens." I recall hearing that phrase a lot when I was a kid, and I confess, I didn't know what it meant.

Again, my frame of reference for cameras was of the consumer variety, the kind my Dad owned, the kind that were sold at Circuit City, Best Buy—and the lenses on those were clearly attached—now and forever—to the cameras they were built onto. To my knowledge, there was no such thing—or need—for "a lens," or the ability to "change" them.

I fear that if I actually knew the benefits of being able to change the lens, if I actually knew that's "how the pros do it," I probably would have bogged down completely, given up, walked away, and never, ever made my first movie. I would have been sucked into the quagmire of price points and glass types. Anamorphic, to me then, was what it meant

TO LENS...OR NOT TO LENS... 135

when you saw the two black bars above the picture. "Widescreen," in other words. Which is what I wanted!

I'm embarrassed to admit it took long into my 20s to discover that Anamorphic is a type of lens.

As I age, I truly begin to appreciate the graces ignorance affords me.

Because if I had known what Anamorphic meant, if I had known that "widescreen" is simply a byproduct of shooting on an Anamorphic lens—and that an Anamorphic lens costs upwards of $30,000 dollars—I would have just given up.

And yet, as you search for a camera, you will see this phrase again and again: "interchangeable lens."

I humbly submit that the "changing of the lens" really demarcates a whole new kind of filmmaking for a filmmaker.

Perhaps it was never meant to be that way.

When beginning filmmakers used to begin with 8mm, they knew that the lens could be attached. In fact, that's how ALL cameras were made.

But, with the advent of home video camcorders, with the discovery that there were people out there like my Dad who just wanted to shoot some home videos, and do a thing called "zoom in, zoom out," then there began this business about "interchangeable lenses."

At least, this is how I explain it to myself.

Because again, it was a surprise to me. And even when it no longer was a surprise to me that you could change the lens of on a camera, it became a point of pride that I bought a camera that didn't have an "interchangeable lens" (Panasonic DVX-100). I suspect I subconsciously knew the troubles—and temptations—that an interchangeable lens would invite.

I broach the subject, however, because there is something available now that wasn't when I was a kid. And that is the advent of photography cameras—known professionally as DSLRs—that can also shoot video. See, it was always easy to find a 'photography' camera where you could change the lens. And photographers, as a lot, were familiar with the concept of changing the lens. Then, one of the companies figured out how to have their photography cameras also shoot video.

Suddenly "DSLRs"—an acronym I'm proud to admit my ignorance of its meaning—caught the interest of filmmakers.

It's a temptation that wasn't around when I was a kid.

And, so... why is this business with changing the lens even a temptation?

It all has to do with getting the background of your image BLURRY. Your subject is in sharp focus, but the background is hazy, gauzy, perhaps totally "blurred."

And that's what the whole business amounts to. Getting that look. Truly. Anyone who tells you otherwise is trying to justify the thousands and thousands—and hundreds of thousands—of dollars they've invested in buying lenses, all in the quest of obtaining that look of the background being blurry.

Of course, they could console themselves—they are getting a better image. A sharper image. And there is a remarkable difference between the lens that comes fixed to a camera sold at Best Buy, and a $40,000 dollar lens (that's just for one lens) used on a Hollywood movie set. There is such a remarkable difference that I even pine for the day when I can just go buy em' all up and retire away to a blissful filmmaking Nirvana.

And yet, a doubt lingers in my mind.

Is it really worth the trouble? Because changing lenses does invite a lot of trouble. It invites a whole host of difficult variables. Price being one of them. If you can get over the initial "sticker shock" of a good lens being $3,000, you'll also be bulled over to learn that "this lens" only provides ONE FIXED VIEW POINT. Industry jargon labels this as a "mm"—24mm, 50mm, 70mm, etc. So, if you buy a 24mm lens, that's it. You only see 24mm worth of a vantage.

What's a 24mm vantage like, you might ask? Well, "it's wide," as a pro might explain it. It's a wide, wide view of whatever it is you're looking at. The higher up the "mm" number, the "closer" the view—50mm being used on close ups, for instance.

So, if you buy a lens—called "prime lens"—then you're stuck at that one view. Unless you buy another lens. And then, even if you buy another lens, keep in mind you still have to change the lens. Meaning, when you're out there in the trenches, and your people are pounding you about time, hurrying you up, and you discover that you want to get "closer in" on the action—and you don't have time to move up from where you have the camera positioned—then you'll have to hold up your hands, pause everyone, reach up, unscrew the camera—and therefore exposing all of the inner guts of the camera to the elements—pull off that lens, cap it (because you don't want the naked end of a lens exposed!); then with your other hand, uncap the other lens (so you're effectively doing this one handed), pop that onto the camera, and screw it tight.

In other words—you can't just zoom in on the action. Whereas you can zoom to your heart's content with a camera for under $1,000, it suddenly becomes way more expensive, or impossible, once you reach the level of the BlackMagic and RED cameras.

There's legitimate, actual reasons, to be sure, as to why this paradox

TO LENS...OR NOT TO LENS... 137

occurs.

But—gee, I don't know; I'm of two minds when it comes to the topic.

On one hand, the purist in me, the guy who was just last night watching MEMENTO and agonizing over which lens—exactly WHICH lens—was used by Wally Pfister and crew to cover the action—wants to demand, demand you only use a camera that comes with the ability to change out the lens.

And yet, I keep thinking of that movie ONE HOUR PHOTO. You know the one? Robin Williams stars as this psychotic, obsessive photographer who insists that all photos be shot on a certain kind of film, who literally goes through a psychotic break when he's discovered and punished for administering such rigorous standards on the photo-developing process on his job at… Wal-Mart. It's called something else in the film, but he essentially works at Wal-Mart, developing photos at the one hour photo booth.

I vaguely remember this one shot where Robin Williams starts tearing out his own eyes. The metaphor isn't lost on photographers in the audience.

At one point, his boss is forced to offer him some friendly advice: "This isn't Neiman Marcus."

This isn't Neiman Marcus.

Sy "the photo guy," the hero of ONE HOUR PHOTO, forgot where he worked. You see, he forgot his purpose. And his purpose was to develop one hour photos for the people who got their pictures developed at… Wal Mart.

Am I suggesting that we're only getting photos developed at Wal-Mart? Of course not. I submit the allegory, the analogy, as a means of keeping perspective.

Which is most important when it comes to deciding on whether you want a camera that can change lenses—or—frankly—when it comes to deciding on anything in filmmaking.

Perspective.

I have no idea on knowing what your particular situation is.

Maybe you're like me at 14—completely bewildered that the notion of a "lens" is even being discussed—"A lens is a lens? They all come with one."

Maybe you've had access to a photography camera, a "DSLR," and you're already well versed in the art of apertures (which we'll touch on), ISOs, ND filters, the fun of "swapping" lenses; you think of photography in a totally different way than I did at 14. To you, a lot goes into achieving a certain look.

Maybe you're like Sy "the photo guy"—a die-hard purist, absolutely refusing to shoot on anything less than a 50mm Anamorphic piece of glass produced and manufactured by Panavision, absolutely refusing to shoot anything less than 35mm film, tossing and turning awake all night in bed, eyes open, fantasizing about grain and aperture, fantasizing the doom and death of film, imagining a world where any and all standards about shooting photography all totally go out the window in lieu of idiots running around shooting pictures on their iPhones. You're nothing short of apocalyptic when it comes to film photography.

You are, in other words, an expert.

I'm slightly embarrassed, slightly proud, to admit that I'm now in the Sy "the photo guy" category.

But just remember: this isn't Neiman Marcus.

If you're a beginner, if you're like how I was at 14, if you're surprised to learn that there are cameras that offer the ability to "change" the lens, if you're a normal person yet unbaptized and neurotic by all the nuances of shooting the perfect image—then I highly, highly, highly... highly... suggest you buy a consumer grade camera.

Answering the lens question is a point where I can confidently point you in one direction or another.

Buy a consumer grade camera, one where it already comes with a lens, one that already affords you the ability to zoom in, and zoom out—and be happy. You will have plenty of time later, later on—like when you master all the other important aspects of filmmaking of dealing with people, securing locations, getting your shots, and actually finishing the movie—to fret and scratch your eyes out over the difference between Anamorphic and Spherical lenses.

The truth of the matter is, the only reason this whole thing ever becomes of interest to anyone, anywhere, is the interest all filmmakers have to BLUR OUT THE BACKGROUND OF AN IMAGE. That's it.

And thankfully, that can be done with a consumer grade camera.

Trust me. You will find a very pleasing result by placing the camera far away from your subject—and zooming in. And I promise, the background will blur out and the actor will remain in subject. It looks "just like a movie." Trust me.

It takes a shift in thinking to even begin worrying about lenses and changing them. If you're like I was at 14, then you more than likely think of film photography, largely, in terms of BRIGHTNESS and DARKNESS. If you think in those terms, that's a sure sign <u>you should just go ahead and buy a consumer grade camera</u>. When you go to shoot, you will either want things "brighter" or "darker." It's important to note

TO LENS...OR NOT TO LENS...

that this isn't how cameras work—but what's even more important to note is how you THINK. Because how you think, if you're in this area, is only going to be slightly better than how your friends and family and your recruits are going to think about movie photography.

In the so-called "professional world," it's the complete opposite. Instead of naturally thinking in terms of "brightness" and "darkness," it's "apertures" and "exposures." In the professional world, when it comes to movie photography, everything is a paradox.

But, if you are interested in learning, if your brain doesn't fog over as easily as mine did—and still does—then we'll get to it in the chapter about lighting. I just want to leave an "out" for the people who are anxious to get to the business of making movies, and not totally intimidate them with jargon that I still don't really appreciate.

Just so were clear, that's an "exit."

If you're still interested, let us segue into the equipment of lighting—and how it's all tangled up with this business about "the lens."

10
LIGHTS!

This being a book about bare bones productions, I'm half tempted to say, "forget using lights!" And even further tempted to say, "they don't matter!"

And yet…

They do. Lighting matters. Professional lights are good. I mean, it's truly miraculous the first time you really see what a good light can do—that is to say, what good they can do when correctly used in tandem with the camera.

But, before you can really appreciate a good light, even before a good light would do you any good, we have to establish a few other things.

I place this section about lighting and lighting equipment right after the section about "to lens, or not to lens" because the two concepts—lenses and lighting—when you get right down to it—are intimately connected. And in a way that may or may not be all that great to get into right now. Understanding movie lighting, and how it works in tandem with what the camera actually sees, requires a profound shift in thinking about "light" and how movie cameras "capture it."

A short story to clarify:

One day while shooting a scene, I needed someone to 'man' the camera because I was going to be in the scene, walking. The scene called for some camera movement. Always a risky proposition.

I recruited my Dad.

He was the only one around, and, usually—thankfully—he's happy to help me out.

I give my Dad the instructions on what kind of camera work I wanted

LIGHTS!

(we'll get more into that later); he nods, accepting the instructions; I go into the scene, and I go through some really complicated ordeal, giving it my all. When I'm finished, when I look over to say, "cut," I see my Father, pinching the tripod handle, squinting <u>not</u> at the viewfinder on the camera, but at the camera itself. His expression is that of someone who just discovered a rat lying dead on the floor. He looks really confused, and really offended.

He looks like he's wondering why he ever had kids.

"Is it supposed to be all black?" He grunts.

I jogged over to "review" the footage, switching the camera into 'play' mode, hitting 'play'—and. Boom. Dead in the water. What I see goes as follows:

The image pops up on screen, just as I'd set it up, just as I had left it framed and composed for my Dad. Then, on screen, the action begins. I enter the frame. And as as soon as the camera begins to follow me—

The entire picture goes black.

I could still hear the soundtrack, the whine of the cicadas, of me walking through the field, but it was all black. Nothing on screen.

Then, all of a sudden, the picture came roaring back in a wash of daylight, and everything, the entire image, looks, as you might say, "blown out." You know the look—it looks as if the sun has completely exploded, washing everything out in pools of absolute white, obliterating all semblance of any shapes, the highlights just eating everything up—

And then it then it went black again.

It's moments like this that will force your interest in things like 'exposure' and 'lighting.'

See, my Dad had just inadvertently discovered the "aperture wheel." Which on the particular model of camera we were using, the Panasonic HVX200a, is located just behind the zoom.

But what's an 'aperture?'

When talking about "lighting equipment," or movie lighting in general, talking right off the bat about the best kinds of lights, the best lighting setups, the best lighting technique, is virtually pointless without a basic understanding of how lighting actually works in tandem with a camera.

Right away, let me just say "movie lighting" is not only complicated, it's paradoxical.

It's hard for me to gauge how you think about lighting. But if I had my guess, if you're anything like I was, then you think about light in terms of subtraction. I.e., you think about lighting in terms 99.9% of the planet thinks about light:

You care about it to the extent that it isn't there.

You think about lighting in terms of "brightness" and "darkness." Something is either too bright, or it's too dark. Yet, the learning of lighting, the dealing with it, the contending with it, the achieving it, is about understanding how your camera views light.

That's where I want to start the discussion about movie lighting. In darkness. Literally. And metaphorically.

A traditional chapter about movie lighting would begin with suggestions on the kinds of lights to choose from—halogen, fluorescent, etc—their various brands, the color temperatures, the accessories, the differences between various kinds of electrical sockets, the difference between AC and DC, on and on. In other words, jargon that you're expected to immediately understand.

I vividly remember reading chapters about lighting with a lot of trepidation. And not just because of my own ignorance. But because I was seeing items I just knew, just knew, would be profoundly expensive. Phrases like "3-point lighting" (you mean I gotta' get three lights?!?), 600 watt, 1,500 watt, just made me hear the ka-ching sound.

A simple perusal of the lighting section on B&H will confirm these suspicions.

So, I want to start the chapter on lighting not from the lights… but from the camera itself.

You have to understand why you would even <u>need</u> to buy—or, worse, rent—those big huge lights in the first place.

Because that's what this whole business of lighting revolves around.

<u>What you see is not what the camera sees</u>. Obvious, yes. But it bears mentioning. I'm sure you've figured out by now: what you see is never what the camera actually ends up recording, and thus, spitting out.

Before we go any further, I want you to go find a dark room with a mirror—probably a bathroom—close the door, look at the mirror. OK? Look yourself in the eyes—and pick a single eye to look at. Take note of your pupil, which is that black part in the middle of your eye. Depending on where you've come from, that black dot, your pupil, is either really big, or it's really small—less like a dot, more like a pinhole.

Just take note of that black dot.

Now, turn the lights off. Wait a few seconds.

With your finger on the switch, with you looking at the mirror, flip the lights on—real quick, try to catch your eye in the mirror. It might take a few attempts at this, but sooner or later, you'll see something you've probably seen before—but never took serious note of: that black dot, that pupil, suddenly shrinks from a large circle, to the size of a pinhole.

If you've never tried this before (you most likely have) it's really amaz-

LIGHTS!

ing to see; literally, you're seeing something happen to your eye with your own eye. And that something is the shrinking. And if you could somehow have a little light in the bathroom, when you turn the light off, you'd see your pupil expand, enlarge.

So, it goes like this—more light, your pupil shrinks; less light, the pupil enlarges.

You have to understand this is exactly how a movie camera works.

Now, try the experiment again. Turn off the light, turn it on. Watch how your eye reacts. It instinctively shrinks! It's truly amazing if you ask me. Your eyeball just does this naturally, without you having to think about it, or operate any kind of wheel.

Why it works like this, how it works like this, all of the scientific stuff, is completely incidental to our needs. You just need to understand what it means. And what it means is that your eye only wants so much light.

Let me repeat that again. Your eye, like a camera, only wants so much light—and only the exact amount that it wants right at that point in time.

Why your eye does this, I'm not sure, and thankfully, as filmmakers, we don't have to know or be sure. But why a camera works essentially the same as an eye, and requires this same shrinking and opening of its own "pupil," is because of a thing called exposure.

You've maybe heard this word before. "Exposure." In real life, it means something being exposed to the elements. In the film world, in the technical part of the film world, it means how much light is exposed to the "film," or to the "recording media." Between you and I, it means… brightness… darkness.

I know, I know. I can just see the professionals shaking their heads. And, well, there it is. Exposure is all about brightness and darkness. If this were a truly technical class, we wouldn't be talking like this. But for our purposes: exposure = brightness, or darkness.

Because it's through understanding this, through grasping the 'exposure' notion, that we can then loop around and confront the true gatekeeper of lighting:

The aperture.

Hold on. Hold on. Aperture. Aperture. A terrifying looking word. At first glance, it means almost nothing. Maybe it has something to do with a camera, or, at best, photography. Aperture. I don't want to talk about this word, I have a vague feeling you don't want to talk about this word. But we have to talk about it. I've wanted to avoid all—or most—jargon in the process of this book. But this is one thing we have to learn about, and understand.

Better to get it out of the way.

First, let me just say that I personally think "aperture" is a silly word. I submit that it's a word that the camera pros believe the great unwashed masses know, or should know. I humbly submit that no one, not even the majority of photographers—including me—really knows what it is. Just look to Apple, and their release of a computer program for photo editing, years ago, called "APERTURE." Since 2014, that program is no longer called "Aperture"—it's been discontinued in favor of a photo program called, simply, "Photos."

Get it? They too figured out it's a silly word! A word that no one knows, or cares about. Just doesn't stick. Doesn't sell.

Truth be told… it's a fancy word for "hole." Aperture. It's a hole. Just look it up. "A hole," "a gap." For our uses, it's an opening. More specifically, it's the opening to the camera. But even that confuses the issue. Because wouldn't that be the lens? No stuff! You might believe that the opening, the hole to get inside the camera, the little hole capturing all the action, is the lens itself! Don't feel bad if you think that. And if you're a professional and don't believe me that someone would make this misconception—just look to Apple and the original box art for Apple's "Aperture 3." Google it. What's that a picture of? Not an aperture. It's a picture of a lens.

Nevertheless, the concept of an 'aperture' is going to haunt you the whole way through your filmmaking. You'll read all these descriptions about the aperture being "open," or "closed," and to what degree, and to what "f-stop,"—and ugh. A common exchange with a film expert might go as follows:

Beginning Filmmaker: "Can we go darker?"
Pro Filmmaker: "Bump it up, yea?"
Beginning Filmmaker: "No, darker."
Pro Filmmaker: "So, add a few more stops?"
Beginning Filmmaker: "Just… darker."
Pro Filmmaker: "So, go up a stop?"

A stop? The terror of the "stop." The terror! If anything'll make you queasy about photography, it's the word "stop." You think, "stop." Like, "halt." Right? So, being a dutiful filmmaking student, you seek out an explanation of what a "stop" is. You find something like: "it's the doubling or halving of the amount of light."

Oh man. Hopeless.

Perhaps, growing fearful, feeling that you're losing control of the situation, you start with, "Just… just… MAKE IT DARKER!" The pro filmmaker, the photographer, throws up his hands, starts with the, "*Fine! Fine!*" And then he just cranks the image and it all goes almost totally

LIGHTS!

black. You can see everything, sure, but it all looks... it's...

"It's too dark now!" You say, starting to worry that you're in over your head. And this could go on and on until the cinematographer, or you, figures out that the crank or wheel can be set at a certain number that makes the picture "look good." Now, what "looks good" is beside the point.

So, while he keeps cranking the dial...

You notice that the turning of this dial correlates, maybe, with a number on the screen of your camera. It lands on numbers like "1.4," "2," "4,"—you notice that the higher these numbers go UP, the darker the image on screen gets. So, alas, you surmise that this will safely control what you perceive as brightness and darkness. You probably find yourself staying away from "1.4," because it REALLY gets bright and "BLOWN OUT," and land on some higher number. If it's a really bright day, you'll probably find you can't GET this number high ENOUGH—16, 22.

What these numbers mean, what they do, understanding them, isn't so important—if you only care about the brightness and darkness of the picture.

And perhaps, you will find yourself, at least in the beginning, being quite content with just correlating these ambiguous numbers with how dark or bright the picture gets. Because you may find, in being a dutiful student and trying to learn about what's happening, that the numbers themselves end up betraying an even more confusing subset of actions— higher is smaller, lower is larger.

What you think of as going 'up,' is actually going 'down,' and what you think of as getting 'smaller,' is actually getting 'larger.'

Suffice to say, you can make a film, can get through the shooting of a movie, without understanding what these numbers mean, how the aperture works, all that—and live to tell about it.

True confession: I cruised through about 4 or 5 shorts, and a feature and a half without really understanding the numbers—or at least, only understanding them in terms of "brightness" and "darkness."

And that's fine.

This is heresy, mind you. And it's not going to garner you or I any speaking opportunities with the ASC (American Society of Cinematographers). But for your purposes, for just getting your movie going, for getting it out there—it's fine.

This is truly a bewildering topic. If anything could send you packing, it's this business about 'apertures' and 'stops,' and these strange numbers.

With all of that being said, with all of that out of the way, with saying that you can "get by" just dialing through those numbers until the picture looks good, let me then go to the next step…

…which is in explaining what you'll be missing if you don't want to understand these numbers.

Simply put, these numbers, all of the hair-pulling about them, all of the fussing, the whole thing with the photographer sticking up that little remote control with the white cueball in it and clicking it at the lights, all has to do, primarily with one, very important thing that may very well be of deep interest to you:

Getting the blurry look.

Yep. We're back to that again. You probably have very little interest in what an aperture is (again, no one was less interested than me!), but I will bet a thousand bucks, will bet the farm, you want to get that blurry look: the actor in focus, everything behind him out of focus.

If you want to get that look, read on.

I'm not even going to try and explain what's "actually going on," because it really doesn't matter. What's important… what you need to know… is this:

The lower that number (f1.4 for example), the more blur you're going to get.

The higher that number (f5.6, for example), the less blur you're going to get.

That's it.

That's what it ALL BOILS DOWN TO.

Real simple, right? You want that blurry look, so you just roll that number down to 1.4. You get the camera down to f1.4, you look at the monitor, and then suddenly you curse me—because—ugh—now it's "TOO BRIGHT!" And too bright to you means everything has seemingly lost its shape; everything is washed out in light, everyone looks like a ghost, and everything has that "BLOWN OUT" look to it. Seeing this, you sense I don't know what I'm talking about, and you real quick crank that wheel, that number, back to something like f/8. There, that did it. Right?

Hold on a second.

Before you roll the camera up out of "1.4," I want you to remember what happened when you went in the bathroom and turned the lights on. Your pupils shrunk. Your eyeballs, in trying to keep correct vision, instinctively "dialed down" to keep the added light out.

This right here, this phenomena, this notion that an eyeball—a camera—only wants SO much light—and that it only wants the EXACT amount of light that it wants—is why, when you see a huge, huge movie

LIGHTS!

crew filming on a city street or in a field OUT IN BROAD DAYLIGHT, that they ALSO HAVE A TON OF HUGE LIGHTS BLARING IN ADDITION.

Have you ever seen that? A picture of it, of course. Huge film set, broad daylight, clearly MORE THAN ENOUGH SUN, and yet, they have these barrel-like spot lamps blazing.

Why do they need even more light? Maybe you figure the cameras just really, really suck. Or, at the very least, you figure maybe they just have a lot of extra money and like the look of all those big spot lamps (you wouldn't be too far off on that one, but no.).

In fact, you would be even more bewildered if I told you—and this will really blow your mind—that the camera man is putting a darkened piece of glass over the lens TO KEEP LIGHT OUT!

No stuff. Can you believe that? Not only is it broad daylight, not only is the sun pounding down—I mean, people are standing around wearing sunglasses it's so bright—but they also have these big, huge lights pounding on the actors.

And the cameraman is essentially putting sunglasses on the camera?

Hello!?!? If it's so bright, turn off those freaking lights!

There's a reason those extra lights are there—and that the cameraman is placing, essentially, sunglasses on the camera. A very good reason. And one that brings us back to why we had to climb down this rabbit hole when we first started talking about what kind of lights to buy.

In reality, what it all comes down to is this: whereas you think it's all about "adding" lights, to the pros...

IT'S ABOUT SUBTRACTING LIGHT.

Notice I didn't say "lights." To repeat—you think, and naturally I might add, that movie lighting is all about "adding" lights. Because, as we said—people care about light in a movie to the extent that it isn't there: "Hey, this is too dark! Add some lights!" But to a camera, it's all about keeping out all but the most essential of light.

Remember, the camera only wants so much light—no more—and no less.

Understanding movie lighting—getting "good shots"—is all in understanding that the action is with the camera—and not the lights.

In other words, how much light you're letting into the camera.

If you were to go out in the sun, your pupils would shrink. Your eyeballs are saying, "Woah. Too much light."

But what if you didn't want your pupils to shrink? For whatever reason, you don't want your pupils to shrink. In fact, you want your pupils to be big and open, but you want them to be big and open out there in the sunlight.

What do you do?

You put on a pair of shades.

A good pair of Ray-Bans.

This is tricking your eye into thinking it's darker than it actually is. And so, your pupils would enlarge.

If your eyes were a camera… your camera would produce a very nice image—one that is neither too bright nor too dark—but that also—and this is KEY—**GIVES YOU THE BLURRY LOOK YOU LIKE SO MUCH**.

Great cinematography, good shots, "great shots," begins with this understanding. *It begins with tricking your camera into thinking it's in a darker environment than it actually is.* This is accomplished by putting sunglasses on the camera.

Except, in Hollywood, on a professional movie set, they don't put Ray-Ban sunglasses on the lens. They use what are, essentially, sunglasses made specifically for a camera. These are called ND filters.

Now, what "ND" stands for doesn't matter. Just "ND." On a professional movie set they will take a piece of glass—an "ND filter"—and slip it over the lens, thereby tricking the camera into thinking it's darker out than it actually is. This bluffs the camera into enlarging its pupils, thereby getting the brightness level just right, but also achieving MAXIMUM blurriness behind the actor or subject.

So, how does this circle back to lighting?

Well, by putting sunglasses on the camera—essentially—by making it darker—you are thereby making the picture darker. And the picture may literally look too dark. And you'll be tempted to take off those sunglasses. And, sure, you can dial that "f/" number up to a place where the image is "just right," is "exposed correctly." But I promise you won't get the blurry look anymore.

By leaving the sunglasses on, by leaving the ND filter on, moviemakers are then forced to put up those huge, huge lights—even though there's clearly enough sunlight already. They're being forced to blast in more light. Hence why those lights are so bright in the first place. They've tricked their cameras into thinking it's dark out so that they can get that blurry look. As a price, they have to ADD in more light, thereby achieving a good look—this, all the while still hoodwinking the camera to keep its pupils WIDE OPEN.

Confusing?

Seem like a lot of work?

You betcha'!

LIGHTS!

And this is the REAL reason why movies use lights.

Yes, true, they want to create a "look." Yes, true, they want to create a "mood."

But this, this process about putting sunglasses on the camera, is the real, end-of-the-line reason why "lighting" is such an issue with making movies.

It's because the moviemakers are trying to get the image "just right."

Again, to re-iterate, movies are not lit, primarily, to create a mood. There isn't a lighting department, a lighting crew, simply to add more of a creative flair to the "cinematography. Movies deal with lighting, primarily, TO MAKE THE IMAGE JUST RIGHT.

And "just right," means, "properly exposed." And "properly exposed," for you and I, means, "not too bright, not too dark." It means, in terms of image, that all of the details are included. You can see the sky, and you can see the person shrouded in shade under the tree. Because, if you've ever filmed anything, and left the auto exposure on, you'll notice that camera alternates between making everything but the sky pitch black—showing everything EXCEPT a totally bright, totally blown-out sky. It's what our eyeballs are doing for us when our pupils shrink or expand—it doesn't want us looking at a world that is far too bright, or far too dark. It's properly exposing things for us.

Movies are lit… primarily… for exposure reasons.

Movies are not lit, primarily, for creative reasons.

If there is this misconception, it's because of that old chestnut that we've all heard: "lights, camera, action." Which literally suggests that a real movie—a real, honest to god movie—actually NEEDS TO BE LIT. As if some de-facto force has decreed any kind of movie that plays in a theater must be lit—and must ONLY BE LIT—with the best and most expensive of lights.

Not true.

You can get by, just fine, without any lights.

Their absence is not a deal breaker.

Most cameras, especially now, can see just fine. And you'll get by, just fine, dialing your image via that "f/" number. Remember—crank it up, the picture gets darker. Crank it down, the thing goes brighter. That's it. And if that's as far as you want to take it—well, that's OK.

I know I did just that—for years.

And truth be told, my movies always, always, always looked very, very nice. Never heard one complaint about the so called "cinematography."

Now, of course, that's not to say "cinematography" isn't important, or that, for that matter, professional lights are way overrated.

No, not at all.

In fact, it took two technically sophisticated people to, so to speak, "show me the light." I will happily admit, because of these two technically sophisticated, technically inclined and smart people, I now only want the best of lights—the brightest, the best, with all the clamps, and those umbrella-like things placed over the lights (the kind you see when you get your yearbook picture taken), and the gels, and the HMIs, and the LEDs, and the proper color temperature, and all the stuff that gets yanked over and falls, and breaks, and explodes, and sets fires, and makes people hot, and makes people whine and complain, and fries electric sockets, and forces a power outage, and snakes about, and hogs all kinds of time—

TIME YOU DON'T HAVE.

I'll happily admit that I love all of that stuff—now.

But when I was "shown the light," when I really took a shining to "lighting," and really understanding it, I'd already done 5 shorts (one of them almost an hour), and grown hungry for more ways of improving my work.

Maybe you want to do that now.

I would argue that good lighting can be achieved without all the hoopla of a massive Hollywood set.

And that can be done in ways other than spending thousands and thousands of dollars on lights. If you want lights, use the ones Dad already has in the garage, or try the utility lights you can buy at Wal-Mart or Home Depot for $50 bucks. Either one of those will give you more light than you know what do with.

If capturing "good cinematography" is of huge interest to you, I suggest you divorce the concept of "cinematography" from the concept of "lighting." Instead of lights, and worrying about lighting, I suggest grabbing a photography camera—one that takes stills—and you go out and you take pictures. Just take pictures. As many you can. Look at them. Are they pleasing to you? Take some more. Get a feel for "centering" the shot, or for keeping it slightly off balance. Perhaps, in your travels, you may come across the "rule of thirds." Which I won't cover here because it's beside the point.

If you take enough pictures, you'll start to develop "an eye" for taking "shots," you'll start to get a "natural" feel for it. "Natural," of course, is a deliberately chosen misnomer. What's happening is that you're accruing an ability to "frame" a scene, and capture it in a reasonably pleasing manner—absent setting up a whole movie set around your endeavors.

LIGHTS!

Sometimes you'll get pedestrian results, sometimes you'll get some real "wowers" that you'll want to hang on to.

In other words, I beg you to separate the business of taking a picture from the machinations of producing a motion picture. You don't want to be trying to learn to do two things at once—because they ARE two different things.

Just remember: movies aren't lit for "aesthetic" or "cinematic" reasons. They're lit to expose an image.

Everything else is… well… extra.

Closing out this section on equipment, I encourage you to really give the subject some serious thought.

Also, just get in touch with me at **camera@tomgetty.com** if you want my thoughts about your potential camera and equipment choices!

PART 3

MAKING THE MOVIE

11
RECRUITING

A cursory glance at the credits of any movie will verify just how many people are involved in the making of any motion picture—major or not.

Outside of the director and the actors, there's the director of photography, there's the producers, the executive producers, the line producers, a production manager, a unit manager, a production coordinator, a first assistant director, a <u>second</u> assistant director, a location manager, a location scout, a set director, a casting director, a sound man, a sound operator, a sound mixer, special-effects supervisors, script supervisors, costume designers, costume supervisors, camera operators, steadicam operators, stunt coordinators, loaders, gaffers, grips, dolly grips, key grips, best boys, illustrators, carpenters, prop masters, on and on, and on—

This doesn't even begin to include the army of technicians who shepherd the post production process.

A cursory glance makes you realize that the subject of cast and crew deserves a lot more than just a cursory glance.

If the previous section dealt with equipment, the necessary tools, the physical "stuff" needed to actually make a movie, this section deals with the more nuanced, the more psychological aspect of making a movie: recruiting people.

For an artist, or anyone inclined toward the arts, few things are more unpleasant. I believe most artists are, by nature, introverted. They spend—necessarily so—most—if not all—waking hours in their own mind, mulling and stewing over the vision of their output. Dealing with people itself is difficult enough. Recruiting them, a whole other ball game.

First, you have to understand what making a movie actually is.

It is moving furniture.

That's it. If you can get your mind around that, you'll be successful in finding help to make your movie. Moviemaking has very little to do with actually making a movie. Picking out camera angles, directing actors, lighting a scene, the actual filming, the fun stuff, accounts for less than 2% of all that occurs during the creation of a movie.

It's for this reason that, when recruiting, you can and should completely bypass anyone who has any aspirations of working in the "film business," in "the biz," in "the industry." Don't even bother seeking out people who appear to share an interest in filmmaking.

The problems with seemingly like-minded folks are many. The biggest problem being that aspiring moviemakers—especially ones in the early stages of their ambitions—are always, always under the belief—or have yet to be *over* the belief—that the movies they love so much were, largely, directed.

It likely still resonates with them that a film was "made by" such-and-such director. The aspiring filmmaker sees "directed by" and believes that the movie was actually made by a single person, only assisted by an army of barely legible names buried in the credits. Yes, a Christopher Nolan film is different than a Steven Spielberg film; yes, a David Fincher film is profoundly different than a Martin Scorsese film—but the differences, for practical purposes, for the purposes of someone aspiring to actually "be a director" or to "make movies," is negligible. The aspiring director has yet to fully realize both intellectually and emotionally how insulated the typical director is by an army of master craftsmen, actors, and technicians.

In other words, most—if not all—aspiring film people believe that their greatest chance of success at creative self-expression is in being a "director."

When in reality, it's the exact opposite! There's few things more banal, more mechanized, more rote than filming a motion picture.

Let me repeat that again. There are few things more mechanized, more brutally repetitive, more banal, more manufactured, more CONSERVATIVE, than the making of a movie.

Movie director Alfred Hitchcock (PSYCHO, NORTH BY NORTHWEST) is famously noted for saying that actors should be treated like cattle. While being cheeky, what he was really saying was this: **movies are made long before they're ever filmed**.

Success in moviemaking is found in cooperation—not collaboration.

Execution—not expression—is what's needed at this stage.

RECRUITING

The true quality of a movie is not the product of its director, but rather of the individual technicians and crew members who realize the prepared vision of one person—the director.

That's what you're seeing when you watch a Steven Spielberg movie, a Christopher Nolan movie, a Scorsese movie. That great camera work? A cinematographer was hired; he hired an assistant, a camera operator, a lighter, grips, etc—a whole department of people pounding the pavement to realize what the director is trying to describe. Without these people, there is no great camera work.

A film director's fundamental skill is in realizing he has no fundamental skill.

He or she is in the business of selecting people who are more talented than he or she is.

That is what a director actually is. Someone smart enough to recognize that they can't possibly realize mastery in all the individual positions that make up moviemaking.

An aspiring director, however, believes that a film is good simply because of the good taste and aesthetic of the film director.

Not true.

When you reach out to a fellow filmmaker you are reaching out to someone who has even less skill than realizing they have no skills (self-recognized incompetence, believe it or not, is a slowly recognized skill)—and even more disappointment to bear when they learn what moviemaking actually entails:

Waiting. Standing.

It's recording sound. It's setting up lights. It's loading up a camera. It's taping down actor's marks. It's focusing a lens. It's serving food. It's driving cars. It's memorizing and reciting lines. It's pushing a camera. It's carrying heavy equipment. It's moving furniture. It's a collection of positions that, in and of themselves, bear no resemblance to actual moviemaking.

Recording sound is recording sound. Lighting a scene is lighting a scene. Gaffering is gaffering. Doing stunts is doing stunts. Virtually no one on a movie set ever gets to actually make a movie. And if any one person did—they'd never want to do it all themselves ever again.

That's the true beauty of getting 100% creative control: you'll never want it again!

But that's something an aspiring director has to learn.

It's something *you* have to learn.

Now if you can get "get" an actual, professional technician to perform their job on your film, do it! But more than likely, a professional—especially a highly paid one—will not want to stand around day after day on your set, pro bono, when they could be making real money elsewhere. They are paid "top dollar" for their services—and that is something you do not have to offer.

You have no dollar.

Rather than reaching out to like-minded folks in your field, you instead recognize that you just need people—period—and that the town you currently live in more than likely just so happens to be filled with them!

Your life, as it stands today, is already filled with enough, worthy people.

Start with them.

Family is, hands down, the best place to start your recruiting efforts. The best aspect being you can, arguably, hold them hostage for hours on end. There is some strange rule in our culture that you have to go a little further for your family. A lot further. They're helping out family. Mom and dad are great. While you might feel a little reluctant to work with and hang out with your parents, they will always come through for you. If both work a 9-5 job, that's OK. You just can't have access to them from 9-5. You likely won't have access to yourself then anyway.

Siblings are gold mines. Not only can you get them to work for hours on end, but you've seemingly multiplied their efforts because you now have access to your brother's and sister's rolodex of friends. Depending on your sibling's relationships with other people, you could very well cast an entire film just from a few of their contacts.

Relatives are the next logical step in this—and they're almost as good, if not as good as mom and dad. Grandparents, uncles, aunts, cousins. All are great, and all are usually willing to chip in and help their budding entrepreneur (that's you, the filmmaker).

Friends are on the next level down. This is where things get a little shaky. Some friends are great. Some friends who you think are great, are actually terrible. Some friends who you wouldn't trust with a 3 dollar bill, end up being the best people. It's something of a crapshoot.

Another good and obvious place to find recruits is school. Whether that's junior high, high school, or college. Of course, there are limitations. Junior high and high school students only being so reliable—*the junior high kids being the more reliable of the two*. College students, of course, being even less reliable than their younger counterparts. Young people hit peak reliability at about 12, maybe 13—and then it's straight down hill until they're 30 or have their firstborn—whichever should occur first.

With college students, you can increase your odds at choosing correctly by looking at the person's chosen field of study. Their degree. Engineers, for instance, are perfect. They are some of the best people to ask for help. If an engineer agrees to help, he or she will actually help. And the help will be consummate with their studies—logical, orderly, practical, and useful. Conversely, help from an art major will be consummate with their studies—***utterly useless***. Not because of the content of their degree. But because the type of person who picks to major in art is generally unreliable.

That's the real test of the degree.

The kind of person one degree or another attracts.

An engineer's studies are rigorous and demanding, tending to attract students prepared to meet that standard. An art student's studies, on the other hand, are vague and abstract, and tend to attract students unprepared to meet any standard. Both sets of studies tend to reflect the performance of the person studying. I'm not saying that lazy, useless people major in art. I'm saying that lazy, useless people tend to major in art because, forced to attend college by their parents, or felt pressured by society, they pick the area of study that appears to offer the least amount of resistance in obtaining an actual degree. 'Appear' being the key word. Because there's no more difficult field than the creative field, the art field. Breaking in, almost impossible. Keeping up a life long career at it? Tough times. But a so called "creative" person doesn't—or can't—see it that way. Either they are fundamentally and intellectually lazy, or, like I was, have not been exposed to this truth:

Art requires the most diligent and persistent person, someone who has transcended believing that they are either "right-brained" (a creative thinker) or "left-brained" (a practical, logical thinker) and mastered the ability to pull both hemispheres together. It was only after that I learned to go beyond thinking only with the "right side" of my brain—the creative side—and transitioned to my so-called "left brain," slowing myself down, actually thinking problems through in an orderly fashion, that I ever started to have actual artistic success.

Frankly, I always thought the teachers who diagnosed me as a "right-brained" thinker were simply just trying to be kind.

Stick to picking and recruiting people from degrees ordered around logic, analysis, and hard work. Engineering, computer science, finance (not business!), the sciences, nursing, medicine, etc. Avoid recruiting people from degrees ordered around creativity and the humanities—English, Art, and especially—ESPECIALLY(!)—Theater.

<u>Especially theater majors.</u>

Kids in high school and college theater clubs, in the musical, young people professing an interest in a career with acting, or modeling, or whatever, are generally less interested in the actual craft of the acting—the doing of the acting—the actual becoming of the actor or actress—and far more geared toward achieving some sort of acceptance, some sort of immediate sense of approval from their family and peers, and the community.

These are the kids who, in addition to being in theater club, in the musical, in their interests to being an actor, are also in literally every single extracurricular club possible, and are also involved in any activity that operates under the halo of a non-profit (doubly so for actresses). I'm not saying there is anything wrong with charity, or being a community person. But you have to recognize what these kids are ACTUALLY doing: padding their resume.

You believe they actually want to be in theater, that—gasp, gasp—they actually hold some sort of inclination to acting. No. They're, if still in high school, cushioning their resume for college. These kids would never do anything that couldn't be written down and packaged on a resume to whatever Ivy League school they hope of being accepted at. If still in college, they're keeping themselves open to their "big break" in the movies. Which means keeping themselves closed off to acting in your movie. In both cases, you and your movie just won't move the needle much for them.

The vast majority of the kids professing an interest in acting, or working in theater club, or on the musical, could never handle the ostensibly off-road nature of, every weekend, showing up somewhere, to film a movie that may, just may, never see the light of day.

If you look to someone who majors in theater—acting—you'll more than likely find problems manifesting when it comes to them actually showing up. They're generally exasperated people. When you propose locking down a time, that exasperation skyrockets, their fretting soars. Whatever neuroses they have—and to be sure, creative people are rife with them—will rear their ugly head and become YOUR neuroses.

You will, in a effect, be turning yourself into a babysitter. And no other time will you feel like more of a babysitter, more of a parent, than when you're ready to film and the actor or actress hasn't shown yet, and you're on the phone with them, trying to negotiate with them the importance of your film production versus the eight zillion other activities they've committed themselves to. You can just see the actress: wiping wild strands of hair from her face, battling the wind, trying to balance a drink carrier of Starbucks lattes (not because she's working there, but because she's loading up on Caffeine), doing that dramatic waddle to choir practice, to the Habitat For Humanity meeting, to the nursing home, to the this, to the that—

—Maybe I've just met too many divas.

Mind you, there are some actors in training who are phenomenal people. You can generally spot these people in their demeanor, their humility—and their actually having a side job/side-training for a totally different profession. They're professional enough to train at acting, but sober enough and practical enough to actually provide tangible service to society. If you can find an actor or actress like that—hold onto them for dear life. They're going somewhere.

Remember—successful movie making requires diligent, orderly, hard work, and therefore requires diligent, orderly, LOGICAL, hard working people. Not what the schools pass off as "so-called" creative types.

Out of this matrix of people I've just described, how should you go about your recruiting? Of all the people you know and love—and may not so love (we can't be picky at this point)—how do you go about qualifying who your best chances lie with?

It seems like a subjective call, a sliding scale dependent on how desperate you are, how adventurous you're feeling, on what you want, what you need, and ultimately, what kind of risks you're willing to take.

For instance, you might make your choices best on how comfortable you feel with the person. You may love your Mom, but you may not want to sit around with her in the confines of a film production. She has that way of acutely judging you—especially how you wear your hair. You may love your Dad, but you may not want him around when you start dragging furniture across his refurbished hardwood floors. Sis' may be fun some of the time, but other times, she's downright moody. Friends are a whole other bag of worms—some work well with others, some not so much. You may have noticed that personalities of "good" friends shift dramatically when other "friends" are present.

You may personally prefer certain qualities over another. You may prefer looks to talent. The one girl, if she'd drop the compact mirror she's always gazing into, is gorgeous—but she couldn't act her way out of a paper bag. Or—you may prefer talent to reliability. Perhaps you've noted a Brando-esque magnetism in the one guy at school, and that he'd be perfect to play that one bad guy in your script—but at 16, he's already an alcoholic-in-training. Or, you may prefer competence to talent. The movie world, after all, is replete with talented artists who moonlight as walking disasters.

So, what's the correct way of picking your recruits?

You flip the whole business around.

You skip casting and crewing—recruiting—based on skill—and go right to casting and crewing based on a person's professionalism.

Or, put in other words, **a person's character**.

Read: you recruit people for your films based on character—<u>NOT SKILL!</u> NOT TALENT!

When you cast and crew your movie, when you recruit, you stop looking at it as a creative project. You remember what you actually need: reliable people.

Because there's no one worse than someone who doesn't show when they say they will. If you ask me, someone <u>not</u> showing up is worse than someone who can't act, worse still than someone who didn't remember their lines, worse than someone who doesn't even know how to turn a camera on. Someone who doesn't show up—when they said they would—is the absolute, bar none, hands down, no questions asked, **worst**.

That's the first, perhaps only, problem you have to surmount. And it's a huge one. Finding reliable people to just show up.

It requires, in large part, having a lot of trust and faith.

It all, really, depends on a person's word.

Nothing else. Not money, not favors, not owe-mes, not contracts.

A person's word.

In our world… a person's word is everything.

I'll pick a person whose words match their actions over someone with inordinate talent—or inordinate bankability. Integrity, integrity, integrity.

Does the person in question demonstrate a habit of integrity? Do they keep their big commitments—as well as their small ones? If you were to make a date at the movies with this person, would they show up on time? Or would you find yourself sitting alone in the theater, receiving a text at the last minute reading, "Sorry, can't make it."

The best test for this is simple: does this person have a job? If the person has a job—then they'll more than likely already demonstrate at least a partial habit of integrity and showing up. If they didn't, they wouldn't have the job. They must be in a certain place and time, ready to go, and ready to work.

Any job will do. Waitress, waiter, cashier, salesmen, lawyer, doctor, CEO, mechanic, whatever.

Of course, some jobs guarantee reliability more than others. That's why my favorite people to work with are emergency medical technicians (EMT), law enforcement, and the military. There are no people better

RECRUITING

to work with. They are quite simply the most disciplined, the most focused, and the most depended on in our society to possess strong character. Discipline, duty, and honor! George Lucas, for instance, made his short THX-1138 exclusively with Navy men. Doesn't it stand to reason? Making a film is almost like invading a small country. Who better to do that with than people who actually have the character to run straight into danger?

You'd think that this method of choosing someone with a job or in the military wouldn't work. You'd think it would be the other way around—you would think that if they have a job, they'd more than likely not have the time to be in some movie. But, the old adage is what holds true:

"If you want something done, give it to a busy man."

Because if you follow your instinct and pick up someone who doesn't have a job—well, you're then dealing with someone who has previous problems that not even you will be able to solve.

But what about picking an actual actor who has an actual JOB acting? Too many problems. Not because there's anything wrong with the character of professional actors (they are generally professionals of the highest quality), it's that they usually belong to a union or guild of some kind that bars them from any kind of work that pays anything—ANYTHING—less than a standard rate, and a standard package of benefits. Most professional actors belong to "SAG"—the Screen Actors Guild. As far as I've always understood, as far as my experience in requesting professional actors, SAG absolutely prohibits its members to work for free. Frankly, it's complicated, and I've never seen it really work out well for independent filmmakers. Read: that's <u>actually independent</u>—meaning, no money.

It just compounds your legal problems.

Truthfully, your hang-ups in picking "only professional" actors is in not understanding the actual art of acting. You think and believe that it's only actors who can act. When in reality, EVERY professional has to act. Literally, every profession requires the professional to, one degree or another, act. Nurses act. Surgeons act. Lawyers act. Judges act. Doctors act. It's been said that the most difficult aspect of being a doctor is in not laughing at the patients.

The higher up the professional ladder, the more the act.

For our concerns, the quality of their acting is really only determined by three skills: **speaking ability**, **memorization**, and **concentration**. These are not easy skills, mind you. The people who can do all three are a rare bird indeed. But there are greater numbers of people who CAN do all three better than you might at first believe.

You should look to jobs that require the professional to do a lot of public speaking. Salesmen. Managers. Public relations folks. Spokespeople. Lawyers, for instance, have to spend the majority of their day in the greatest theater of them all: the courtroom. Without being cynical, lawyers are great actors. If only because they have to basically memorize complex legal arguments and present them to the average juror (which, incidentally, is your average moviegoer). The ability to speak, to articulate words and complex ideas, to carry a rhythm, a cadence, is really the chief instrument of an actor's trade.

FIRST RECRUIT

But before you look to recruit anyone else, there is one person you must first recruit: yourself.

Before you start anything, before you shoot a single frame, just go ahead and plan on doing everything yourself!

That's everything.

That's operating the camera, recording the sound, fixing the lighting, focusing the lens, moving the camera, driving people around, finding the locations—doing all the jobs listed at the opening of this chapter.

And plan to do them all yourself!

Everything from the catering and clean-up all the way up to the most crucial of movie jobs:

The acting.

At our level, you must play one of the major parts, if not the starring role.

Frankly, I highly suggest you play THE starring role. Not out of any sense of egotism, or self-promotion—although, that's a fringe benefit—but rather as a matter of insurance.

Whatever happens, the film will get made.

By casting yourself in the lead role you ensure that your actor always, always, shows up. You won't end up shooting half a movie around someone else, and then have that someone else up and decide it's "just not for them," leaving you with a hard drive full of random video clips.

Imagine such a terrible fate. You shoot, say, half the movie, and the actor or actress—well "things change." They stop returning your phone calls.

It could happen.

RECRUITING

Happily, you can avoid all of that by just casting yourself as the lead.

Starring in the movie yourself will provide you with a number of benefits. First and foremost, it will force you to learn acting from the inside out. It will force in you an interest in the study of acting. From Stanislavski to Strasberg; from Stella Adler to Sanford Meisner. More so, you'll come to intimately understand the pains of memorizing lines (something all directors should be doing of their scenes anyway). Then, you'll personally, emotionally, understand the terrors that await the actor after the film comes out: criticism from people who've never acted a day in their life. You'll never again give some poor sap the speech about "being a good sport" or having a "thick skin" about criticism. You'll come face to face with the terrifying insecurity every actor has has to deal with and overcome, over and over and over again, on a daily basis. You'll learn what actors need most from a director: empathy. Because when you're a professional director in Hollywood and your lead, one of Hollywood's most in-demand leading ladies pulls you aside and says, "I'm not so sure about this one line," you'll be able to hear what's she's really saying: "**I don't trust you**. Not yet, at least."

Directing actors and actresses is about earning their individual trust.

When you act in your own film, you will someday have an easier time at winning that trust.

Easier because you'll understand what you're really asking of an actor or actress: "Will you let me expose you to the entire world?"

Furthermore, there's something about learning acting that improves and sharpens all the other duties of a director. By acting, you'll go about thinking from another person's point of view more easily, of feeling what they feel, of seeing life from the vantage of another character, of "getting in to character." As a bonus, acting will dramatically improve your abilities as a writer. Because after all, writing is the act of imagining the world through another character's eyes. Some of the greatest writers were once great actors!

Doing this and everything else on a film set will force you to learn it all. Even more importantly, it will force you to appreciate everything that IS done on a movie. So, when you become a famous movie director, you'll have a deep understanding—a depth of gratitude—for the people who can actually do all of the different things that need done on a movie.

Doing everything drills into your head how hard all the jobs on a movie set actually—ACTUALLY—are—and therefore teaches you the absolute most important quality a director can posses: respect.

No, not the respect coming from the cast and crew. Rather, the respect coming from YOU toward <u>all the people helping you</u>, the people who, for all intensive purposes, are far more talented than you.

It's the kind of respect that moves mountains.

This is fixing a certain attitude in your mind. This is believing that every single person you meet is the most important person in the world. And believing that this might be the last time you ever see of them.

This is a respect for literally ever single person, and every single job.

I learned this the hard way. On one of my recent films, I needed an actress for a very quick, very small part. It was at the end of production, and, having filmed myself into a corner, I needed someone to just sit there on the other end of a phone conversation, look professional, and hack out a few lines of dialogue. I stressed "quick" and "small" to her because I believed that this would alleviate her anxiety in getting involved in some big, complicated activity. I stressed it so much that she got my real message: "This is such a quick and small part, I reserved it specifically for YOU!"

Think about that for a moment.

You get people in your movie by being respectful to them, by valuing their time—and valuing that time in a considerate way.

If you treat any part as small, if you treat any job as small, then the person you're asking to do that job will sense so, and more than likely resent you for it. "What's this business holding this stupid mic?" They'll think. "Why'd he get me to do it? Because he thinks I'm stupid? Well, I'll show him!"

Listen up! Every person is important. Every job is important. If it weren't, you wouldn't be going out of your way to ask someone to do it.

Whoever you do get to do it—they are, simply, gold.

If there's any profound irony in being a successful director, it's found in a director knowing his place: right there, just below everyone else.

Without these wonderful amazing people, the director would be out of business.

When the film's long over, when the years pass and you watch the movie again, you'll learn the real truth: it's not the making of the movie that brings its maker the most joy, it's the memory of all the loving people who made it so. It's seeing their names in the credits, and remembering their sacrifice. Remembering that for a moment in time, some very wonderful people—the best people—thought enough of you to give you their time, their energy, their love and support. The credits of all my films represent such people.

The greatest reward of being a movie director is the humility it teaches you.

RECRUITING

If you treat everything and everyone with respect, if you treat every single person like a king, you will never find yourself alone when it comes time to storm the perilous shores of filming a movie.

12
PRODUCTION

You'll never get more excited about filmmaking than when you think about the actual shoot, the loading up of the camera, the readying of the lens, the angling of the lights, the turning of the knobs, the pacing of the actors, the pacing of the crew, the rising of the energy, the being right there...

You realize that this thing could actually happen.

It's becoming real.

It's a heady moment.

If you've never done any filming before, if you've never actually ever shot a scene, have no experience, the night before a film shoot is like Christmas eve.

But if you've made a few attempts at filmmaking, your brain will be clicking away: Will the actors show? Will the crew show? Will such-and-such actor clash with his co-star? Will you "make the day?" Will it rain? Or, will it be too sunny? Are the batteries charged?

There's an enormous amount of anxiety.

If there's anytime a filmmaker who has made a few films wants to throw away the production, it's the night before the cameras roll, right when the train is about to leave the station.

If you've ever done even the smallest production—I'm talking even the smallest, tiniest shoot—you know what I'm talking about:

D-day.

This mix of excitement and anxiety is the enormity of the task ahead dawning on you. It's understanding one simple fact: movie production—of any kind—is hard work.

PRODUCTION

Really, really, hard work.

Exciting at first. But then a few shots into the shoot, a different energy descends. Enthusiasm wanes. Then it plummets all at once. The shots aren't turning out as you planned, the actors are forgetting their lines, the "set" isn't as big—or nearly as epic—as you remembered it. The sun isn't cooperating, peeking in and out of the clouds, giving you no real way to set the "exposure" of the camera, or, in your case, the 'brightness' and 'darkness.' The wind goes from a stand-still to hurricane gusts that knock anything on three legs over, including the tripod and lights, dropping them with an unceremonious bang.

You notice the energy turning darker not only with the setting, but with the people. You can literally feel your friends growing impatient—and downright hostile, always inspecting for the slightest lull in your behavior.

The air goes from creative to desperate. Things are harder than you planned. Time is running out. And, if not time, then your own energy. You just barely got that last shot, and well, it wasn't even that good, and well, it sure did take a lot out of you, and wow, you realize you've got about 100 other shots you need to make the so-called "day." You start to wonder why you made it so complicated. You become downright primitive, like a dumb animal rattling the cage, throwing finesse and grace out the window, your single goal becoming all about just "getting the shots in the can."

If you ever wanted to see this on display in a professional environment, just look up the many videos of famous actors, news anchors, entertainers, caught on camera, near the end of the day, in the midst of a full-on meltdown of frantic rage, the vanishing of their usual calm persona, their demons emerging. I always feel sorry when I see those meltdowns.

It's called desperation.

And it's what happens when you've strayed from The Plan—or when you find you didn't have one to begin with.

Movie production is war.

I'm always weary when movie production is looked at as a stage for creativity. That it's somehow akin to the renaissance painter, tucked away in his warm studio on a cold day, considering the blank canvas before him, brush pinched in his hand like a conductor's wand, no possible plan or notion but the impulses of his spirit. On a movie set, this manifests itself in "trying things out," or "experimenting," or "trying something different," or fretting around with camera angles, or otherwise "groovin'."

If there is creativity on a movie set, it's in solving problems (which there will be a lot of). If there's any creativity involved in shooting a movie, it's in managing the unforeseeable. And by unforeseeable, I mean the stuff that will seem completely obvious in hindsight.

The truth of the matter about movie production—especially a beginner's movie production—is that most moviemakers don't plan correctly. They have something in mind, but that's not planning. They discuss, but that's not planning. They storyboard, envision camera angles, but that's not planning. Doodling storyboards is fun and somewhat useful—but it's not planning.

It's not a set-up.

Movie production should really just be a matter of work, of rote. It should be a matter of execution—not creation.

Sure, movie production should be enjoyable. Laughs, fun, exhilaration. Don't get the impression from me that a movie production should be like Pink Floyd's "Another Brick In The Wall," with the the conveyor moving along faceless children. But to a certain extent, you want movie production to be a matter of firing up the engines, releasing the break, and setting off down the railway.

You want production to be fun, enjoyable, and to a large extent, a good time—for everyone else. You might be under a lot of stress. But that's fine, so long as your recruits are enjoying the rather pleasant fruits of your prior designs.

A battle is either won or lost long before it's even fought. And that battle is usually won or lost based on the planning—or lack thereof—that took place long before a single shot was ever fired. When the seams of a production bare and unravel, when the shouting starts and the tension ratchets, when that primitive, dumb animal behavior takes over—it's because something wasn't thought out before.

You don't want to be standing there, trying to solve impossible problems while everyone else taps their watches. Even on your type of movie production where there isn't any money involved. There are still significant resources at play—and at high risk. Energy, patience, morale, to name a few.

Having a plan, thinking things through prior, seems obvious. Seems like it doesn't even need mentioned. That's why they call it "pre-production," right? And yet, what's called "pre-production," or what goes on during "pre-production," amounts to little more than picking actors, picking out locations, drawing storyboards, having discussions with the cinematographer, the editor, and the actors—the creative aspects, in other words. But these obvious, attractive efforts don't even begin to scratch the surface of actually laying out the architecture of a successful movie production.

PRODUCTION

The problem with "pre-production" is that it suggests a single phase that begins and ends by a certain date, and then segues into the next phase of production. When in reality, beyond completing the script, all of the remaining phases of making a movie will blend into one. You'll be shooting while you cast, casting while you shoot, editing while you shoot, casting while you edit, special effecting while you cast, location scouting while you do special effect work—and location scouting even as you begin to market.

Believe it or not, the marketing of the film begins right in tandem with the commencing of production—perhaps even earlier.

The problem placing each one of these phases into compartments is that it suggests all of the complicated tasks of completing a movie can be done with some sort of sequential cohesion.

Of course, some cohesion would be nice.

But you have to remember that you're going to be at the mercy of other people's schedules and moods (more so their moods), outside events, forces—and worst of all, your own instinct to procrastinate. Don't forget, this is work. And with any work, there's a huge amount of procrastination to overcome. If you think filming a movie exempts you from the throes of delaying the inevitable miseries of true effort, think again.

Successful planning for a movie production requires an entirely different way of thinking. One that goes beyond the creative, and lies somewhere in the realm of the mundane, the mechanized, the engined. It's creating a force that will carry itself. It's about creating a chain of events that will keep a certain tempo, keep a certain meter, keep a certain flow of time.

It's about catching momentum. And it's in that momentum that the so-called creative spirit will come alive. This isn't "making the day," or beating some kind of arbitrary deadline. This is about crafting a sequence of force, a certain propulsion that ignites a series of carefully placed charges. When a demolition crew blows up a building or bridge, they don't do it in pieces. They do it in the press of a single red button.

In your case, it's the flashing of the proverbial "green light."

Pre-production *is* production!

This is about recognizing the truth of movie production: the production itself is what's actually in charge. Its own "weight," its own nature, predetermines—whether you know it or not—the outcome.

Inertia, really, is the key.

The following chapter is about artificially creating that inertia so that it will guide you through the rocky roads of shooting a movie, and allow you to actually enjoy the ride. There's a reason why, in any movie about a heist, the actual planning of the heist takes up so much of the film's runtime. It's not that they have to "plan the heist," it's that the heist itself is the plan. The last thing you want is to plan out an entire production, shoot a day, and then find your efforts stopped by some unforeseen—or seen—event! You would lose the most crucial fuel to production: momentum!

You have to understand that, after a certain point, momentum wanes and slows. Days turn to weeks, weeks bleed into months, months crawl into years. Time marches on, leaving you with the creeping awareness that your time on planet Earth is being marked away by a 20 minute movie, a 2 hour feature, a whatever-length the film happens to be. It's really terrifying, actually. Watching life notch the cavern walls of your life: graduations, birthdays, engagements, marriages, firstborns, divorces, deaths. Life can pass you by when you're "making a movie."

So, production needs to be broken down into its smallest of atoms. The details, in other words. Because that's where it all falls apart. Right there, in between the millions of atoms that make up a production, right there in the millions of cells that collect together to eventually form a complete motion picture. It's in not overlooking these tiny details. It's here where everything begins.

Take for example the scene I shot where the general gets a glass of water. At the beginning of the scene, he is reviewing some "classified" military documents, shaking his head, gritting his teeth, going through all of the cinematic gestures of someone reviewing some serious top secret documents. Trouble is, you can clearly see there is NOTHING on the papers. Even though we, as the audience, are looking toward his face as he looks at the documents, you can clearly see there is nothing even printed on the paper. And not only can you see that, but you can tell—you can feel—there's nothing there. The paper documents he's flipping through look too clean, as if they were just taken out of the printer tray.

Because they were! Just opened the family's printer and swiped a stack of blank printer paper.

I figured (correctly, I'd add) that creating real documents, actual, weathered documents with text on them, would take some work. I believed I could "get away" with just putting some blank sheets of paper in the folder. And I didn't even put some kind of gibberish, "Lorem Ipsum" text on it.

This is a very small thing, of course, but in the movie, in that one

PRODUCTION

second, it's a horrible blow to the story's credibility.

I somehow knew that creating actual, real documents would mean doing a whole lot more work. For one, it would mean slowing down, stopping, and focusing on one single detail. I'd have to do the research, for one. I'd have to find actual, real document-binders, folders, and take a look at how they're assembled. For another, I would have realized that documents—especially "top secret" documents—are not neat, are not tidy, but have a certain wear and tear. They don't look like a 14 year old just grabbed some folders, crammed in some printer paper, and marked it "TOP SECRET."

I digress. (My laziness then still pains me today.)

You could say that was a maturity—or immaturity—problem, and I would agree. But I would submit that there was something deeper going on. If there's any major problem in my earlier movies, the problem itself can directly be traced back to a rushing attitude of, "It's not that important, so let's cut a corner here."

I felt that I didn't have the time to really focus in on that one single detail. I was in the 8th grade at the time, with a whole set of classes and homework for each class, and my weekends and free time were buffered by hockey practices, games, and the requisite social events. I couldn't have stood the anxiety of sitting down and devoting so much thought and care to a seemingly "insignificant" prop that would only occupy the time of a single shot.

And yet, that's exactly what you need to do.

Make every little, seemingly insignificant detail COUNT.

And not just with props. But in your global attitude toward all the mundane details of a physical production: getting equipment into a location, getting it out, setting up the lights, taking them down, laying out the props, setting up the camera, breaking it down, setting up the audio, unplugging the audio, setting up whatever special effects you're going to need, readying the wardrobe, dialing in focus on the camera, setting up the tripod, blocking, rigging, gaffering, on and on, and on.

All of these are a hotbed of details just waiting to be overlooked.

Take for instance the issue of transportation. The not only GETTING to the location, but the GETTING in, and then, the GETTING out. Simply, how do you move around all of the physical aspects of production? At first blush, that may seem easy. But somewhere in your heart, you know that this single facet is just a can of worms waiting to spring loose. Will you drive? If you're young, that won't be an option. You'll have to walk. Or bike. Or, you'll need Mom or Dad to chauffeur you. Who drives? What schedule is the driver on? How far are they willing to drive—and drive back? What car? How much storage in the rear? Can you fit all of your gear? And fit it neatly? Then, once you arrive at the location, how difficult will it be to get your materials into the location?

This is yet another seemingly simple activity that becomes anything but simple.

Are there stairs that need climbed? How many sets of doors must you pass through before you get to the actual location? Will your chauffeur feel compelled to help? How much complaining will Dad do? How about Mom? Do either one of them like or get along with the "owner" of said location? What if they see one another? What if they don't see one another? Where will the car—or bike—be parked during all of these hijinks?

Seemingly small questions.

Seemingly endless.

All tempting your negligence.

Because, at some level, you sense answering any of these questions is likely to exponentially lead to still even more questions—and ultimately, consume your life.

If there are to be problems in movie production, it's in these questions.

It's in the answering of these questions <u>where successful movie production lies</u>.

The general response to these questions is to kind of glaze over and just "wing it," hoping for the best.

Not a good strategy.

How do you answer the questions? Further, how do you make the answering somehow manageable?

First step is to forget you're actually trying to make a movie.

Counter intuitive, I know. But.

When beginning a production, you don't "cast and crew," recruit, and raise money. Rather, you seek out situations.

That is, situations that will be agreeable to the momentum of a motion-picture production.

A great situation, for example, would be a "group project." If you're still in school, you will notice that teachers like to assign a great deal of these. Sometimes, if you're lucky, you get to pick the group, and the activity.

What's more, group projects—especially in secondary school and college—are hot beds for abdicating authority, work, to one person in the group. You've been there before: one member does all the work, while the rest pray no one notices.

This is perfect for you.

Arguably, there is no better situation for a young filmmaker than to find a school project, a group project, where everyone in that group wants to do the least amount of work for the best possible grade.

Additionally, most kids—all the way from elementary to college to graduate school—are enchanted with the idea of "doing a video" for the chosen project. Especially if they know <u>you're</u> interested in movies.

Read: they know you'll do all the work.

Which is fine by you.

By dovetailing your production with a group project, you've effectively hitched your movie to three or four other people, and the credibility of whatever institution is sponsoring the project. You have, at your beck and call, people who hold a vested interest in the project reaching completion, and reaching completion in a timely fashion—and, on your terms.

There's something about saying, "It's for a school project," that opens many doors. Parents stop nagging you when they learn "it's for school." Fellow group workers aren't so reticent about getting their hands dirty and making a few sacrifices: "It's for school."

A kind of pleasant sanity drapes over the entire production. There isn't any of this, "What am I doing with my life?" attitude. You won't have any of your friends standing around, growing a brain and second guessing how they're wasting their lives. After all, they're "doing it for school."

Still of me playing F. Scott Fitzgerald in AMERICAN WRITER, circa 2003. Movie done via a school project, allowing me to focus on actually making the movie for a change. Passion-wise, this is probably my best film because of that freedom.

There's no greater justification when you're young. It's for school! If smoking dope improved your grades, you can bet your parents—even the U.S. Department of Education—would be pumping it through the school's ventilation ducts. It's for school!

When you schedule a "shoot," and one of the group members doesn't show, you suddenly have credible leverage to move mountains, and make them show. No longer will you hear excuses about soccer practice, or about visiting grandma, or raking the yard, or going to the movies, or whatever lame story people dream up when the "bell tolls for thee."

It's for school!

And when you're in school, you're in school. School is king.

Keep that in mind.

Look for a situation where the situation itself propels the filmmaking forward. It doesn't even have to be "school," if you should be passed that age. Consider again the George Lucas example of him making his first film, and using the Navy men to get it done. He recognized a "situation"—or, put another way, he recognized an "opportunity": Since World War II, the US Navy would send their men to the USC film school for extra study. Part of this involved a film class that NO ONE at USC wanted to teach. Presumably because the professors at the school had rigid pre-conceived notions (gee—what a surprise!) about people in the military. Of course, Lucas not having yet been fully indoctrinated could see the opportunity, the situation: As per the Navy's agreement with USC, the Navy would pick up the tab on all of its student's efforts—including color film. Which, in the 1960s (and still today), costs a fortune. And, UNLIKE USC—and I stress UNLIKE USC—the Navy didn't put any chintzy restrictions on how much color film. I don't know which is more amazing. That the Navy offered such a great deal to aspiring filmmakers, or that a film school DIDN'T offer the same deal to its very students PAYING for that very education. Anyways. George Lucas, whom I would call a genius for this very reason, saw the light, and asked to teach the class.

Genius.

Not only did the young director tap into an endless supply of color film, he was able to garner access to a host of locations that none of the other filmmaking students could even dream of. Then, of course, the added bonus of being able to have a team of Navy men. Who most likely had far less interest in film, and far, far less ambition to be movie directors, and who would have probably been thrilled to be doing a project for a guy so enthused about the effort at hand—unlike the professors in the past who probably droned on and on about what a shame it was

PRODUCTION

that Orson Welles never got another shot after CITIZEN KANE. When a group of men and women are engaged in actually doing something, actually executing a goal, there is this amazing sense of camaraderie and direction—regardless the content of the objective at hand. This engagement, this shared purpose among the people trapped in the situation (Navy students, for example) becomes a powerful force when harnessed by an ACTUAL leader. It's the kind of energy and passion that gives you justification for the late nights, the pacing, the tremors that creep in during the twilight of filming a movie. When someone—your Mom, your Dad, whoever in authority—says they're worried about you (and eventually, they will), the other person can just shrug and say, "Well, it's for school."

Because without this this external justification to point at, to blame all of your stress on, people all around you begin to wonder why you're putting so much on the line…

For a silly movie.

It's just the way people think. Few people understand doing something for the sake of doing something, of becoming possessed with some kind of idea, of taking it all the way to end of the line—hell or high water. It's a rare person, usually a successful person, who can understand and empathize with the lone crusader who treks through the tundra of any kind of long term project where there's no income, no immediate accolades, no immediate gratification, and no short-term pay off.

The reality is 95% of people never experience—nor could they tolerate—the kind of mental, physical, and spiritual exertion (anguish?) required in making a motion picture—or any long-term project.

You will find, with profound shock, that the majority of people you meet in life are unwilling to do what it takes to be a success—at anything.

Read that again: "to do what it takes…to be a success."

Short of breaking the law or compromising your own morality, success—in anything—demands, COMMANDS, absolute obedience, commitment, determination—and heart. Nothing worthwhile in life is easy. No surprise there.

But you will be absolutely floored by how few people actually ever engage the iron cauldrons of "making it happen" (whatever 'it' is)—and see it all the way through to the bitter end.

Finding a project of some sort to shelter your production in will protect you from the prying, curious eyes of others, of why you're going to hell and back, and putting yourself through it all, for something that does not generate any income during the production.

Find some situation in your world that could shelter a long-term project.

If you can't, then you'll have to rely on good old fashion curiosity. In the 21st century people are still curious about the "wonders" of moviemaking. They, thanks to media, believe movie life is a glamorous circus with good looking people looking great, and average people looking even better.

People still hold out hope that the movies will save their soul.

This is literally all you will have beyond "doing it for school," or some other situation in your life.

By my estimation, it takes the average person approximately one movie-shoot to figure out moviemaking isn't going to solve their sense of vanity, instead discovering that it's a lot of hurrying up and waiting. There's not anything wrong with this, and god bless them, because this is a person who is helping you, but no matter how good natured, no matter how spirited, artistic, altruistic—they will figure out how much making a movie sucks!

And they will back out.

The key is to string the initial interest out as long as possible.

Finally, if there is no situation to shield your work, if you exhaust people's very shallow curiosity about moviemaking, then you're left appealing to people's emotions. There's appealing to their goodwill—which is a terrible thing to rely on. There's mercy—of which only goes so far. And then, there's guilt. Which works best in a pinch! You'll end up using all three of these emotions—and at great personal and emotional cost. But there must be some current and momentum beyond your own passion for moviemaking!

Find it!

13
PREPARATION

Now that we have the script ready to go, now that we have potential recruits in mind (getting them will be an ongoing process), now that you have some outside situation, momentum, to keep you going and shield your work, it's time to forget everything else—including that script you've spent so much time agonizing over.

Yes—forget the script!

Your first inclination, in regards to the script, is to make a bunch of copies and hand it out to every person you hope to have appear in your film, or hope to have work on the film. This is a futile, if well intended, misconception. The misconception being that 1) people actually read scripts, and 2) that people enjoy reading, and 3) people anywhere, ever, actually read scripts.

Reality is, people hate to read. I mean, they hate it. Absolutely resent it. Especially scripts. And no one hates reading scripts more than people in Hollywood.

If a hundred people on a movie were given the script, maybe, maybe, 10 people—maybe—would give it more than just a cursory glance. Frankly, I think the number is smaller.

If a hundred people were given the script, maybe 2 or 3 would actually do what is really required with a script: read it again. And then again. And take notes.

Your scoffing at this because you've been led to believe, at least, when it comes to moviemaking, that the script is king.

It is, to be sure.

But in reality, few people even bother. Especially in Hollywood. Few people—save for a few of the key technicians and people who actually take their job seriously—actually read the screenplay. Perhaps they glance at the parts where they appear. But you're expecting they, the actors, your potential recruits, whoever, will sit down, like you would, like any professional director, and pull the tome apart, reading it five or six times, enough times to internalize it, to understand it, to achieve a "vision of it."

The reality is… the people making a movie already have "a vision of it." It's called the paycheck.

Beyond that, most people involved garner a sense of the movie from what gets said about the project itself, from the director's storyboards, from the guidance of agents and producers, from pitches, from the highlighting of their character's name, wherever it should appear in the script.

If you've ever wondered why there are so many bad movies—and I'm talking, "Wow, I can't believe someone O.K.'ed that," this is why. No one—sometimes not even the director—no one—but whomever wrote the actual document—actually even read the script! Happens every day. Regardless of how many millions of dollars are at stake.

Did you think it would be any other way? Consider this—almost 20% of American high school grads haven't even developed "basic reading proficiency."

Then consider this: **most actors and actresses aren't <u>even</u> high school graduates**. One highly paid, highly sought-after actress recently confessed to never even having finished middle school—*that's middle school*. Newsflash: she's the one who determines what movie is made and what movie is not. It's not an executive with an MBA at Paramount, it's not an ivy-leaguer VP of production at Warner, it's not the Harvard grad president at Universal; it's NONE of the people who pose and posture to have the power to green-light a film. **It is a middle school dropout**. Given today's public education system, that might actually be a good thing. But I assure you, someone who can't even bear the reading material required of a sixth reader will do everything in their power to avoid the day-long project of reading a script.

This is all over—in Hollywood, across the country, all the way to the nation's capitol: bills, legislation passed, without even so much as the person who endorses it reading the thing. Do you honestly believe your congressman, your whomever, any of those people with the suits and the ties and the microphones, is actually reading those labyrinth, thousand page bibles that appear before whatever committee on a daily basis?

People—of all sorts, of all creeds, of all levels of powers—especially the powerful—hate to read.

Or, at the very least, you have to assume this.

PREPARATION

If a top-paid actress won't even read the script, you have to assume no one you know will even know HOW to read a script. Which is fine.

You don't really need anyone to read it anyway.

Sure, if someone reads your script, great.

But just assume no one will read it, and that you had better know where it is you're taking the picture.

Instead, just chuck the script aside.

A script, in most respects, is fairly worthless.

Important to you, yes. Important to the movie—even more so. But in making it? How is knowing the dialogue of the characters even loosely connected to securing and locking down locations, to dressing the locations, to scheduling people, to making events happen on a particular day when the cameras are ready to roll? The notion that this document is the main "programming," the main plan for actually making the movie, is silly.

The script is only the basis for the actual script.

THE ACTUAL SCRIPT

What you're going to do first is break your screenplay down into a series of notecards. Each scene receives its own notecard, listing what location it takes place in, whether it occurs night or day, how many characters are involved, which characters are involved, and what necessary props are needed.

A typical script—a feature length one—will render something like 40-50 cards.

Next, you organize these notecards via <u>first</u> who is in each scene. The people take precedence here, not location. I know, in Hollywood, it's reversed. They want to shoot everything at one location, finish it up, then move all the trucks and equipment to the next place.

But here, not so. Here, people take precedence.

They're really what's of most value.

In fact, I'm going to have you get beyond even thinking in terms of shooting via locations. I want you to start thinking in terms of filming people.

So that's 'people' first, 'location' a close second.

Since you're playing the main character, you can be flexible on when those scenes, the scenes with your main character, are shot.

What's not so flexible are the other characters.

You'll list the scenes in order of difficulty. And difficulty is gauged by how many characters are together in one scene. More characters, more difficult. Scenes with lots of characters have to be carefully coordinated, and must happen within a certain time frame, or must be prepped with the utmost accuracy. Less characters—less difficult. These scenes are far more flexible in terms of when they can be shot, and of who actually has to be there.

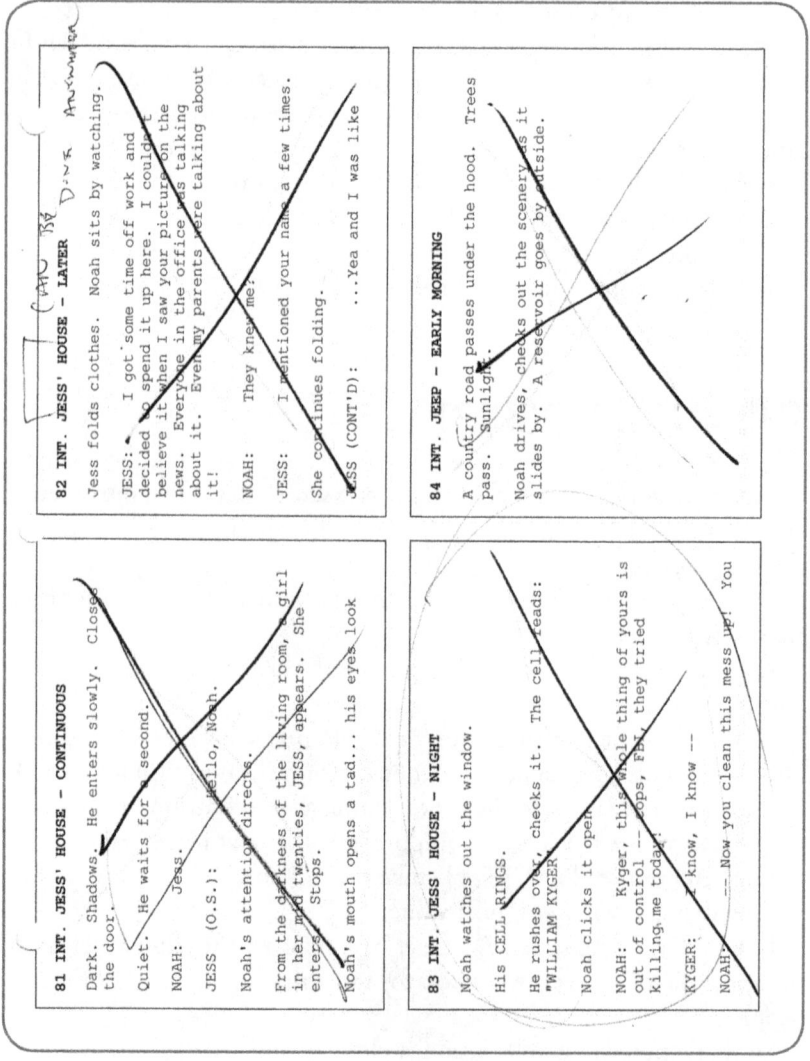

Put all your scenes on individual 3x5 notecards, and then 'x' the ones you complete.

PREPARATION

On any given movie, there's always two or three scenes that are a real pain. In my film RISING FEAR (AMERICA HAS FALLEN), the big scene that worried me was the one where I'm tortured by the FBI agent. Worrisome because it involved many different characters, all interacting in the same time frame, and many pages of dialogue, all requiring a certain momentum in and of themselves. You'll have two or three such scenes—or sequences to be more exact. You'll notice that there is no cutting them out, no re-writing them, no re-shuffling them, no economizing of them, no MOVIE without them.

So, you start with planning those. They will be the big shoots.

Which characters are involved? Where do the sequences take place? What time of day? Can the set-ups be broken apart, all the while maintaining continuity?

This is where some real creativity on your part comes in.

Do you really need all these people to be in the same shot? Maybe yes, maybe no.

I submit that not every scene *can be broken up; that it necessitates multiple people actually being in the same space and time to make it happen.

These are the scenes you set your initial efforts on.

And you really look at these scenes, realizing that when you watch a movie, all you're really seeing is a person on screen, and a background behind them. The goal here is to keep things simple. That is to say, to keep the schedules from getting too complex, from trying to coordinate too many people's differing availabilities. Usually, you can get one guy one day, and the other guy, the next.

This is why starring in the movie is so helpful. You're always available.

There are scenes and sequences, however, that *can be broken up into multiple shoots. Many of them scenes and sequences that take place at the same exact time, and in the same exact space. In RISING FEAR (AMERICA HAS FALLEN), toward the end, when the tech squad is switching the heart monitor from Agent Carter to the president, all of the people in the scene were filmed at separate times, when they were actually available. I shot the tech stuff on one day, my Dad on the next, and then, when time permitted, and when I could get him in, Curtis Caldwell, on another. He sat on the bench—with my Pops in the background (because I can ALWAYS count on my Pops)—and went through the scene as if someone were on the other side of the scene.

That took some planning. Rent or buy RISING FEAR (AMERICA HAS FALLEN), cue up that scene toward the end of the movie, when the tech is switching the heart monitor from Curtis to my father, and watch with the knowledge that none of those people, except my Dad, were there at the same time. There's about a week between each setup.

There's many scenes like this in my movies. Another example is in EMULATION; cue the film up to a scene toward the end where the one FBI agent has captured my character, has brought him to the bad guy's "lair," has set him down "in front" of the bad guy, "in front" of the other captured girl as a major scene proceeds. There are 4 actors in that scene, including myself, none of whom were present when the other person was filming. When it came time for "my close up," I set the camera up myself and essentially talked to a series of pre-marked points I set up about the room that would represent where the actors were. In fact, the concrete wall behind myself, and the one behind the girl is actually the same exact wall. In reality, my parent's garage (where we shot it) only had one such wall. I just shot against it twice, but switched the eye-lines around (having the actors look right to left, then, opposite, left to right).

Pictured above: three shots from the "basement" scene in EMULATION. Neither Jeff, myself, nor Jocelyn were present at the same time. Also, the same wall was used three times. Note the circled electrical outlet.

PREPARATION

I highly suggest watching that scene and, knowing what I just outlined, figure how you could do the same, for similar complicated scenes.

Then, once you start thinking in this manner, this manner of recognizing that not everyone always has to be in the same location at the same time, and recognizing that not even the same location in the story must all be shot at the *same exact* location, you realize that the main obstacle to filming the movie is in the scheduling of your recruits.

SCHEDULING

So, you look at your notecards, you see you have a character named "Steve," and you have a vague notion, a vague hope, your one buddy is going to play that part. So, you list all of the "Steve" scenes, list them in order according to the location they happen at—warehouse, bedroom, street, etc...

And then you proceed to ask yourself how you can shoot all of it in one day.

Get it out of your mind that directors on a Hollywood movie will "only have 30 days" to shoot a movie; just totally forget it. Realize that you will essentially have a *day* for the "Steve" stuff. Maybe two.

Maybe three, if you really fight. If this is really a nice, kind, compassionate person. Maybe.

But best to keep your designs to a single day.

And it is possible.

You do it by recognizing "the day" you get with your friend who is playing Steve—we'll call that friend "Rick"—will only be 2 hours long. Yes, that's right—a day, in this world of filmmaking, must be made in about 2 hours—and it must occur on a Friday, Saturday, or a Sunday.

It goes like this. You can't shoot all week because that's when people are at work; so, that leaves Saturday and Sunday. But you can't begin shooting until noon on Saturday because people have been out the night before at the bars, and they're going to be hungover the next morning, and you wouldn't want them there even if they could make it. They mope like nobody's business.

And since people don't skip meals, that means you can't start filming until after, at least, 1 PM. And because meals, at least in the United States, always end up dragging out into social situations, lunch takes an hour and a half; that bumps you up until 1:30. Then, factor in all the dickering with the tip, all the dickering with the coats, all the dickering with the toothpicks, the check, the USA Today paper, the flirty friends and flirty waitresses, and just all the general dickering everyone must do—you're looking at 2 PM.

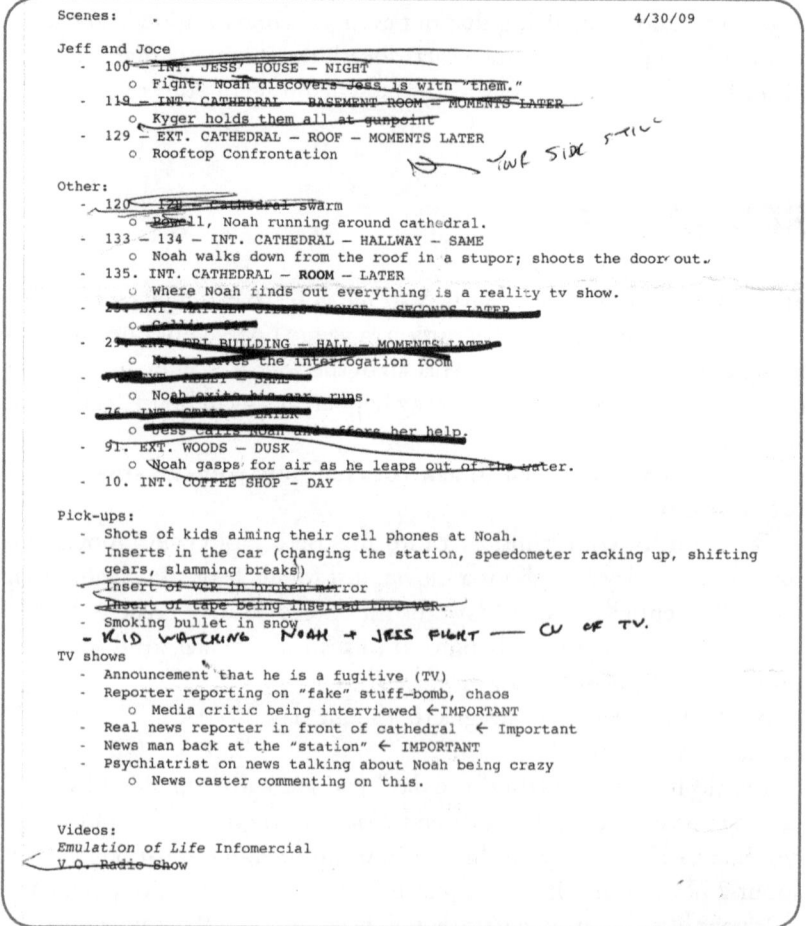

Scheduling is an ongoing tug-of-war between locations, people, and your own laziness. I wrote out the above set of notes in late April 2009—five months after we began filming on Emulation!

And then, getting to the location? Now you're looking at 3 o' clock.

That's what you get. If it's a day shoot, on the weekend, you get, on average, from 3-5 PM to work your stuff. That's it.

Because at 5, it's time to eat again. And then that lasts until 6:30. And then, maybe, maybe, maybe, maybe if you're lucky, you can squeeze another hour in between 6:30 and 7:30, when it will be time for people to go back to the bars.

PREPARATION

In America, outside of their jobs, people don't work. That is, unless there's some money involved. And that amount of money can be anything from 5 dollars to 100 dollars. It really can be as small as 5. Just so long as money is being changed hands. But then if you pay them 5 dollars, you have to pay everyone 5 dollars. And if you can pay them 5 dollars—they won't want it, because, remember, they're helping you as a friend.

Help from a friend gets you 3-5PM.

If you can't do your shots in 2 hours, then you can forget about ever making a feature film. Or even a short.

And that's if there isn't a sports game that weekend. If there's a sports game. Forget it. You're dead in the water. When there's some kind of sporting event, the region just shuts down. Perhaps that could work in your favor if you're in need of locations where no one will be around (kind of like a 28 DAYS LATER post-apocalypse type scene). With RISING FEAR, I shot all the dangerous Jeep/Apache helicopter scenes in downtown Pittsburgh on a Sunday during a Steelers game.

From here, I want you to park yourself in front of the computer. Pull up a text document. And with all of the aforementioned in mind, I want you to write out what this day of filming will look like. You don't have to timestamp it or anything so restrictive. You just sit there, and start to imagine what the "day" will look like.

This is thinking on paper.

You allow yourself here to dream and imagine, knowing that this is where the real creativity comes in. You write how the "Steve" character appears in a living room. You think about your family's living room. Then you remember your friend Rick, who has vaguely agreed to play Steve, also has a living room. Would he be friendly to shooting it in it there? Would his mom be friendly to this? Could it be shot in his bedroom? How about his back yard? A scene doesn't always have to take place in a living room.

OK, you realize. Rick hasn't invited you over to his house in years. Not to mention, his house is all the way over yonder, and there's no way you could hustle up there on your bike with a camera in tow (if you don't drive). Rick's living room is out of the question.

Maybe.

So you settle on shooting the scene in your own living room.

You write that down.

Then, you write <u>how</u> you will shoot in your living room. What do you see yourself needing to accomplish this work? Props? Cameras? Lights?

Where will you get these items? Where will you put them? Write all of this out, and—*write all of this out*. In your mind, it's just an errant thought, swept about in the millions of thought-debris that barrel through the human consciousness on a daily basis. Written down on paper, it begins to penetrate your subconscious, begins to germinate its own ideas and its own plans. Writing it down, like writing down goals, enacts what's called "The Law of Attraction." By writing it down, you're sending out a message to the universe, demanding these things happen. What's really happening is that your subconscious, by you writing these things down, is being signaled to take note and be on high alert.

You're making it real.

So, you write it out, and write it out in great detail.

You write out how you'll need the one light stand, because, as you write, you suddenly realize that the lighting in that room is always "just right" around that certain time of day, and so, you'll want to augment it. And when you write this down, you'll remember that lights—lights you plug in—don't really match well with the lighting outside, so you'll need to plan for that. Maybe you won't even need to light.

You just keep typing. Writing down whatever solution comes to mind.

You write out how you'll need a tripod, and then, as you write, you'll realize you're not sure where the characters are going to stand, where their "marks are going to be." So, you go into the living room, you pace around, you act out the scene, and you find yourself seeing exactly where the characters will stand. You write this out. Perhaps you jot it down as a storyboard.

I prefer writing it down.

You remember things like your Dad comes home at a certain time, and that might be of conflict. Maybe. You note it down. You think of where your Mom will be. You remember the scene needs a gun, so you write down, "I have the prop gun placed on the living room table. And the gun must be a 38.!"

Then, you imagine your friend there, standing there, waiting to be told what to do, and you proceed to imagine what you'll say to him. You'll realize that you should have already had the equipment set up, and you plan for that, and decide to do it the night before, and so, since that's out of the way, you tell him to do such and such, and then—

—Here's the important part to all of this—

You imagine his possible reactions. Will he object? Will he acquiesce? What do you plan on saying to him? If he objects, then what do you say? What if he can't memorize the lines? What will you do? There's a solution to that, and we'll get to it later. What if, outside, the neighbor's

PREPARATION

dog starts barking? What will you do? This'll get you thinking.

The point to all of this is to literally script out the entire shoot that day—down to the smallest detail.

Sure, it sounds intimidating at first glance. But I promise you, if you sit down and do what I'm advising for even a few minutes, you'll find yourself being sucked into tangent after tangent, anticipating the unanticipated, readying contingencies, and amassing almost a god-like omnipotence to your future film shoot.

As you write this script out, as you move onto the next scene, a scene that takes place outside, say, a pizza parlor, you realize that there is also another scene in the movie where Rick, playing Steve, appears, offering a few lines of dialogue, and that this scene takes place in a basement. You remember that you were going to shoot this scene in your one friend's basement, in a basement that looked just like what you imagined a basement should look like—but then you realize that while your own basement wouldn't suffice, you have that one wall in your garage that more than gives off the Feng-shui of a drug dealer's crypt. A few cutting of the lights, a few re-workings of the eye-lines, and you realize you could knock out that one scene—at least his part of the scene—<u>before</u> you head over to the pizza parlor.

Then, as you write out all this stuff, your mind drifts to what you'll need for that shoot in the garage; and you write all this stuff down too, amassing page after page of planning.

And by now, again, you're probably feeling like this is a little intimidating.

But what you might not yet know, what you have yet to find out, is that if this is done right, if you actually do this in good faith, you won't need to re-read it, you won't need to re-analyze it. You will have ingested the entire battle plan, finding your subconscious is already guiding a great deal of your energies.

What's more, this plan isn't something that's being cast in stone. You're not constructing a bridge of explosive charges that must detonate one after the other (to borrow the earlier analogy). You're simply exploring all of the options available to yourself, igniting your creativity, all the while confronting almost every single thing that could go wrong—or, more importantly—could go right.

Truth be told, you will probably find a lot of better ways of doing things than if you had just gone into the whole process blind.

By writing all of this stuff out in such great detail, you're effectively living through it once already from the comfort of your own computer. You're effectively already confronting one of Murphy's Laws that directly applies to what we're talking about: "There is never enough time to do it right the first time, but there is always enough time to do it over."

Nothing is ever done right, until it's done twice.

Write it all down, print it all out. Then call this document, "Steve's scenes."

In effect, it has become it's own movie. Steve's Scenes.

You do this then for each subsequent character.

Perhaps you even find a very agreeable moment in time where you can have "Steve's scenes" actually correspond with another person's scenes. Because, who knows, luck might be on your side, and because the whole operation is running so smoothly, the other person who is playing the other character might just be there, and because you've thought all of these things through, you can easily integrate him or her into the shoot.

Then, you take all of your notecards, the notecards representing each scene in the movie, and you tack them up, or pin them up, or tape them up, to a wall or a board of some kind, on some wall where you can see the entire movie at a glance. And as you make your way through each scene, you cross it off, thereby marking the long odyssey to having an entire film in the can. You keep going until everything is "X'ed" out.

14
ACTUALLY GETTING LOCATIONS

I say "actually" getting locations, because there's a difference between scouting out a location, and then actually showing up there, day of, cameras in hand, people at your side, ready to shoot. Those are two profoundly different moments. One is full of creativity and hope. The other, desperation and anxiety.

Which is why you always plan on NOT getting the location.

Just assume, right now, that whatever you have in mind won't be available when it comes time to film.

Of course, this is a personal call. How worth it is it to you to shoot outside of the pizza parlor? Is it worth re-scheduling, possibly never getting back some of your actors?

Do you actually have to shoot outside this pizza parlor? Or, could you maybe go grab a few still-pictures of it, then back in your driveway, on a green screen, shoot the scene?

When picking locations, there's always the issue of "obtaining permission." And I'm always amazed when an audience member asks if I got permission to film in a location. As if it matters at that point. It's in the film.

That's how you have to think. Do you want to get permission... or do you want to get the location on film? Again, that's your call. And I can't advise illegally trespassing, or, doing anything illegal to procure a location—but, hey. I'll say this. It's far worse to not ask permission and just shoot the scene, than it is to ask for permission, get a 'no,' and then do it—knowing full well you're prohibited from being there.

I'm not a lawyer. This isn't legal advice.

But I will also say that the topic about locations brings up this amateur business of 'being a professional.' Again, it's the old thing with the filmmaker wanting to appear like they're making a movie. That includes drawing up papers, fancy looking documents, presenting them to the proper authorities, garnering proper access and authorization, obtaining some kind of permit—whatever such a thing actually looks like (I've never seen one)—and waving it at the police when they inevitably show up.

By doing this, by doing what you're prescribed to do, by going to the proper authorities, by presenting them the script, requesting authorization, you're more than likely to arouse needless fears and concerns by the people in charge of the location. You have to understand, whoever is legally in charge of a location has to worry themselves about liability and all kinds of legal knots and ties, and just who—AND WHAT—they're signing off on. What, because—are you a corporation? Are you an LLC? Are you a sole proprietor? Are you insured? Are you, x, y, and z?

It's the old, "What momma' don't know, won't hurt her" adage.

Frankly, I violated this rule once, and I ended up wasting time and putting myself in needless jeopardy. I won't say what movie it was on, or what location it was, but there was one time where I decided to do everything completely legit. Procure the right forms, find the right people. After much questioning of what office to go through, after battling through much bewilderment from its own employees that such an office or function would even exist in their organization, I tracked down the necessary authorities, and requested permission.

When you make a movie, you will find that seldom do you ever deal with the "top brass." No. For you, for your requests, the powers-that-be will supply their main sentinels: the secretary. The assistants. Whatever is their particular euphemism for "person who keeps all work from the actual person who should be doing the work."

I sent the script in to the right official. After a week, the official deemed that the script was too graphic and "bloody." I argued that she didn't read the entire script, that the "bloody" aspect was just a ruse by the bad guys. That didn't hold water. I then argued that said location had already been featured—prominently so—in a slasher movie that depicted many, many scenes of horrific mutilations. No go.

ACTUALLY GETTING LOCATIONS

Back and forth, all a waste of time.

I was trapped really. I had to use the location, and that was that. I snuck in one night, did the scene—was even caught by security—even caught while I was waving a 9mm handgun around—and, well, the scene WAS SHOT. And was shot in that location. And it's in the movie. And everyone escaped OK.

I'm not a reckless person, and I abhor taking risks, and you'd never get me going sky diving or anything that would put loved ones or myself in physical jeopardy—but this is film we're talking about.

This is film.

Frankly, the whole business of asking permission to use a location invokes the other old adage of "letting sleeping dogs lie." If I hadn't asked for permission then the location owner could have in good faith denied any knowledge or authorization. If I had asked permission, and they had given it to me, and something had gone wrong, then it's not on me—it's on them.

And if it ends up being on you, so be it. For all legal purposes, you're essentially judgement proof. Meaning, you have no assets. Meaning, when the lawsuit comes, it'll be quickly dropped because there is nothing for the other lawyer to sue for.

The reason the location supervisor was giving me the business about the "inappropriate content," when there already had been a movie with inappropriate content filmed there, is because that movie was a film produced by a major corporation, capable of providing a fee, and capable of shuddering a law suit, if one should come about.

Money talks, in other words.

The key to the whole location business is in looking at the location's nature. How accessible is it? Within driving distance? Walking distance? Is it locked? Is it unlocked? Can one come and go freely? Or does entry—and exit—require a series of procedures, say, like in an airport? Is it a building that's busy all week, and then sits there, dead, unattended on the weekends? What kind of traffic graces the area?

My old high school, for instance, was a wonderful location. Busy all week, dead all weekend. Then, inside, one could move about. But, again, notice I said "nature of the location." Nature includes your relation to the location. My old high school was a wonderful location... when I was in high school. I was a student there and had a legal, if not quasi-moral, right to parade about the campus, wielding cameras and doing whatever business needed doing. At my age now? Forget about it.

These principles in choosing a location operate on a very subjective, relative scale. For instance, I used to have unfettered access to a wonderful apartment in Oakland, Pittsburgh, right down there on good old Neville Street. But, of course, those days are long gone, and I wouldn't even think to film there again. It was great at the time, because it was great at the time—because I had immediate access and didn't have to go through a lot to use it.

Consider all these things.

MINIMIZING VARIABLES

One other thing you're going to have to think about is transportation. How you will transport not only yourself, not only your "cast and crew," but your equipment to the choice of location. This is one of those intangible problems you don't think about until it's too late. Until you're trying to wrangle doodad after doodad up two flights of stoned-flagged steps, through doorways paneled in fragile wood, over couches and sofas and everything else on two legs. The obstacles, just in regards to transportation, are endless. Ostensibly, a whole book could be written on the whole concept of "moviemaking transportation"—indeed, entire departments on a film set are devoted to this very topic.

I'll simplify.

With your gear, you want to keep everything—and this is an obvious point—to an absolute minimum. The bare minimum. The essentials, and nothing more. The essentials being:

— 3 camera batteries
— battery charger
— the little thing that connects the camera to the tripod
— tripod
— memory cards
— lens (if you're using interchangeable lenses)
— XLR cable (2)
— XLR mic
— notes
— **and that's that.**

Anything more, in regards to the actual filming equipment, and you're begging for problems. Ideally, you could find a backpack where all of these things can be neatly stuffed. Obviously, having the backpack will free up your hands to carry whatever else, and, more importantly, to hold open doors. Again, I know, an obvious point. But you don't know how crucial it is until you're trying to get through the many doors you'll

ACTUALLY GETTING LOCATIONS

have to battle in your travels.

Doorways, in filmmaking, are the worst!

The physical transportation, the getting to the location, the—even more important—getting back from the location, the "getting everyone else there," is another challenge, and one that deserves some extra thought. You might know how you're going to get there. But I promise, your helpers, your recruits, won't. In fact, when it comes time to getting your recruits to the location, all of their previous knowledge of travel will fly right out the window. Don't blame them. They're giving themselves over to you and they just want to do you right.

So, to keep everything simple, let's run down a few parameters. If you can drive, ensure that the location is no more than, say, 20 miles away from where you—and your recruits—sleep. Any further and you bring in a host of other problems. Becoming a human GPS, for one. Lessening your chances of getting help, for another.

If you can't drive, if you're too young, or whatever, then, obviously, your location picks should probably be no more than, say, five miles beyond where you live and sleep. I pick five just as an arbitrary number. The real number is: how many miles your carless friends would be willing to travel. People will drive long distances, will even sit in cars for long distances; but walking or biking, no way.

Take for example, filming in a spot deep in the woods (and I'm using that because it's the most commonly available location for young filmmakers (me, you, anyone who has ever held a camera [and for good reasons too—no police, no immediate authorities])). You take your friends deep into the woods for the sole purpose of making a movie, you get into a "Blair Witch Project" scenario where every miserable thing on the trek becomes solely the fault of the movie—and therefore, the fault of you! That is to say, the actual traveling to the location is, in your friend's mind, time spent "on the job."

Time spent traveling, is time that could be spent filming.

The sad fact about going through all the trouble to film in an exotic locale (whether that be a foreign country, or something as mundane as the local landfill), is that when all is filmed and done, movie directors quietly realize that they could have achieved similar—maybe even better—results by just choosing a more accessible location. They look at the footage and realize that they're not even "seeing" a whole lot of what it was that initially attracted them to the location. That swamp deep in the woods, later, on video, suddenly just looks like any other mundane backyard. That really gothic basement two hours away, with all of its labyrinth walls, and pipes and garbage, when filmed, looks like just another basement.

The location business is always up for debate. On one hand, you have the Warner Herzog school of thought, the, what he calls, "voodoo of the location," where a certain... a certain... 'je ne sais quoi'... is achieved on film merely just by actually doing the filming on that location. See the documentary BURDEN OF DREAMS for an autopsy of this theory—and it's price. Then on the other end of the spectrum, is the Alfred Hitchcock style of shooting virtually everything from the comforts of a movie studio. There's one scene in THE BIRDS where—for whatever reasons (more than likely, technical)—the two actors on location are getting out of a boat; and then when they reach the dock and the editor cuts to the next shot, you can clearly tell they're suddenly walking in front of a rear projection screen that's projecting footage of an actual dock. That's how much Hitchcock despised shooting on location!

Neither is a better approach. Both extremes come at a high cost.

My advice is to wait a little bit before you try dragging a 320-ton steamship over a mountain. And wait a little while before you try to start faking locations via green screens (THE BIRDS—except they did it with rear projection and blue screens). Both ends of the spectrum demand money, both demand even more skill. Both demand good reason for doing so.

Personally, I want you to be perfectly content filming in and around your parent's home. It may seem like a dull location because you've lived there for years, but once on video, once seen through the lens of a camera, once photographed and compressed in the digital realm, you'll suddenly see it in a different way. You'll begin to see a lot of places differently. Especially after a few bad filmmaking experiences!

15
FILMING THE MOVIE

So, you get there, you arrive on location, you have your helpers, or helper (I shot my first movie with just one other person), and you're ready to film. You're ready to finally shoot your movie. Your first instinct is to set your bag down, pull out the camera and set it up.

Not a bad instinct. It's not entirely incorrect. It's always the first thing I did, all the while talking with the helper, pointing at far off, invisible points, rattling off my agenda, trying to quell my initial nerves.

What you're thinking about, at this moment, are your shots. Specifically, you're thinking in terms of how the scene is "going to look."

This is a movie, so it's only natural to pull your camera out and then proceed to "film a movie." What you don't realize is that the camera, what you see in the viewfinder of the camera is completely warping your brain. What you see stops you from thinking about all the other important details. You stop thinking in words and start thinking in pictures. You are thinking, in other words, like a cinematographer.

You are not a cinematographer.

You are first and foremost a <u>movie producer</u>.

But what does a movie producer actually do? If there's any more commonly asked question about the business, it's the question of what a producer actually does. The easy answer is that a producer acquires the finance, and packages the nitty-gritty business deals together.

If that's the case, why then are producers seen on a movie set? And why do you hear all these stories about the producer and the director clashing? Because, a movie producer's actual work, actual business, when it comes time to the <u>actual</u> filming, is not to produce, but rather to entertain. His real business is making sure everyone's happy, making sure everyone's "having fun." He looms, he floats, he gathers with the key players, telling jokes, listening to jokes (more importantly), listening to stories, and ultimately using his or her importance to distract attention from the fact that there's nothing else going on at the moment.

With all that money at stake, with the vast resources being burnt through on a daily basis, the producer is there to make sure people aren't absent purpose, meandering about, drifting here, drifting there, ensuring that his or her film doesn't become a case in point in proving one of the great, ancient axioms: idle hands do the devil's work.

A producer's main job is to make sure the people he or she has hired aren't staging a mutiny against the director.

So, what, as a movie producer, a movie producer without any help, crew, cinematographer, grips, etc., a movie producer who is also playing the role of all these other things, supposed to do? You, again, forget you are making a movie. Because… you're not! This is where you realize why it's a blessing—not a curse—to NOT have unlimited resources. In this case, unlimited help. Unlimited people. Because the more people helping you, the more people you have to watch. Which is what the producer is really doing when he "entertains." Having less people means you have less people to entertain (to babysit) (to manage).

So, you combine the work of a producer with the work of a movie director.

And what does a director really do? He directs actors.

So, your first order of business, when you arrive on a location, when you arrive at the set, is to <u>recognize what filming a movie is all about</u>: capturing an event.

That's it. There's no such thing as moviemaking, truth be told. Or, at the very least, actually making a movie is just an infinitesimal fraction of "moviemaking." You are simply with this crew of people, at this location, at this time, here to capture an event.

And that event has to be orchestrated by someone—you, the director.

A director's true job is in <u>orchestrating the event that's to be captured</u>.

This is why I stress avoiding the business of first picking up a camera, and then from behind the camera, defaulting to that famous director position of pointing to those heretofore places off in the distance. At this nascent moment, there is literally nothing to film.

FILMING THE MOVIE

So when you first arrive, you take your actors—your crew—out to wherever they're going to be in the scene, and you begin orchestrating the scene. Forget about the camera, the lights, all that stuff.

Just think of it like you're making a play.

Your "set" is the stage.

Why do beginning filmmakers never do it this way? Why is there a natural inclination to start from "behind the camera" and work forward?

The reason why beginning film directors shy away from the business of "orchestrating the event," of getting out there with the actors and making a scene happen, is not necessarily because they don't know how to deal with actors—as is usually cited—rather, beginning directors shy away from working with the actors because beginning directors tend to work with beginning actors—and the beginning director thinks the beginning actor is not going to be very good.

It's an acute, insightful observation for the beginning director to note. Insightful because he just somehow instinctively knows this. Acute because there's literally no getting around it and still being able to have the fun of getting "behind the camera."

It's for this reason most filmmakers, most people claiming to be filmmakers, tend to just default their careers as so-called movie directors to making music videos, filming "ambient" style footage of crowds and nature and the like; or, if they're a little more aggressive, being a documentarian. Not that there's anything wrong with any of those jobs. In fact, being a real documentarian takes a whole lot _more_ work and patience than just conjuring up a performance and capturing it. Being an actual, legitimate documentarian requires finding the performance, rather than creating it. No easy task.

To re-iterate: being a movie director has very little to do—if anything—with making a movie.

Thinking in terms of camera angles, in lighting, in lens choice, in camera moves, <u>is not directing.</u>

It's photography.

Which is generally the director of photography's job. Ostensibly.

This is a painful fact that you will have to face as a director. You've gone through all of this work and preparation, and sweat, and blood, and pain, and anguish, and drudgery, and despair, all to get these resources and people to this one spot—and you're essentially relegated to doing what a theater director does from the comfort of a theater.

One wonders if it's worth it?

I say yes. Whole heartedly. By reading this book you're starting to see that there's an entirely different subtext to making a movie—one

I would argue is a whole lot more interesting than picking out camera angles and throwing light on a scene:

As a movie director, you are creating life.

But to do this, to do it correctly and successful, you have to work through actors.

This is exactly why beginning directors are really uncomfortable with their real duties.

The simple truth: **the actors they're working with can't memorize the lines.**

Let's pause here for a second.

I'm hoping that hit you with a thud. The actors can't—and won't—memorize the lines. Most directors give up because they secretly know there's no humanly way their helpers, their actors—even professional ones—will ever know the lines.

If you want to know what makes a good actor, look no further than back to when you were in the second grade and had a spelling test. You either memorized, to the tee, the words, or you perished. Knowing this, you sat and re-wrote the word, again, and again, trying it blind, failing, then re-copying it again and again, having someone quiz you, trying it yourself—again and again.

Memorization is one of the hardest mental skills.

And you can be sure your friends—who have never acted before—will be unable to memorize anything.

Further, you can be certain—to a major degree—your friends, your helpers, whoever you're going to put in the scene—hasn't even read the lines.

In fact, you have to count on it.

As a beginning movie director you have to essentially teach the scene to a group of people.

Nothing more painful.

My early attempts at filmmaking were mostly me trudging through this business of "teaching the scene." It was like pulling teeth. I'd begin orchestrating the scene by, "OK, so you're going to stand here, and then you're going to say this line, OK?" I'd place my lifeless friend, "And then I want you to look at—hey, Carl, Carl. Quit picking your nose, come here. You're going to look at Carl—and Carl, you're going to be here," and I'd place a frozen-stiff Carl in some unmarked location, and then I'd tax my memory trying to remember the next line. But then I'd realize I didn't know the lines either. So, I'd have to pull out the script, then have to realize I didn't have the script on me, then I'd have to scramble away, find the script, tear it open, flip through pages, panic, fumble, race back, then read to them, "OK, and Carl, you're going to interrupt and say 'x,' and then, John—oh man, oh man—where's John!?"

This would go on for about five minutes, this teaching, this lecturing. All the while my friends were respectful, silent, receptive, and completely terrified. Imagine how you FEEL when you have to remember a phone number.

To make things worse, I believed at the time that I could assuage their memory lapses by just sticking out my hands, assuring them it's OK, while I'd flee back to the camera bag, grabbing the camera, shouting over my shoulder something about, "Just try…and…just you know, get into character! You'll get it!"

Keep in mind also, this environment you've selected to film in is already changing. The sun is shifting and the location, just five minutes later, doesn't look exactly as it did when you first arrived. If you're sensitive to such things, you'll noticed the color has shifted a bit; the shadows too. Perhaps it's the sudden gust of wind. Perhaps it's the massive field of clouds rolling in front of the sun, darkening everything, desaturating all the colors.

This is time running out.

I'd tell my friends, "OK, let's do a take!"

I'd hit the record button, I'd give them a quiet "action," (I know enough not to scream ACTIONNNN!!!—nothing makes a person more nervous)—and then—

My two friends, oh my poor two friends, standing there. I would watch them through the viewfinder. Both frozen. Eyes unblinking. A moment stretching into a century, a century stretching into an eternity, the world and everyone in it waiting to see which of my poor friends would break first.

"I'm sorry," the one would finally sigh, "I have no clue what my line is."

And so, this is why most directors never become actual movie directors.

It's not because of studio interference, it's not because of a lack of money, or lack of connections, it's not even because it's so hard to find a good script.

It's because, "I have no clue what my line is."

No matter how many gizmos and gadgets are invented, no matter how much money you throw at the process, no matter how many cranes and jibs, and this and that are swirling about your production, if you hear that fetid "I don't know my line," it's all for nothing.

I'm embarrassed to admit that I often resorted to standing off camera, holding the script and looking at the actor who was going to speak, and instructing: "OK, now say '(whatever the line was)'." And the actor would repeat what I said. Would keep staring where I told him to stare. Then I would say the next line. He'd repeat that.

Then, later in editing, I'd cover this fact up by just cutting back and forth between close ups, isolating the individual lines, using the footage of their stares to sometimes play over the other person "saying their line."

Doing this, I could usually save the scene. And frankly, it wasn't that bad. I never—never, ever—heard any complaints about 'stiff' acting or whatever.

But it was a chore, and very ungainly.

Thankfully, there's a better answer to all of this.

There's a thing called a "teleprompter."

You don't even have to buy an actual teleprompter—which is generally a few thousand bucks. Thankfully, you can download a very cheap "teleprompter" app on your iPad or tablet. You enter in the lines, then have them scroll on the tablet in big, green letters that can be read from a distance. The tablet is then secured on a stand, and, get this, placed in the eye line—or completely substituted in for—the other actor.

It works like a charm.

What I want you to do is find a teleprompter app you find agreeable, write out all the lines in a text document, upload it to the iPad or tablet of your choice, and just tell your actor to <u>read</u> the lines.

This is going to raise a ton of red flags with acting fans, teachers, and film enthusiasts in general. It flies completely in the face of what's supposed to be happening: an actor, standing there, creating a character, in a scene, channeling some other persona, interacting with some other persona, and creating life.

Which, when you think about it, is kind of overrated. Not that I don't love great acting! In fact, I'd rather have the man or woman who <u>can</u> memorize the lines, who can ingest the character, who <u>can</u> channel and mentally create the character, who <u>can</u> disappear into the person they're playing, their previous self just vanishing before the camera. Think DeNiro in TAXI DRIVER. Think DiCaprio in WOLF OF WALL STREET. Great, total performances.

But those are multi-million dollar movies. And sadly, achieving that level of acting at this level isn't really feasible.

Personally, I don't think it's possible, at this level of filmmaking, to make a movie where you're able to capture a performance like DeNiro's in TAXI DRIVER. Not only did DeNiro train and train, and train, and train, and really, really work hard for his performance in TAXI DRIVER—

He also had already won an Academy Award before doing it.

When someone saw that famous performance DeNiro delivered in TAXI DRIVER, they were already aware of him being a great actor; they were already positioned—I'd almost say 'hypnotized'—into expecting him to be great. Vis-a-vis just the trailers being on TV, vis-a-vis the critics already having championed his work (they weren't ascribing those glowing accolades to his earlier performances—nor are the critics ever ascribing those accolades to any other actor's earlier performances).

What I'm saying is that: what separates GREAT acting from mere GOOD acting, or, further, COMPETENT acting, is a vast external system of marketing priming, and you, the audience member, being prepared to say, "Wow, this guy is a hell of an actor!"

Past a certain point with acting, you reach what's called "diminishing returns." I can't recall a single time there's a ever been a movie production like the one you're going to embark on making where the critics, or any critic, sat down, watched the movie and said, "You know, it was a bad movie—but, woah, that one actor. He just—he just did everything I've always hoped to see in an actor."

I'm not saying GREAT acting isn't important. No. There is much, much to be said for DeNiro in TAXI DRIVER. Same with DiCaprio in TITANIC. Pick any actor you really admire.

There is something special to what they offer.

But that's <u>not</u> what they're being paid 20 million dollars a movie for.

Major actors and actresses don't get the big bucks because of their acting skills. They get the big bucks because of their name.

THEY GET THE BIG BUCKS BECAUSE OF THEIR PREVIOUS ACCOMPLISHMENTS.

Really consider this when you get a little down that you can't get Javier Bardem to play the killer in your movie, and instead, have to settle with your…

Uncle.

Your uncle, who has seen NO COUNTRY FOR OLD MEN, who really loved NO COUNTRY FOR OLD MEN, who is really just doing an impression of Mr. Bardem.

Don't feel bad.

Past a certain point, your uncle is going to be almost as good.

Again, this isn't to take anything away from professional actors. Believe me. You're uncle will never win an Academy Award. But with him there, with him reading the teleprompter, he's going to at least give you the lines, and he's going to consistently deliver them with ease and finesse, and therefore give you the life you need to fill the screen of your movie.

I emphasize this not to denigrate the actors, but rather, to get you passed the hang-ups of "oh, I gotta' have a star in order to make a movie." Or, "Oh, my Dad really stinks at acting." No, your Dad doesn't stink at acting. You just aren't setting up the conditions in which your Dad can zero in on what he's doing.

Because the secret to any great performance, including the great performances all your favorite actors give, is attention.

At the root of all bad acting is not a lack of talent; rather, it's a misplacement of attention and concentration.

When someone in life is a "bad actor," it's not because they're not "selling" whatever it is they're trying to sell, it's that their attention is on something other than what they're trying to sell. Usually it's on themselves.

That's how you can spot a liar. He or she is closely monitoring their own mannerisms. Their intent is not to say what they're saying, but to distract you from what they're <u>not</u> saying. It's why, if you're a man, and you're talking to a woman, and you're looking to court her, and you're trying to "flirt," the encounter seldom amounts to a success.

The attention is directed at the wrong person: yourself.

The key to great acting—in life—and especially in movies—is successfully directing the actor's attention. For example, getting their thoughts, their emotions, their feelings, off of themselves and onto something else.

Anything else.

Anything other than their own self.

Bad acting, even the bad acting of your friends and family, stems right from the person in question thinking about how they look and trying to recall lines (which is why memorization is so key). They're betraying an awkwardness that's borne out of the focus being on themselves.

Using the teleprompter solves this every time. Instead of their attention being directed on trying to recall lines, it's pulled away from their own self, and deflected onto reading the teleprompter. Their attention is relaxed because you're giving the poor guy or girl something to do. <u>That's</u> acting. Giving the actor something to do.

With professional actors, you can give them a bit of direction of, "OK, here, your character is trying to persuade the other character." And that's good direction. But your recruit, your actor, untrained in how to translate verbs into actionable acting, is unlikely to really glom onto being able to even <u>take</u> good direction.

But reading the teleprompter? If he or she can read—he or she can do it.

That's what you need. You need it done! You need it "in the can."

For a more in-depth education on actually directing actors—outside of your purposes of ensuring a performance actually gets on screen—I highly recommend reading Judith Weston's *Directing Actors*. She wrote, what I think, is the masterpiece on how to actually direct not only actors—but direct a movie. She's a genius, and knows her stuff. Read that book!

16
SHOOTING WITH CAMERAS

Before you actually set up the camera, I want you to consider what it is you're actually doing. Your brain might tell you that you're setting up "for your shots." But in reality, you're actually locking yourself into a set place. I used to always make this mistake: set the tripod up, set the camera up, turn it on, then use the viewfinder to pick out what shot I wanted.

While it wasn't too late to set up the tripod again, to move it somewhere else if I didn't like what I was seeing, it became very, very cumbersome to move the tripod around once it was set up. It may seem easy to just pick up the tripod and move it a few feet, but over time doing so becomes a hugely draining activity.

Better to realize that camera work isn't something done with the <u>actual camera</u>. Better to realize that real camera work begins with the <u>support rig</u>—a.k.a. the tripod—and where it's placed.

So before you do anything, look at the scene you're going to be filming as if your eyes are already the camera. It takes some training, but once you get good at it, you can just look at a scene, mentally tick through the lens choices, the zoom length, and be able to mentally anticipate the set-up that will be most beneficial to what the shot will ultimately look like.

I say the phrase "set-up" because that's what's of most importance. The "set-up." Placing the tripod somewhere, unraveling it, locking it somewhere, locking the camera on it, dialing in all the settings on the camera like the focus and aperture—that's a "set-up."

And "set-ups" are the name of the game.

Because once you get one set-up, a certain inertia takes over. It takes a lot of work to "get out" of that set-up, to break it down, and move it elsewhere.

Let me pause and say that a successful set-up is golden. A successful set-up is a set-up where you have the framing of the picture just where you want it, you have the focus dialed in just perfectly on the actor, you have the aperture (brightness, darkness) set just right, you've got the audio set up, you've got your actors in frame ready to deliver the lines—and ready to repeat the lines at a moment's notice. Because when those actors, or actor, starts reading those lines, he or she is going to get into a groove and you'll want to capitalize on that groove.

Because from there, things start to fall apart.

The wind blows. The batteries drain. The clouds roll in. The sun goes down. The actor's energy fades.

Everyone's energy fades.

And once you pause things to "set up" again, it becomes that much more difficult to re-capture that initial groove and initial inertia.

The goal is to keep time between set-ups to an absolute minimum.

It's for this reason why I want you to start thinking in terms of "set-ups," not camera angles. Because once you've "got" a successful setup, I want you to lock it in and film the hell out of whatever it is you're filming. That means getting a "wide," that means getting a "close up." That means getting enough so-called coverage so that when you're, months later, sitting in your bedroom editing the movie, you'll have more than enough footage to weave together.

Because it's there in editing, at that moment, when you're watching the scene, just desperately looking for that right moment of footage, that you'll be so happy, so thrilled, that you didn't fuss about with the camera angle once you got it set up. That you'll be so relieved you just let the whole thing run on the subject, and then let it run some more to just get a few extra seconds.

That's professional filmmaking. <u>Getting stable coverage that can be woven together later.</u>

Don't fuss with the camera angle once you get a decent "lock," don't spend endless time tinkering and looking for the perfect shot. A perfect shot is one that gets the character in frame, and keeps him there until the lines are all said. THAT'S great cinematography! Don't mess with the camera once it's rolling, once it's "capturing the magic." Just let it go.

And when you think it's time to "stop" the recording, <u>WAIT TEN MORE SECONDS</u>. I repeat, let it record for <u>ten more seconds</u>. These will be ten very painful seconds. But when you watch your footage at home, you'll be grateful, and you'll see how those ten extra seconds get you out of a lot of bad spots in editing. Remember—once you go to "cut," wait ten more seconds. You'll be happy when it comes time to edit.

REFINING YOUR SHOT

As you proceed to "film" in this manner, you'll notice that a certain wild inertia settles over everything. You're no longer in control, more or less. The inertia is. The movie gods are. And if they allow this moment to proceed, if they allow your actors to proceed with the scene and "get it in the can," then you should be really thankful and grateful, and know that you've gotten away with something! This is the pinnacle of success in making a movie. Actually getting the footage, with the audio, in the can.

So, then, for more advanced camera work, you will in the future not pick your shots via the monitor on the camera. That'll be to refine your shots. After enough practice, you'll be able to use your eyes to mentally anticipate what the camera is going to see, be able to set it up, and then go for it.

What's more, once you get that set-up, you'll be able to maximize it by getting more angles via zooming in, zooming out, and refining the look as it is right there.

Now, this is all great advice if YOU'RE going to be behind the camera. But I've already advised you to star in the movie. At some point, you <u>will</u> have to get in front of the camera and abdicate the camera duties to a friend.

A typical film book would describe to you the difference between a Long shot (LS) and a Medium shot (MS), or, for that matter, a Medium Close Up (MCU). But it's here I hesitate giving you the definitions—not that they're all that hard to understand. I don't give you the definitions because, what good would it do you? Especially when it's time for YOU to be in the movie.

"Hey, John, gimme a 'long' on that car," you say to John, your best friend, your recruited cameraman for the afternoon. Wanting to help, he'll give you a few reactions. A "Huh?" Or, a flat out, "What do you mean a long shot?" Or, he'll stand there, worrying, not wanting to look stupid, and not wanting to let you down, his anxiety creeping up. That's anxiety you don't want to add to his already strained experience.

Turning to your friend and saying, "Give me a 'long,' and then follow me as he goes from frame left to frame right," is an exercise in futility. Your poor friend will nod his head, ready himself behind the camera. Because he doesn't want to break your very expensive camera, because he wants to be very careful, he'll pinch the tripod handle, he'll grab onto one of the legs, having figured out that the whole apparatus almost tips over when any movement is attempted. He'll give you the go-ahead. You'll hop in the scene, give him a nod, he'll echo back, "action"—and when you review the footage, you'll see all kinds of horrors: The picture jerks the subject left to right opposite to the subject's path, it speeds up, then slows—then sputters—then, the subject of the picture is suddenly forced up against the right of the frame, and then it sends the subject over to the left—and it's just a mess.

It's a mess because you're trying to push your resources too far.

MOVEMENT

At some point, you're going to want to add a little camera movement to your motion picture. You'll dream of having the camera zoom through the air, "push in" on the subject matter, "pull out," "pan," and mimic otherwise professional camera work. But it means whoever is operating the camera will have to know how to do all these things too.

And these maneuvers take skill. And a large knowledge of what any of the camera-movement terms mean. What's a "pan" to you—swiveling the camera side to side—will be to another person something one uses to bake a pizza in. What's a "dolly shot" to you will make someone else think about dolls. This goes for "trucking," "swivel," "crane down," "jib in"—and the worst—"BOOMING." Have you ever heard that phrase? "Boom down!" "Boom up!" In industry jargon it means the camera, on a crane, lowers or raises into the scene. Believe me, your friend will not know that—nor will he comprehend (or care) if explained!

Any instruction involving your friend, your recruits, and a tripod will be meaningless.

For a moment, let's step back and look at what a tripod really is. When people started taking pictures, the cameras, because they were so primitive, had to be rock solid.

So, the tripods didn't move.

They were only meant to stay in one place.

With the advent of motion pictures, filmmakers naturally wanted those tripods—those stands that photographers placed cameras on—to make some movement. To pan—to scan, really—from one locked position, to another. And the tripods weren't all that great; so the pans, or the scans, or the movements themselves, the swivel of the tripod head, was jerky and creaky. But that was OK because audiences had never seen an image 'look' at one place, and then in one continuous movement, scan over to another position.

So tripods became more and more advanced. With hydraulics, and gears, and motors, and cranes, and thousands of dollars of gizmos and gadgets, and now can they glide around in all directions.

In the 21st century, there isn't any place where you can't smoothly move the camera.

Except in your movie.

In your movie, it's 1912. And the tripod you've purchased, likely the one you bought on Amazon for $50 dollars, or the one you've found in the basement (one that was considered expensive when it was bought at $20 dollars), only pans (ugh, I keep using that word), only scans, swivels—left and right, up and down, and there in between.

If you're lucky.

But it will serve your purposes well. It's a tripod. It's a stand with three legs that can be collapsed and moved at a rapid pace. It's to keep the camera where you put it—and no more.

It's only offering the <u>promise</u> of movement. I emphasize the word 'promise.' Sure, after many of your own contortions, you can get a decent camera movement out of it. But that's you. And you're already an above average cameraman. You already know what you're looking for. You know to intentionally brace the tripod down (because the device weighs less than 2 pounds), to grip a leg with one hand while you grapple the tripod handle, to almost pull the tripod toward you a little bit so as to circumvent the shoddy gears of the tripod head, to almost hold your breath as you pan from point 'a' to point 'b' without any jerks. And you already know to start slowing your whole movement before the camera reaches point 'b.' You don't want a complete stop. You want a slow roll off. A decompression. Almost like a fade of energy.

Well, at least sometimes you'll want that.

You see, there are so many variables that go into just engineering camera movements that Hollywood devotes an entire department to doing so. In Hollywood, on a professional movie, they'll usually have anywhere from 2-4 people, all hunched over the entire apparatus, dialing, pulling at knobs, pushing and pulling.

That's 4 people it takes to operate a camera. And if Hollywood could do away with them, they would.

To make that camera move—and to make it move successfully—a Hollywood production must employ: a focus puller, a camera operator, a pusher, and a crane operator.

The camera operator—this person generally sits or stands there, eyeballing the viewfinder, ensuring that the picture he's shooting stays on track. And if that were an easy task, he wouldn't be there.

Focus puller—arguably the MVP. The picture, the filming, could glide like an eagle—but it will be for nothing if the picture is blurry. Depending on the aperture, the difficulty of "nailing" the sharpness of the focus varies drastically. Happily, the industry has developed many devices and gizmos for the "focus pullers."

The pusher—this is the person who gives the camera some movement. He'll either dig in beside the rig (this is assuming the tripod is on a platform) and push or pull. He also makes sure the contraption doesn't fall over.

Crane operator—this person is directing the physical movements of the camera.

This isn't even a comprehensive list. It's very general, only to illustrate to you how many people it takes to introduce just a little camera movement. And this isn't even to get into how many people it takes to get the camera powered up, keep it on, load it up, calibrate it, and ensure it doesn't fall over.

It takes a lot of people just to operate the camera!

Now, instinctively, you wouldn't think that this is the case.

When you watch a movie, you see the camera move. It follows the characters, and that's that. You don't even really notice the movement at first. When you do see it, you become enchanted. You realize how complex it makes the language of watching a film. Something is certainly being 'said' when the camera, the picture, pushes in on the character's face, and holds there. Something is certainly being 'said' in that, versus just having that camera read the actor's expressions.

In fact, camera movement can completely change the acting. The camera moving can, if we may, be almost a yellow highlighter, dipping into a sea of black and white text, and dragging a long yellow streak over a certain sentence.

So, camera movement is important.

But, boy, oh boy. Does it take a lot of people to make happen! Because not only is it difficult to get the movement right, it takes a craftsman to keep the proper framing of the subject.

When I say, "framing of the subject," I mean keeping your subject, whatever it is you're filming, in some logical place on screen. Not too far to the left, not too far to the right, not up in the sky, not on the ground. But right there, on the person's face.

I could write an entire book on this and none of it would be of any help to you. Because you would still have to explain it to others.

Anything beyond just setting up the camera, just hitting 'record' and getting the action, is asking for major danger.

Is "camera movement" worth that much to you?

Just know that any kind of extra, special camera work, exponentially taxes what limited resources you already have. So don't feel bad if you can't even get a simple "panning" shot. Just panning can turn into a huge debacle.

Remember, keep it simple.

The movie gods may shine on you!

RECORDING SOUND

Beyond "getting your shot," I want you to make sure you're "getting your sound." When you're done filming, check the footage, and make sure you're getting audio.

Right here, watching the footage, is probably the moment you're going to hear something strange on your audio. If you're outside, if there's a major gust of wind, you'll notice that the recorded sound ROARS, and that it ROARS and CRACKLES whenever there's a gust of wind. This is happening because the microphone you're using, the one I hope you have set up independently of the camera, isn't covered by a "windshield," or rather, one of those fuzzy looking things you see on professional mics. Make sure you purchase one of those fuzzy looking things. They. Are. Gems. They keep out that roaring sound.

Important: wherever you shoot, whenever you shoot, make sure, make sure, you record more than enough AUDIO of the environment itself. That means, make sure none of the actors are talking, and that it's just the sound of the environment itself. Get upwards of <u>two minutes</u> of what is called "room tone." Because it's going to be more than a life saver later. It's going to be your salvation when it comes time to actually edit the footage.

It's what will make your editing "sound" seamless.

Do this!

AN EXERCISE

Production is one of the most difficult aspects of making a movie, if only because so much is at stake, if only because so many people are involved, if only because…

…there are so few opportunities to really get good at doing it.

Think about it. Even a professional director, one who has directed, say, 10 movies in his career, has really only actually spent <u>less than an entire year</u> "directing movies." In 30 years, the average director spends only a single year directing actual production.

Just imagine if a professional athlete could only do his or her 'thing' for less than a year's time. Imagine if the only time he or she could actually "do their thing" was when it came to "do their thing," when it came time to perform in the game, in the olympics, in the big marathon, whatever.

That would be an insane recipe for total failure. Or at least, it would make for some really sub-par athletes.

You need to practice.

If you were a jet fighter, you'd have to spend hundreds of hours, maybe even thousands, in a flight simulator before the military would let you anywhere near an actual jet. Because anything that involves doing something in a limited time and space, anything that puts a lot of resources at stake—say, a jet—requires a great deal of practice.

And yet, with movie directing, there really is no notion out there about "practice." There's rehearsal, but that's not what I'm talking about. Working with actors is its <u>own</u> thing, and requires its own practice. When I say practice, I'm talking about being in an environment where you can repeat a certain task again and again—away from the high risk stakes of a movie set.

Thankfully, there is such a thing you can do.

Before you do any "official filmmaking," I want you to go down into your basement, grab up a handful of those old action figures you don't play with anymore, maybe grab that Jurassic Park compound play set that's down there too—then I want you to proceed setting those toys up in whatever kind of scene, and film as much of it as you can. Moving the toys around, trying to create different moods and feelings via the lighting of the figures themselves, the figures looking at one another, the figures in the car, whatever. Just create as many "set-ups" as you can.

Ignore anyone who smirks at this exercise. It's a training simulator for the "big game." There is nothing else that so closely mimics the actual stress of making a real movie, of dealing with real people. The camera gives you just as many problems, the tripod gives you just as many headaches, the cables tangle just like they do on a real movie set.

You'll see how difficult it is to move anything when it comes to filmmaking. Setting up stands will show you how fickle and cranky they get. How difficult tripods AND the stands are to move around about one another, setting them in just the exact place needed. Doing everything in miniature, with your old toys, allows you to totally replicate actual moviemaking—without all the risk and expense—and allows you to do so over and over again.

Which is what you need to do.

As a bonus, the figures, the "actors," will constantly fall over at the slightest bump of whatever their standing on. This closely replicates how fast people fall out of the "set-up," otherwise grow antsy, otherwise frustrate your attempts. It will teach you to move quickly, and with great stealth. It will show you to keep things to a minimum, and to think strategically.

Try it now.

If you want to go further with it, I suggest playing the sound of a real movie as you practice, and use the figures to visualize what it is you're hearing on the film's soundtrack. Then, when you get all the "coverage" of the needed shots, use the sound of the real movie scene to edit together your footage against. Doing so will teach you things like pacing, camera movement (how difficult it is), reading subtext, how powerful a simple camera placement can be, and how powerful editing becomes later on.

It's an amazing technique.

If you need your practice to be easier, just subtract whatever is making it so difficult. Place some sticky tack on the action figure's feet. It keeps them up for longer periods of time. Try using one light instead of two. Or, use five lights to increase the difficulty. Add in a second camera to see how efficient it is to have two cameras running—and obtain two set-ups for the price of one!

While you're doing this exercise, keep a composition book by your side. Not a computer. But a composition book. Every time you run into a problem in your practice, you handwrite it down in the composition book, thereby imparting it deeper into your subconscious mind—deeper than it would go if you were just typing the problems out.

You note the problem you've experienced, and then you write out three possible solutions.

Just writing this down will get you thinking. And, if you've been doing your homework, if you've been reading lots of film books, you'll start to immediately come up with your own unique solutions:

> Consider the background of the shot, not just the subject. Must anticipate before setting up camera. This is 'chess,' not 'checkers.'

They might not be very good ideas, but they'll get your subconscious, your entire mind, engaged in solving the problem.

Then, at the end of each month, go back through your composition book, your notes, and put each note on a single 3x5 notecard. For example:

> Shots aren't good. Don't look cinematic enough.

That gets its own notecard.

Then, move onto the next problem. Filling up a bunch of notecards. Then, put them all away.

Then, a little later, you pull one notecard out at a time. Carry the notecard around all day in your pocket, in your backpack, wherever. But keep glancing at it throughout the day. You don't have to get bent out of shape about it. Just keep "flashing" the card at yourself, thinking about it.

You're ingraining the problem, you're asking your subconscious to "mull over" this problem you have with filmmaking. And in doing so, I guarantee you, when you least expect it, probably without you even realizing it, a solution to the problem will just "hit you," right out of the blue.

You may be saying that this is an extreme waste of time, that you don't need to come up with your own solutions to each of these problems, because one day, someone—a professional—will be doing these things for you. You might be asking, "Ever hear of delegating, Tom?"

And that's very true.

Maybe some day someone, some professional may solve this problem for you.

But that's SOMEDAY. For now, YOU HAVE TO DO IT. You have to solve it, because you have to re-invent the wheel to suit your own,

<u>particular needs</u>.

The professional world, Hollywood, is on another planet as far as you and I are concerned. You have to approach your work, your filming, as if no one has ever filmed before, that there is no set methodology, and that it's all up to you.

<u>You'll be better off for doing so</u>.

Trust me.

Doing all of this will re-map your brain and get you actually thinking like a <u>real</u> director, not somebody who thinks they're a director because they lucked into the position via some sort of nepotism or lucky break. You'll be a <u>REAL</u> director.

This business of directing movies is all about how you think. Not just in your attitude, but in how you strategize out the physical mechanisms of planning a movie shoot. For example, the reason an electrical cord is never long enough to reach the outlet isn't because it's not long enough, it's because you failed to anticipate just how much cable was actually needed.

When you look at a room, you'll be able to just intuitively grasp all of the disadvantages of shooting in that particular room—and all of its advantages. I promise, whatever solutions you come up with, you will begin understanding and knowing every nook and cranny to being an actual filmmaker—a professional filmmaker. Like a general, you can mentally map out a location and be able to do everything in your mind before you even set up a tripod.

You'll have, in other words, a "vision."

At a certain point, you'll get beyond the petty frustrations, and elevate your mind out of the nuisances that plague even the great directors throughout their entire career. You'll get your mind out of the mundane and elevate it to where it should be: thinking about the actual movie.

PART 4
FINISHING THE MOVIE

17
HALF-WAY THERE

A professional movie production, at some point, ends. The cast and crew complete all the shooting, a wrap party is called, and all involved celebrate the end of a long journey. But for you, the process will be very different. For you, so-called "production" won't end.

There will be no wrap party.

You will be filming right up until you "print" the final movie for public viewing.

Truth is, all of the phases of production—from here on in—will begin to blend together.

Nothing will separate "pre-production" from "production," and "production" from "post-production." If anything, you'll drift from one back to the other. With "post-production," it might arrive sooner than you think.

For instance, when you finish the first day of shooting you might be tempted to review all the footage, upload it to the computer, and begin editing. Which isn't a bad idea.

Because the truth of the matter is… it's going to be a very long time before you get to the second day of shooting.

Once you start filming the movie, a metaphorical train pulls away from the station. Slowly at first. Then it gathers momentum. The tracks lead through some very deadly, war-torn, famine poached territory. Sooner or later, the tracks will run out, and the conductor must start the train again on another track. You, of course, are the conductor. You had a lot of energy and enthusiasm at the beginning of the journey. But somewhere, back there, maybe right out of the station, the tracks started to get bumpy, the engine crapped out, and the chimney began vomiting out a strange black soot. Sure the footage once looked promising. But after repeated viewing, it all somehow seems…

…stale.

It was good at the beginning, sure—especially after that first promising day. But now it seems bad. Maybe it's the acting? Maybe the camera work? Maybe the lighting? Maybe it's the audio?

You start to get a sense that you're making a bad movie.

And so, things grind to a halt.

Your friends stop returning calls, one of your actors goes missing, and you find yourself quietly relieved when one of your recruits has other plans. It certainly lets you off the hook for the weekend, right!?

All of this compounds by one simple fact that's beginning to eat away at you: you're only half done.

Do you remember that scene in THE DARK KNIGHT RISES where Bane breaks Batman's back and throws him into an underground prison? Beaten and crippled, Batman can only ask why Bane hasn't just finished him off.

Bane simply replies, "Your punishment must be more severe."

That's how the mid-point of making a long movie feels. A severe punishment. Not only do you feel beaten down by the months—maybe even years—you've already poured into this project, but you now know—you now fully realize—you have just as much—perhaps even more—punishment ahead.

You somehow know your punishment for embarking on this ambitious journey… must be more severe.

I can't emphasize what a low-point this is. I probably shouldn't, if only to avoid scaring you off. But I do so anyway. I believe it's important not only to warn you of it, but to let you know that you're not abnormal for feeling down once you get in its throes. Around the half-way point of making a movie, you'll feel lifeless, tired, agitated, frustrated, miserable, and unhappy. Worse still, others will not understand! You wanted this, right!? This is your dream, right!?

Yea—well—few people ever push so far with their dream to see how quickly it can turn into a nightmare. Especially one you can't wake up from.

You'll look at every conceivable excuse for walking away: the movie isn't any good. You're not even being paid. No one else cares. No one

HALF-WAY THERE

will notice. There's no market for it anymore. You'd rather get a real job (whatever that might be)! You'd rather get any other job! It's just a nothing movie. Walking away would be for the best.

Other projects start to look really appealing.

But you pause, because you know you've already sunk so much into this project. It would be a shame to just throw it all away.

So, you feel completely torn.

This is truly, truly, the point of NO RETURN.

It wasn't when you began filming the movie. No. You were still excited then. It wasn't when you wrote the script. You can always dump a script. In comparison to making a movie, not a lot goes into a script. Only time.

But here? At this point in the filmmaking process? You've not only "wasted your time," but you've wasted the time of others—and they're gonna' be on the lookout. They're going to want to see that scene they were in. They're going to want to see THE MOVIE you told them they were going to be in. Worse still—everyone you told about the movie will be asking the same question: "When's it going to be finished?"

That might be the worst part.

"When's the movie going to be finished?"

If anything turns you anti-social, it'll be this question from every single person you know, repeated over and over again, every single time you see that same person.

This is where your commitment will be tested the most. Not in the beginning when your natural enthusiasm carried the day.

But here.

When it feels as if it's all conspiring against you.

Because of the truth of the matter—and get ready for this—the real truth—is that no one and nothing is against you… except you.

If there will be any great, great challenge at this part of the project, it will be in overcoming your own natural tendency to do everything but succeed. Don't feel bad. Happens to everyone. Whatever's most important to the person will end up slowing them to a crawl, and doing everything in its power to stop them from actually conquering it.

It's called procrastination.

I urge you, with everything, with all of the energy I can muster via my writing, I scream, I chant, I holler and rant: DO NOT GO GENTLY INTO THAT GOOD NIGHT!

DO NOT QUIT.
DO NOT QUIT.
DO NOT QUIT.
Keep pushing.

Accept this purgatory as a natural course of doing anything worthwhile in life. You won't hear that from anyone else—because truth be told, they may just be hoping you WON'T finish the movie.

Maybe.

Maybe not.

Good people, still.

But you have to understand. At this point, you're in a fight for your soul. And everyone is watching, whether you know it or not. They've taken note of your attempts at this obviously ambitious project, and secretly—even unbeknownst to themselves—kinda' hoping—or at least, very indifferently hoping—you don't finish.

Your failure would let them off the hook.

So, you go on. You keep going on until you reach the finish line. Because people ARE WATCHING. They—caring as they are—helpful and supportive as they are—and appear to be—believe deeply in their hearts…

That it can't be done.

"I told you…" the doctor in THE DARK KNIGHT RISES scolds Bruce Wayne after his first, failed attempt at climbing.

"It could not be done."

Most everyone in your life, perhaps everyone, will believe it can't be done.

In fact… there's someone even more important who isn't quite so sure it can be done.

And that's you.

Deep down, that doctor from the Batman movie is somewhere inside you, reminding you, "I told you… it couldn't be done."

And it's here where you'll really find yourself.

Which is why I say, "Never, never quit." Because if you do, you'll be haunted forever. Sure, maybe one day you can go back. Maybe you could go on and do another project. Yes—maybe this project really is that bad—and well, maybe this _was_ all a bad idea.

But until you finish _this_ movie, you'll never know.

For those who do continue, who press on and fight the good fight, they'll be rewarded with the similar gift Batman finds when he's finally able to make the climb: courage!

True courage!

That is what you need to get to the end. And you will only get it when you reach the end. The trick is to find it, to create it… within yourself.

There's another reason I urge you to fight past this dark period of stagnation and self-doubt: you will never, ever, ever know if you've made a bad movie, or a good movie.

Never.

Not until the movie is playing in front of an audience.

And even then, eh. Not so much.

Basically you'll never know if you've made a good movie or not.

One of my favorite movie stories is how Scorsese was at the premiere of GOODFELLAS, sitting in the front row next to editor Thelma Schoonmaker, suggesting to her all the ways the movie—the movie they were currently showing to ALL of Hollywood—<u>needed</u> to be re-edited.

Just think: that's Scorsese with GOODFELLAS! One of the greatest films he ever made. And he still wanted to change it even at the premiere.

Imagine that! Being Martin Scorsese, having made one of the greatest films of your career, arguably one of the greatest films of the 20th century, and wanting to re-edit the entire picture!

When it comes to the movie you've directed, <u>your</u> own opinion of it is the least important—and most biased.

So, if not the satisfaction of knowing whether you made a good movie or not, what is the point in finishing?

To learn more for the next one.

The greatest reward from finishing a movie, beyond the money, beyond the fame, beyond the glory, is the quiet knowledge that you can do it—and that you'll do it even better the next time.

There is no greater joy than *the next movie*.

But for now, before you reach that profound satisfaction, you must fight through *this* movie. You must earn whatever rewards—tangible and intangible—that may or may not lie beyond the horizon of this movie's completion. You have to claw into your own heart and conjure up a courage that might not at first be there, and you have to push forward—hell or high water!

The rest of this book is about the tools that will get you through to the end!

18
SAVING THE MOVIE

"Movies aren't finished—they're abandoned." — Unknown

You've written the script, you've shot the footage, now only editing remains; maybe find some music, market it, and put it out there. This is typically called "post-production." It's a rather intuitive process.

At least, at first sight.

The four year degree film schools teaching it in such a logical manner suggest that, for you, it will unfold in a similar, logical fashion. You'll edit the movie (or an editor will), you'll score the movie (or a composer will), you'll add special effects to the movie (or a VFX artist will), you'll add sound to the movie (or a sound engineer will), you'll mix the sound (or... the sound engineer will), you'll color correct the movie (or a colorist will), and you'll cap off all your efforts with a big premiere for friends and family.

Teaching it this way suggests that not only do these things happen—in some far off universe—in a logical orderly fashion—but that they happen and are completed by skilled professionals—expensive, skilled professionals—in an orderly, logical fashion.

The traditional teaching suggests that post-production is a series of jobs—tasks, really, "to-dos"—that <u>need</u> to be completed.

Rather than seeing those tasks and "to-dos" as a series of <u>tools</u> that can be deployed to salvage a movie that is, 99 out of hundred times, a seemingly unsalvageable wreck.

I stress the word "seemingly."

That's how it works in the real world. A movie is never just edited—as if there was anything actually there requiring an "edit." A movie is saved. A movie is never "scored" by a composer—it is saved by a composer. A movie is never mixed—it is saved by a mixing engineer. On, and on.

Post-production is a battery assault of tools; tools wielded by master technicans against an unwieldy, cumbersome collection of images and sounds.

Editing is a tool.

Music is a tool.

Sound mixing is a tool.

Color correction is a tool.

Special effects are a tool.

Take it a step further—they are all deadly weapons that may or may not be unleashed against the mutated freak of a monster that is your so-called movie.

And like deadly weapons or deadly tools, they can be overused—and—underused. You're not trying to kill the enemy (the unfinished movie), you're trying to conquer it, you're trying to save it.

To abruptly switch analogies—you don't want to throw the baby out with the bath water.

You have to see editing, special effects, music, sound, color, as tools—as weapons—that are there to save a movie.

Rather than seeing those concepts as steps to fulfill in completing the movie.

The difference between the two mindsets—between the two schools of thought—is that one actually gets you alert, ready, and in a state of scanning for opportunity and possibility; while the other lulls you into a false sense of security and entitlement. The entitlement, for example, leading you to believe that there's actually a finished movie within all the loose ends, all just waiting to be magically coaxed out by other, trained technicians.

You see a glimpse of this in the many behind-the-scenes videos of famous directors attentively sitting by the editor, eagerly pointing at the editing screen, or making some gesture that signifies "Eureka!"—or sometimes he's lounging on a black sofa, arm rested over his head, using the same hand to point at some indiscriminate part of the display that's positioned half-way across the room, a display that's looming over the editor who supposedly knows exactly what the director is indicating at; you see the director laugh, clap; you see him patting the composer's back as they both stand in a mixing studio; you see the director all throughout, with all the top flight craftsmen, him just smiling, and cradling a cozy cup of coffee—all of these images giving you the impression that the director is just thrilled to be along for the journey, just enjoying the realizing of his vision as done by other, less famous people.

That's all marketing hype.

Works nothing like that in real life.

Whereas film production was an outward battle with the world, post-production is an internal siege between the director's rapidly waning interest in the project—and his own knowledge—or, rather, belief—that the movie sucks.

It looks as if the director is trying to finish the movie. He's actually try to salvage it.

This is what whoever said "Movies aren't finished, they're only abandoned" was getting at.

I take it a step further.

A movie is never finished—but it can be saved, and salvaged, and done so through the tools of editing, sound, special effects, and music.

And not necessarily in that order.

Let the notion of logic and procedure go.

Post-production will not be orderly. You will go from step 1 to step 3, to step 2, then step 5—then realize that was too premature, but not *too* premature, so you'll go back to step 2, then step 3, then step 5—realize the same thing again, but this time seeing you have to go all the way back to step 1, where you will start again, but then this time skip step 2 and 3, and then remember you didn't do 4.

It's chaos.

And this isn't just with low-budget movies either.

You would be amazed at which big-budgeted movies entered their post-production phase in a state of tremendous uncertainty—and were ultimately saved by deploying the tools of post-production. These are famous movies that were, at the end of filming, pronounced dead-on-arrival. Such was the case for Steven Spielberg's JAWS. The makers, for their horror movie that was completely dependent on the eponymous shark, had very few—if any—usable shots of said shark. But when master editor Verna Fields deployed her skills against the hours and hours of odds and ends shot by Spielberg and his crew, <u>she</u> brought to life one of the scariest films ever made. Simply because she knew that less was more—especially in the case of a horror movie. Whereas, conversely, the filmmakers, like all filmmakers and executives today who produce similar horror movies, wanted to get their money's worth out of the very expensive monster—and believed—as all filmmakers do to this day—that more is more. JAWS was saved in editing.

Or, take another 70s horror classic—John Carpenter's HALLOWEEN. The investors and producers, upon seeing the first assembly of the film, believed they had a dud.

But then John Carpenter composed the music.

Then the film suddenly came to life.

Even the immortal, seemingly meant-to-be STAR WARS was on life support as it entered the so-called "post-production" phase. The movie certainly wasn't in the footage—in spite of the footage containing the iconic performance by Harrison Ford. The movie would be found—or, rather—achieved—in the special effects. Which, mind you, the makers were almost unable to even do!

Of course, that was not all that saved STAR WARS.

Obviously, the John Williams score and that brilliant blast of orchestration that signals the film's opening titles. That almost goes without saying.

But what ultimately saved STAR WARS—its masterstroke—was in a very simple choice with the sound. While moviegoers are very familiar that actor James Earl Jones is the voice of villain Darth Vader, what's not so familiar is that 1) this choice was only made after George Lucas realized the voice of the original actor who is actually playing Darth Vader, David Prowse, didn't match what the character needed, and 2) that George Lucas actually wanted Darth Vader to be voiced by…

Orson Welles.

And George Lucas decided against it only because Welles' voice—allegedly—was too recognizable (if you study the film world for any length of time, you'll discover that Orson Welles and his film CITIZEN KANE, at least when I was growing up, are held as the de facto standard of great moviemaking. Don't worry if seeing the movie confuses this hype for you. CITIZEN KANE was only successful because it picked on the Donald Trump of its day—William Randolph Hearst)!

Frankly, I believe this post-production choice alone is what ultimately made STAR WARS the blockbuster franchise that it is today. If not for the choice of James Earl Jones (and the casting of Harrison Ford)—forget about it.

Don't believe me? Just look at the reactions to the STAR WARS movies where James Earl Jones' voice isn't heard (or at the least, where Harrison Ford isn't making up for the absence). Confusion, disappointment.

The voice is what literally defines the entire franchise.

STAR WARS was saved in post-production.

That's how key the choices at this junction are.

It's the difference between a… "ehh… decent" movie, and a franchise that Disney laid out a whopping $4 BILLION dollars for.

This example isn't the only one, by the way. An entire book could be written on famous, successful films that were almost lost in post-production—if not for some key decision in the deployment of post-production tools. In the case of STAR WARS, it was the sound that carried the day.

I detail all of this out for one reason:

There is a possibility of "losing" the movie.

It's true.

Many movies are lost during this phase. Most, unceremoniously so.

That possibility is greatly increased for your movie. Not only because you WON'T be aided by the technicians who are always waiting to assist Spielberg and George Lucas—but because of your mindset.

Not only won't you have professionals deploying the tools, you're saddled with this thinking:

Whereas you began the film with a hopeful, glowing view of what your movie "could be," you're now seeing (if you're reading this after production), after all the acting, all the camerawork, all the sound, after attaining all the materials you've acquired up to this point…

What the movie "will be."

Bad.

If there's any point during filmmaking where you're convinced of having made a flop, it's right here, at the cusp of post-production.

Thankfully, I can push you past this mindset:

Take it from me, **ALL movies—EVERY SINGLE ONE OF THEM—are terrible as they enter post-production**. I don't care which movie it is. They're all terrible—or, at least—all seen by their makers as terrible. Don't believe me? Just look to all the stories of major studios playing musical chairs with the film's director role. A studio, nervous solely by the footage, swaps out one director for another. Happens all the time. ESPECIALLY on major studio movies. The Disney-era STAR WARS films are a great example of this.

The movie you're seeing now (if you're at the end of shooting) looks terrible.

But it can be saved.

Seen this way, post-production becomes less about having to actually check off the boxes of editing, sound, music, color correction, special effects, and instead continually reaching back and forth between these various tools—these processes, really—in order to, hopefully, get it to a point where the movie comes alive and speaks to you, or, at the very least, salvage what you thought was going to be a masterpiece.

Tools—not to-dos.

The processes involved are the tools; the application is a result. But the real siege is played out in the metaphysical—the mental. Whereas production was physically demanding, the "putting-together of the movie," the so-called "editing," the "readying" of the film, will be the most mentally taxing thing you ever do.

I would akin the whole process to the readying of a <u>very</u> long term paper.

Looked at in this light, "post-production," as written about in this book, is about the structuring of thoughts, and the organization of ideas. Thing '1' goes before thing '2', because thing '2' will mentally—at least, with the audience—open up expectation for thing '5'. The re-ordering of shots, the re-structuring of scenes, acts, the pulling back of music, the addition of it later on, the yanking apart, the stringing together, the last second improvisations. The process demands both logic, care, empathy, and above all else, a final surge of emotion that hopefully will guide your final creative choices.

It's a mental process that does not respect cohesion and sequence.

It's this because you, as a filmmaker, as an editor, as a practitioner of all the skills listed above, will have to answer one single, central, and profoundly elusive question:

What is the movie?

"Post-production," the arc that bridges a movie in pieces to a finished work of art, as practiced in the real world, is all about the answering of this question. What is it?

Not in a genre sense. But in the sense that each and every movie takes on its own unique and special qualities—whether those qualities are good or not. "What is the movie?"

Unfortunately, you won't know until it's done.

There really is no way to know until it's done. No way. Doesn't matter if the movie had a one dollar budget, or a one billion dollar budget.

There really is no way of knowing what the ultimate context of the movie is until it's done and playing in front of an audience.

The answering of this question… is found in the post-production process.

What is the movie?

19
FIRST ASSEMBLY

The first step: NOT EDITING
The first phase in post-production is usually called "editing." Which is grossly misleading. That word 'editing' is a misnomer. It suggests that something is already completed, and that it only need be "edited" down to an appropriate length. "Appropriate" meaning: people can actually sit through it without falling asleep.

'Editing' is putting the cart before the horse.

So called "editing" is a stage all unto it's own. One that occurs long after special effects, music, and maybe even long after the marketing. It has less to do with swapping about video clips, and more to do with shaping the expectations of someone else: the audience member.

Before a movie even reaches the stage of editing, it has to first be assembled, and built up into a much larger artifact.

'Editing,' 'assembly.' What's the difference? The difference is that one infers something is already there.

When in reality, there is nothing there. At least, not right now.

Nothing but a collection of video clips whose true meaning would elude even the most informed person. Shots of people saying disparate lines, hinting at vague plot points, endlessly repeating the same line, over and over again, all of it excruciating to watch, all of it a lame horror show of insanity and inanity—all of it this because everything is out of context.

This is why you will constantly be asking, "What is the movie?" It's a question that can only really be answered by you—and the choices you make.

But how do you make the "right" choices? You somehow sense there's about a billion possible choices to make, all interlocking, compounding on one another, all shifting in some opaque matrix like the cells in the movie CUBE.

How to pick one 'take' over another? And then do so in the correct order?

FLYING AT 10,000 FEET...

First, you need to get an overall assessment of the movie. You need to get up 10,000 feet so you can look down on it all, enabling you to assess the damage.

The first thing you're going to do is watch all of the footage. Perhaps you've already done so over the long stretch of shooting the movie.

I want you to watch it again. To sit there, and just play through everything again. Excruciatingly boring, I know.

But the viewing is not for you.

It's for your subconscious.

Because by watching the footage, you will start to feel emotions one way or another, and these emotions will stir the deeper realms of the subconscious, which, in its infinite nature, will already begin to answer some of those billion questions and concerns talked about in the previous paragraphs. Really, your subconscious, that deep underbelly of your mind, is the true editor of the movie. And it's in watching the footage again that you're allowing the real editor to get to work.

I say "real editor," not to disparage actual, real life editors. No. They are a god-send—if you can find one. Having an informed, skilled film editor—and they work super hard—is a truly wonderful thing. Objectivity, at this stage of the game, is grace.

But you don't have an editor. Or, at least, frankly, I don't think you should.

I know, I know. All of the books you've read, all of the instruction you've received says you need an editor. And you do. But you won't have one, and if you did use one, you would truly never grasp why an editor is so useful, and how he or she best fits in with the process.

As I wanted you acting in the movie so as to garner a true compassion for the professional actor, I so too want you to garner a true compassion for the professional film editor.

As you sit and "flash" the movie at yourself again, watching all those countless hours of footage, listening to all that sound (can you see why I wanted to have all the sound and picture synced while shooting? Imagine doing that now!), studying all the nuances, letting everything wash over you.

You're already hard at work.

You don't have to take notes or jot ideas down. I personally don't like taking notes and jotting things down in a tidy little log. I think that defeats the process and invites another function of the brain in.

When you're finished, you will have a wealth of emotions. Some of the stuff looked good, a few shots looked PERFECT (shots you probably won't end up using), some of the shots looked really terrible (shots you'll probably have to end up using, again and again), and the majority of it, though, felt very uninspiring.

Very off.

Don't worry. This is simply a matter of projecting your old expectations onto what's actually there—combined with your ignorance of what the movie will actually be.

Truly, there is something good within all of the seemingly endless parade of bad material. Just not now.

Once you finish watching, reflect on everything. Maybe let a week go by. Do something else. Get your mind away from what you've felt—although, you'll more than likely be unable to. But try. I once read somewhere that a director, after watching all the footage, would go skydiving or mountain climbing—i.e., something that would force his mind off all the emotions from the film.

When you return, I suggest, perhaps, if you can stomach it—if, if—and this is a cautious suggestion—watching all the footage over again. It's not necessary, but. I just can't resist making the suggestion. You would be giving your subconscious, and yourself, a truly objective look at the footage.

But, perhaps by this point you will be too anxious to sit through everything again, and will be eager to just get to work.

But where to begin? On what scene? With what take?

You'll more than likely gravitate to the scene you know will look good "once edited."

I suggest pausing that impulse for a moment.

Instead, I want you to organize everything. Depending on what editing software you use—and really, they're all the same—I want you to come up with some coherent, personalized way of editing all of this footage.

FIRST ASSEMBLY

Whether the software offers "bins," or folders, or whatever, I want you to have this footage organized in some coherent way. Because as you go to work completing the movie, the organization—however it is organized—will become so second nature to you from constantly accessing and re-accessing the same data.

So, make it a little more tidy.

Make a folder for "scene 1 [whatever scene 1 is called]" put all the footage shot for scene 1 in that folder, then proceed with doing so for the rest of the movie. How you name these folders is up to you, and really dependent on the camera's set-up and how the camera itself names the video clips.

Of course, it would be nice if the software you're using had a place within the program where you can organize out the slew of video clips you will be importing from your camera, and hard drive storage.

On a side note, I highly suggest having gone through whatever editing process at least once prior to doing it on the scale you're about to, and then sticking with that system. Truly, at this point, this whole project is about to take on a life of its own. Try to stay on top of it as best as possible.

When you're done doing all this, it's time to begin assembling the actual movie. You will do this scene by scene.

But, remember. This isn't editing! Not yet. Assembling differs from editing in that, at this point, you will only really be selecting takes and then purposely adding in a lot of extra "fat," a lot of extra time, intentionally making the first "assembly" 3-4 hours long.

There's lots of reasons to do this. Pacing being among the big ones. Reactions, another. But the chief reason to go about your "editing" in this way, by first assembling a bloated cut of the movie, is to force the material itself to tell you where it wants to go. Rather than trying to prescribe your vision to the material, the material will transmit back to you what it wants—and needs to be.

Let me explain. By creating a bloated mass of an 'edit,' you will see exactly what WON'T work.

A funny thing happens when you begin to assemble the footage. That is to say, when you cut back and forth between two characters (or however many are in the scene). You will realize that a whole other kind of energy, a whole other kind of life springs into action once you start "juxtaposing" the shots, cutting from Character A, to Character B. Suddenly, after you make that first cut between two people, a whole new energy erupts.

This new energy is the film's subtext.

Subtext... is the film's main context.

It's the subtext, you will discover, that's the entire backbone of the movie. It's what the footage is really saying, in spite of nothing being said. This is what it actually means to say that movies are a "visual experience." Not the camera angles, lighting, etc. It's the meaning expressed within these juxtapositions that emerge once the cuts are made. A look and a glance that went unnoticed in your first or second review of the footage, suddenly, when paired up with another shot, becomes shockingly profound—betraying almost. If you've written the script correctly, it's here, in the cutting, in the assembling, that you'll begin to see an inner life behind the actor's gestures and lines.

When you're assembling a scene, I want you to do this. When Character A speaks, I want you to let him say his or her line, then... allow the film to continue, right up until he or she is about to say the next line. If you have off-camera dialogue, if the other actor is speaking, you should hear it off-camera, or, if you solely used the teleprompter, the silence will be coming from when the actor on camera is waiting for the next line to appear.

Then, just before the character says his or her next line, I want you to "cut." Cut right to the next character. But here, here I want you to start Character B's 'side,' 'cut,' duration of cut, just before the other actor off camera would have been saying his PREVIOUS line. Meaning, if:

CHARACTER A: "How are you today?" (off camera dialogue: "I'm good").

//**// CUT ** //

CHARACTER B: (off camera dialogue: "How are you today?") "I'm good."

//**// CUT **//

If it seems confusing, just remember the point is to pad the REACTIONS from each character. You know you're doing this right when the scene triples, quadruples, in length.

If done right, the scene will seem excruciatingly awkward. It will be filled with long, drawn out pauses—characters blankly staring, then suddenly speaking, then the other person blankly staring, then suddenly speaking. It <u>should</u> make you feel awkward. That's the point!

Because this is the movie TELLING YOU what it wants to be.

That feeling of awkwardness you get, watching the performances, watching this long drawn out "assembly," or, if you please, "edit," is your subconscious throwing out billions of warrantless choices, tangents, and dead ends. That feeling of awkwardness is your inner editor, discomforted by all the pauses, becoming aware of THE REAL SUBTEXT OF THE MOVIE.

So, then, what you do next, is continue on with the next scene. Making this scene as bloated as you can. Then, you go to the next scene. You could go in chronological order, or you could skip around and assemble to your heart's content: maybe start assembling the ending, working your way to the middle, or from the middle to the beginning, or whatever. It really doesn't matter.

The only product you need at this point is a rough assembly of everything you have. Warts and all.

Potential gems and all.

This is flying at 10,000 feet, this is getting a true overview of the movie you actually have—not the one you envisioned. This is reality!

So, when you have this rough assembly, I want you to "print" the entire "mess"—if you want to call it that—on a DVD, or some kind of official medium that will give you a sense of finality. A sense that, "This is the movie." I want you to "print it out" on DVD or Blu-ray, because the ritual, the process, will trick your subconscious into thinking something important is happening.

Really, I just want you to have the experience of <u>not being able to fiddle</u> with things as you watch the movie. I don't want you to be watching the first, rough assembly on a computer monitor. I'd like you to take the DVD, or the Blu-ray, or the thumb drive, or however you should ultimately "get it out of the computer" (and we'll talk about that a little later), just so you feel as if the movie is "out of your hands."

The truth is, it's the movie's turn to speak. Not yours. You've had your say, now it's the movie's turn to finally instruct and dictate.

When you sit down to watch, you are an observer. Not a director. Not a writer. Not an editor. Actor. Whatever. A whole cascade of thoughts will hit you, and that's fine, but they don't matter at this point, as you sit there in the chair, or laying in the bed, or wherever you should find yourself reviewing the film—because you are now the student, and the film is the teacher.

It's OK if all the materials needed for your film aren't present at the rough assembly. I'm assuming you'll have missing shots, shots filled in with oblique title cards ("insert: clock"), audio that clicks in and out, terrible sound, missing special effects. In fact, I would advise NOT having any special effects at this point. We'll get to that later.

The point is to simply take in the movie, and let it teach you what it wants to be.

As the three or four hour version of your movie begins, you'll start to immediately understand what the movie is communicating. Don't worry. You'll hear it, you'll see it. And you'll begin to see what the movie is really trying to say, deep within the subtext of all the edits, cuts, and scenes juxtaposed. You'll want to jump up and start editing, start scribbling on a notepad. Don't. Just sit there and let it play. Trust me, you'll remember all of the necessary ideas when it comes time to really hone this thing down.

Truthfully, watching the first assembly can be a rather disappointing experience. If somewhat filled with despair. A sinking feeling may hit you a few minutes into the movie—maybe the whole time.

That's OK. The sinking feeling is part of your subconscious figuring out what to do. It is the editor within you, the lifelong movie fan, springing to action, accepting all of the work that is still ahead, and readying a battle plan.

I stress: don't feel bad if you're not seeing THE DARK KNIGHT when you're watching this first assembly. Please, please, please, don't feel bad. And please, don't you dare compare this first assembly, what you're watching, to an actual, professional, POLISHED, FINISHED motion picture. Doing so is unfair to yourself, and a recipe for unnecessary depression.

A finished movie, one that you see on screen in a theater or on TV, has gone through many people and processes between the time they finished shooting and the time the movie reaches its audience. Things you wouldn't even think of. Things beyond the scope of just "editing," sound mixing, and special effects. Things the professionals do, beyond even those things, to really work the movie into shape, to really give it that "WOW" feeling. It's unfair for you to make comparisons to that.

And, yes, I'll cover all those "extra things" that will make your movie pop.

After you're done watching the movie, you should probably take another week off. Just to let things sink in.

I can promise you this: you are going to have a lot more ideas about the editing than you did when you began. More specific, cogent ideas. Not grand, vague ambitions having to do with music choices or whatever. But actual, real ideas that'll see you across the finish line. Ideas having to do with character, whose movie it is, theme, and subtext.

The content people are actually going to respond to.

FIRST ASSEMBLY

Now. Are you with me? OK. Now, hold on tight. You and I are about to make a sudden shift in topics.

Are you ready?

Pause on the assembly for a second while we talk about…

20
MUSIC...

I imagine you're just dying to put music to the assembly of the movie. I know I always was. Just dying!

I believe music is the most important part of a movie.

I personally think movies are a musician's game. Because without music, 98%, maybe even a 100% of all movies with music, would be totally "out of business." There's an interview on YouTube with Phil Spector talking about the film MEAN STREETS that I want you to watch. In it, he talks about how Martin Scorsese, the film's director, used a Phil Spector song called "Be My Baby," which is an enchanting song if you haven't heard it. And it's even more enchanting in the movie. It's what grabbed me when I first saw it. And Phil Spector wanted to file an injunction against MEAN STREETS because the song had been used illegally. That is to say, it had been used without Spector's permission.

However, thanks to John Lennon's urging, Spector let it go in lieu of collecting royalties, and MEAN STREETS exists today with that song.

But it was a close call, and could have totally destroyed the film. Not to mention Scorsese's and DeNiro's career.

Not just because the movie would have been yanked from theaters. But because without that song opening the movie, without those opening booms of the drums, the movie would have been, as Spector says, "out of business."

I found this to be a shocking, yet stilling claim. Shocking because I'd never considered Scorsese's movies without the music. Without Pietro Mascagni's "Intermezzo" (which Scorsese's mother brilliantly suggested to him) playing over that shot of DeNiro shadowboxing at the beginning of RAGING BULL. Without "Layla" playing over that montage in GOODFELLAS. Without the Rolling Stones blaring throughout CASINO. Without the song "Shipping Off To Boston" in THE DEPARTED. On, and on, and on. I've never considered any of his movies without their music, and you probably haven't either.

Taking it a step further, imagine all of your favorite movies without the music. THE DARK KNIGHT without Hans Zimmer's and James Newton Howard's work. Imagine TITANIC without the music by James Horner (and Celine Dion!). Imagine DIE HARD without Michael Kamen. Imagine GHOSTBUSTERS without its eponymous song by Ray Parker Jr. Imagine RAIDERS OF THE LOST ARK, JURASSIC PARK, ET, STAR WARS, all without John Williams.

Personally, I think Phil Spector makes a compelling case. Scorsese might very well be "out of business" without all the music. And I suspect, if you're honest with yourself, if you think about all this, you'll feel the same way.

This isn't to knock any of Scorsese's films. It's just to show how crucial, how important music is to a movie.

Literally, a movie is nothing without music.

Are there movies without music? Sure! And nobody watches them!

Music... is absolutely necessary.

And yet, what are you to do? It's doubtful Phil Spector will give you a pass in using "Be My Baby" (if you played "Be My Baby" over anything, you'd have a hit). In fact, it's extremely doubtful any music producer at any level will give you such a pass to use their music in your work.

The music issue is a toughie because I know, when I began making movies, before I even understood the whole idea of first assembling the movie, the first thing I would do was lay down a track from some favorite movie score of mine. THE FUGITIVE by James Newton Howard was always a favorite. And I would usually cut the movie to that music. And the scenes always, always came alive when I used it—or anything by James Newton Howard, or Hans Zimmer, or Danny Elfman.

Then those scenes would come alive not only for me, but for anyone I showed the scene to.

For a time, I would be in director heaven. Pats on the back. My friend grabbing his hair, amazed at the one scene where I played "Why So Serious" from THE DARK KNIGHT. "You're a genius," he shouted, the Joker theme ringing out of the speakers.

Sadly, there would always come a time when I'd have to make a choice. Was this a movie I wanted to sell? Because if it was, I'd have to get rid of all that music. It's copyrighted music, and it's owned by Hans Zimmer, or James Newton Howard, or Warner Brothers, or whomever produced the CD, and it effectively made my movie theirs. The same concept will apply to you. If you were to couple your movie with other musician's music and then put the film on YouTube, you would immediately be notified of the video being muted, or removed, or de-monetized, or re-monetized in favor of whoever owns the music.

What's worse, no movie distributors will touch it.

You no longer own the movie when you use other people's music.

In fact, the movie itself drifts into a no-man's land where <u>nothing</u> can be done with it.

This may or may not be a good, or a bad thing. It really depends on where you are in your career. I confess, a lot of my earlier movies—all of them, really—have copyrighted music. I was learning and felt the movies needed it. But, the problem was, when it came time to possibly remove the music, I would be devastated by its absence. Because, in truth, the movie had become about that music. It had become about Hans Zimmer, about James Newton Howard, about the Joker, about Batman, about Harrison Ford in THE FUGITIVE, about all of <u>their</u> choices, and about <u>their</u> stories.

Taking the music away was like leaving the movie a soulless corpse.

Even big time movie directors aren't immune to this. In an interview, Hans Zimmer shared his experience in being called in to score a movie that was already "temped"—that is, temporarily scored—with music HE DID from another movie. He confessed, in the end, even *he* couldn't couldn't top himself.

This isn't a matter of skill, either.

Not even Hans Zimmer himself can top Hans Zimmer. Not even he could re-conjure the energy that another movie conjured up.

That's *that* movie's music. That's THE DARK KNIGHT'S music, that's Heath Ledger's music, designed and constructed to bring alive the subtext of that character. And to try and apply it to your film, my film, whoever's film, whatever film other than THE DARK KNIGHT, is going to do that other movie a grave disservice.

At the very least, it's setting you up for a lot of heartache.

If you're wondering why we've made such a sudden shift into music, it's because, with the assembly, you're stuck in a catch-22. You want to start "cutting" (assembling) to some good music—but:

You don't have any music!

At best, maybe you have a library of what's called "stock music." Admittedly, stock music has gotten a lot better in recent years. Andrew Kramer, many years ago, produced an album of music called *Pro*

Scores—a phenomenal work, filled with actual, great orchestration. But the problem is, it's literally been used to death. And beaten to death. I should know—there's a lot of it in my movie EMULATION.

In a pinch, stock music will work OK.

However, say the stock music feels off, or repetitive, or just not "in sync" with your movie. Maybe you just don't want to use it and would prefer a unique sound for your movie. What then? What do you do?

Thankfully, there's another approach.

I want you to make your own music.

I can hear what you're thinking: "Gasp, I've never even so much as held an instrument in my life." Don't worry.

First off. Take comfort in the fact that you are already in a musician's medium. You're already making movies. There must be some music in you. Otherwise you'd never have wanted to be a director.

Second, technology has taken us far, far from the distant days of the wigged man hunched over his harpsichord, clutching an inked quill, dashing down lines of musical notation.

I want to introduce to you the concept (codec, really) of MIDI, which stands for "Musical Instrument Digital Interface." Do yourself a favor and download a free—yes, a free—program called Synthesia. When you have it booted up and you're playing one of the many songs already loaded into the software, you'll notice that a series—a sequence—of scrolling bars will sound out the notes that make up the song. These bars are MIDI notes.

They are what will enable you to compose your own score.

The scrolling bars, all placed on a list of notes from 'A' to 'G,' activate their respective tones.

The yellow bar on the 'A' key will play the 'A' key at a specific velocity—velocity being how hard you have hit that respective note. Here's the kicker: those little MIDI bars will play the notes through whatever instrument you choose. Don't like the sound of the piano? Switch it over to a violin. Nope? Try the strings. How about the drums? The list is almost endless.

You say, "But yes, those 'virtual instruments' suck!" And I would be quick to agree. However, again, thanks to technology, there are pre-recorded libraries of certain instruments, with every note played, sampled, and processed into a program called Kontakt, which I want you to look into immediately, that will play the samples of the selected instrument. You get it? A professional records an entire arsenal of notes on a violin, all at different velocities, and then a tech has them programmed into a neat little package where all you have to do is hit a key on your MIDI keyboard (which is a keyboard that hooks up to your computer via a USB cord). Suddenly, you're hearing an actual violin.

Do you get why this is significant? For all intensive purposes, you don't have to learn any instruments other than the piano.

And frankly, you really only have to learn the piano to the point where you understand the various notes. You can, on any MIDI creation software like Logic Pro, Garage Band, Pro Tools, Ableton, etc, open what's called the "piano roll" that presents to you a kind of grid where you just "paint" in the notes in whatever order you should desire. Even if you don't know or understand the notes, you can still do a rough guesstimate by moving the MIDI notes about on the piano roll until you get some kind of sequence to your liking.

The MIDI notes themselves are almost like video clips, making the whole experience a lot like video editing. The entirety of music production, in fact, is a lot like video editing; and if you have any experience with that, then you'll feel right at home.

I highly suggest first tracking down the "MIDI" covers of some of your favorite songs. Then download and study them in Synthesia. Not all of the songs you want will be available. In fact, a lot of them won't be. But you'll be able to find something that's similar to it. YouTube is replete with users playing Synthesia covers of many, many songs. Study the patterns, and feel free to augment the tune.

As a bonus, you have at your disposable hours and hours—and hundreds of years—of classical music—all on MIDI. If you wanted to score your film with nothing but classical music—and with the instruments of your choice—you could do that too. Because classical music, any music before 1922 is in what's called the "PUBLIC DOMAIN." Meaning, it's free.

It's free, and more importantly, legally unfettered. Which means you can use it with peace of mind.

So, when you're assembling your movie—and you're finding it a little dry—instead of reaching out for your favorite soundtrack of music, just go and make your own. Don't even travel down that alley of using "temp" music. You can get by, you'll find, very easily by just pecking in a few notes, extending them this way or that way, and creating, in essence a tone or a drone sound. By opening this door, you effectively eliminate any concerns about what you're going to do about music.

Now. Hold on.

We're about to shift topics yet again. Not back to "assembling" the movie. But rather to another tool that will fill in the missing gaps of your assembled film.

21
SPECIAL EFFECTS

The word "special" in "special effects" is a misnomer.
It suggests that they're included in and for themselves, as attractions apart from the feature you've paid to watch. Like a geek show at a circus, like the one-eyed man, the phrase 'special effects' suggests something special, or odd, or something that should stand out.

When they were never meant to be that way.

Of course, they have in large part become that. A lot of special effects in modern movies—mid 1980s onward—exist like the vast assortment of biological oddities in a freak show; there for the sake of attracting attention to their very uniqueness.

If moviegoers, movie fans, filmmakers both professional and amateur, hold a resentment, a suspicion, a distaste, for the grandiosity, the mass saturation of, the almost gaudy-like excess of special effects, it's because somewhere around the 1980s the whole notion of "special effects," the art of adding and extending on to a movie, was hijacked solely as a means of exploitation. Someone, somewhere in the 1980s, read the box office receipts of films like RAIDERS OF THE LOST ARK, STAR WARS, GHOSTBUSTERS, and said, "Eureka! These movies are all hits BECAUSE they have special effects. So…if we just add some more."

So, as the 90s began, movies just became absolutely saturated with exorbitant special effects, only there for the sake of being "special." There's no one particular movie you can point to that was a great offender of this. They all, in general, suffered from it.

In other words, special effects became tools that didn't need to be deployed in the first place.

JURASSIC PARK, TERMINATOR 2, GHOSTBUSTERS, STAR WARS, RAIDERS OF THE LOST ARK—weren't so successful due to the special effects, but rather, their success was due to those films' **need** for the special effects. Those films succeeded because the maker needed moviemaking to go a little further.

Dan Aykroyd and Ivan Reitman needed the technique of rotoscoping (a technique for a later time) to work, because without the proton packs firing the beams, there's no GHOSTBUSTERS. George Lucas needed the technique of rotoscoping to work, because without it, there are no light sabers. Steven Spielberg needed the computer generated imagery to work, because without the dinosaurs—and the ability to film them in really dynamic situations (like chasing a car), JURASSIC PARK is stuck re-treading the familiar ground of 1970s disaster movies like KING KONG and EARTHQUAKE.

These movies, in other words, couldn't have been made…

Until they were made.

Special effects are less about adding things, less about "effecting" something, than they are a process of bridging and sewing back together the frayed edges of a production, of an idea; a process of patching things together, a process of blending, and making whole.

It is a process of making something invisible.

Special effects are literally the movies themselves.

Therefore, a primer on moviemaking deserves—demands—a detailed look at the topic of special effects.

You may not feel the same way. Because you may prefer the quiet, the subtle, the more dramatic. You may be interested NOT in the tent-pole special effects show, but rather only in the small, the quiet, the indoors, the indie aspect, and therefore, a dissertation of special effects would be of no value to you.

Not true.

The following section on special effects will be of great value to you.

Special effects… are all about further realizing YOUR vision. Not the story's, which can always be fluffed up to include more special effects. And that's not necessarily a bad thing, by the way. But the whole issue of special effects begins with what you're seeing in your mind, and the virtual bridge you must cross into reality. Special effects will become of deep interest to you to the extent that they are, in fact, done, and that, more importantly, can be done. Your interest in special effects will

SPECIAL EFFECTS

correspond directly with your awareness of them, and your knowledge of how they're done. Like all the fields in filmmaking, an interest in it begets an even deeper interest.

I remember buying a book called *Special Effects In Film And Television* by Jake Hamiliton; reading it opened an entire pandora's box of questions and thoughts for me:

```
Those big cat-like, AT-ATs in EMPIRE STRIKES
BACK were just models? You mean Gotham city
exists only as a painting? You mean they can
just dress a guy up in blue spandex, and then
can erase him and make it look as if he were
invisible? Why blue? Would any other color
work? You mean the spaceship in INDEPENDENCE
DAY emerging from the clouds is just some
model in a tank? How do you film a tank and
make it look like it's on top of a city? Why
film in a tank? You mean the White House in
INDEPENDENCE DAY was just a model? You mean…
they didn't actually blow it up? The T. Rex
in JURASSIC PARK was made in a computer? Can
the computers at my school do that? Why is
this girl wearing all these dots on her? How
do they get that into the computer?
```

If the book was even more insightful, it was in its illustration of movies I had no idea used any special effects. For instance, how much of the Sylvester Stallone movie CLIFFHANGER was just filmed on a sound stage, using wind machines, fake snow, and sets designed to replicate mountain cliffs. Amazing!

The usage of special effects extend from achieving the fantastic, to the realistic, all the way to the mundane: the feather that lands at Forrest Gump's feet in FORREST GUMP, for example, is completely generated in the computer. Which, when you know that, makes complete sense. But it takes seeing the shot without the feather, then with it added back in, for the whole notion to even occur to you. As a young boy, I honestly believed they had just filmed that feather floating down from the sky and landing perfectly at Tom Hank's feet.

Frustratingly, all of these insights—seeing that these "effects" were indeed effects, were indeed tricks—left me pondering how all of them we're done. And frankly, the absence of an answer kind of left me cold to utilizing the effects. For the longest time, I didn't really care about so-called "CGI," just simply because I could barely even edit a movie on a computer, let alone force it to generate imagery.

I include all of this to kind of bridge the gap between being awed by special effects, to understanding them, to implementing them. I have no idea of knowing your level of knowledge of special effects. But I do know how a lack of knowledge can leave one with a kind of coolness to using them to their full force. I do know how one can be kind of tricked into delaying the "learning" of special effects, because one believes there exists a team of magical wizards in Hollywood who do the impossible. That's partly true. But at one time, those magical wizards were right where you are.

Special effects are possible to learn. Especially for you. They're even more possible to implement.

You may feel that all of the special effects "have been done," you may believe that the pros, the elite special effects artists, have all but pushed the boundaries as far as they can be pushed, and that therefore, there's no real reason to get terribly excited about the possibility of any sort of discovery on your part.

I have news for you. Not only has it not "all been done," but that it "might have all been done" has nothing to do with anything. The key is… you haven't done them yet.

The message is clear. There's a lot of untapped power at your hands. Power that is not being leveraged by other filmmakers.

The topic of special effects is so vast, so expansive, that I would need to write an entire book—a lengthy one—to even begin to exhaust all of the possibilities, and what's needed to fulfill them. I'm going to do my best to condense a lot of it down to the essentials, and point you in the right direction. It's very important you being aware of these possible tools, and being interested in learning about them.

So, where do we begin?

Before anything, before I even get into the fundamentals of special effects, the number one rule is this: you must know how to do the effect on your own before you even begin the movie.

"On your own" is key.

Because "on your own," is what you'll be when it comes time to complete your film. All promises from others about, "I do special effects," will vanish faster than you can blink. By the time you reach the ending phases of a movie production, very few people, if any, will be left.

In fact, I suggest knowing how to do the effect <u>long before you even do the script</u>.

Because it's the knowledge of what you "can do" that's going to most influence your script. You don't want to create plot points that hinge around effects you can't possibly do.

And don't think you'll "write it out now," then figure it out later. Yes, it is possible to have a helicopter flying over your scene. It is. But you don't know that. Not yet.

Not until you see that it can be done, seeing the effect done in a movie, or in a video on YouTube, and then seeing a step-by-step instruction on how to do that particular effect.

But that's putting the cart before the horse.

COMPOSITING

To really gear yourself up for all things special effects, and more importantly, all things related to "computer" special effects (which is where you'll be doing the majority of your effects), you first need to learn any one of the many so-called "compositing" softwares.

This point personally caused me a lot of needless confusion when I was young. Anytime I'd get a foothold in learning special effects, I'd get pointed in a different direction. I would see a video, say, of a GHOSTBUSTERS fan shooting lasers out of their proton pack, and I'd want to do the same thing. I'd then hear something along the lines of, "It was done in After Effects."

Which left me confused—and a little intimidated.

I believed "After Effects" was the name of the actual process in painting on the proton beams, or painting on any kind of electrical beam, onto the footage.

Naive, I know.

But I illustrate it to get everyone on the same page.

First off, let's look at the acronym C.G.I. "CGI." I always, always have to explain and re-explain to my Dad what this means. So many times, with such great detail, that I'm starting to suspect a lot of people don't know what it means. Any skirting of the special effects realm will yield this phrase. "CGI." It stands for, "COMPUTER GENERATED IMAGERY." It's a term that was used to sell the field back when it started in the early 90s.

Any effect that is done after the movie is shot, especially now a days, is a digital effect, is CGI. The helicopter flying through the shot, the monster knocking over a building, the blood spatters, the erasing of wires, the adding of titles and credits, the removing of green screens, are all digital effects. They are all CGI—computer generated imagery.

Let's get that out of the way.

For all the effects done in computer, it then breaks down into two types of special effects. This is where things get slightly more confusing, and a little needlessly intimidating.

The first type of special effect is called "**compositing**." Now, don't worry if that word chills you a little bit. Please, don't let it. "Compositing," while an apt description of the actual activity, is yet another piece of jargon that's needlessly confusing. What's "compositing?" What does it mean? Why is it done? Where's it done? How do you do it? A ton of questions, I know.

First, if you want to add anything to the image of your video, if you want to put anything into—or, better still, onto, your image, your video, your film, your clips, your whatever-you-call them, that's so-called "compositing." To "composite." The definition of the word "composite" means a "blending," and that's apt for this. It boils down to addition. Anything that's adding to the image—that's compositing.

Again, needlessly confusing. But bear with me.

If, for instance, you've seen a behind the scenes video of a favorite movie, and you see the actors standing in front of a green screen—this has to do with compositing. The green, which is very prevalent and no where seen in the final film, is there because the compositing software can remove the green, and then allow something to be added in behind what's left.

Think of compositing like cutting up pieces of paper, sticking them on a canvas, a big piece of poster board, and then arranging the pieces of paper to your liking.

Compositing, compositing software, allows you to literally cut away at your image—and not in an 'edit' kind of "cut," but in an "X-Acto blade" kind of cut—and re-arrange it on another piece of video.

If that sounds interesting to you, if you would like something that would allow you to virtually take an X-Acto knife to your image, cut out things, re-arrange them onto another video clip, then you need to find a COMPOSITING SOFTWARE.

After Effects is a compositing software. In addition, there's Nuke. There's Apple Shake—which I understand is now defunct. There's Apple Motion. There's MovieRide FX, Combustion, SilhouetteFX, and many more.

Anytime you hear those names, or read those names, know that the person is talking about "compositing," about taking a virtual knife to the image, about adding things in, and about "re-composing" the desired shot.

It is highly recommended you seek out a compositing software.

Truth be told, I didn't do so until about six years into my work. And I regret it. Again, I had always had an interest in special effects, in digital effects, but the field just remained this elusive, heretofore concept. Which is a silly notion to have.

There was another reason: price.

Somewhere, somehow, I saw how much After Effects cost—and wretched. $3,000. And as a teenager, I was awfully intimidated about finding that kind of money. If I have any regret, it's that I let this big number get in the way of something I needed to know.

Let me emphasize. You need to learn compositing. If only for the sake of knowing what is possible, if only for the sake that it teaches you a completely different way of thinking about visuals and how you plan, write, direct, etc.

As far as that $3,000 dollar sticker price, Adobe (the maker of After Effects) now does a monthly fee, rather than an outright purchase of the software itself. You rent, rather than buy. I'm not a huge fan of doing it this way, but, that's beside the point. You can now rent the software, which is really, really awesome for you! As of this writing, it's $19.99 a month for just After Effects, or $49.99 for the use of all of Adobe's products. Pricey, sure! But think of all the stuff you, or your family, or whomever supports you, spends in monthly fees. Netflix, anyone? Amazon Prime? The family's cell phone!

I strongly, strongly, strongly—STRONGLY—urge you to do the opposite of what I did when I was a boy, which was to wait. That is, wait until a time when others—experts—wizards—would do the effects for me. A profound, foolish error on my part. Assume that you will never get to work with the technicans you see being interviewed in the behind-the-scenes features, assume you'll never work with anyone from ILM, or Scanline, or whoever is the big special effects house when this should find you. Learn compositing.

Learn compositing.

Because by learning compositing, you discover a catalog of what is—and what isn't—possible.

There's so many wonderful, rich, inspiring(!), resources out there, that I just want to take the time to point you in in their direction for a full scale understanding of "compositing" movie special effects. Here's a list of names you should Google: Zach King, Freddie Wong, Lynda.com, and above all, Andrew Kramer and his wonderful website VideoCopilot.Net.

A quick review of VideoCopilot.Net and Andrew's many tutorials will reveal just a fraction of what's possible:

— Replace the sky in your shots.
— Artificially shake the camera in post.
— Add a totally new background to your shot.
— Create the BLACK HAWK DOWN look (known as Bleach bypass).
— Have someone's head explode.
— Create a light saber effect from STAR WARS.
— Add in fake blood.
— Create the effect of someone getting shot.
— Create realistic gun fire.
— Make a meteor crash.
— Create a lightning strike—and one that can explode a person.
— Create missile fire through a city.
— Create amazing trailer titles.
— Create realistic explosions (Andrew Kramer is the EXPERT at this).
— Create an airplane crash.

I highly suggest, urge, looking up the names I've mentioned, viewing their work, taking in the inspiration, and learning from the videos they've generously made available to the aspiring filmmaker. Go through all of Andrew Kramer's tutorials, watching them once, then following along, then practicing whatever skill he is describing, and finding a way to make the skill your own.

3D GRAPHICS

We've already established what "compositing" is in regards to visual effects, now it's time to make another distinction. The distinction of 3-D graphics. Just to clarify, the kind of 3-D I'm about to refer to has nothing, in any way, to do with when you go to a theater, and opt to go see the "3-D" version of a film like AVATAR. That's something totally different than 3-D graphics.

We're about to talk about 3-D graphics in respect to, for instance, creating the dinosaur.

The kind of 3-D we're going to talk about, the kind of 3-D that's related to visual effects, the kind of 3-D that is being talked about when someone says, "Oh, that's a 3-D effect," isn't even really an effect, but rather an object. When anyone refers to 3-D effects in regards to the creation of visual effects, they are not talking about the actual compositing, the actual doing of the effect, but rather referring to an actual object that is created WITHIN the computer—the dinosaur, the helicopter, the car, the "CGI" person, the whatever needs to be structured up and modeled for whatever will ultimately be "composited into" the shot.

The 3-D moniker comes from the fact that the object, the asset, whatever the thing, is created in 3-D space on a computer.

That's it. That's all it means.

With all of that being said and clarified, the whole issue is a bottleneck that slides into an entire field. Which is the field of creating assets, virtually from nothing, within the realm of a computer. And it's created in the computer because creating it outside, in the physical realm, is all but unfeasible, or downright impossible. For example, creating the dinosaur. Sure, an entire mock dinosaur could be erected—and one was for JURASSIC PARK—but once you need lifelike movements—like making the T-Rex race after a speeding Jeep—you need the aid of digital forces.

This is about creating assets in 3-D space.

And not only creating them, but breathing life into them, making them move, walk, soar, dance, whatever.

Then, it goes even further than objects. It goes into creating <u>elements</u> that will interact with these objects, like smoke plumes, explosions—the majority of which are today just created in a computer.

If I want to achieve anything with this suggestion, it's for you to have the knowledge of what's going on here in this area of special effects. So you won't be intimidated by them. So you'll have correct knowledge on where these subjects are on a theoretical map. Not knowing exactly what was going on with 3D, how it was different from compositing, kept me from learning special effects.

Because, I assumed 3D *WAS* CGI.

Which, again, was a mistake. A mistake based on a misperception I don't want you to share.

I want you to know what 3D is, so you can say, "Well, that's that, and even though it's a whole other thing, even though it's all the way over there requiring a whole bunch of new skills, I can still focus on this other part of visual effects, and indeed succeed on this other part."

Because 3D effects are really, really hard to do. Or, rather, I should say, really hard to create.

Really hard because it requires so many different skills. Because first, you have to know how to model. Whereas effects artists used to sit at a bench and finely craft a monster (sometimes, they still do), they now sit at a computer and finely craft the actual item needed. And knowing how to model entails a whole host of skills that, well, you may not possess at the moment.

Then, there's the technical aspects of modeling, of understanding wire-meshing, of "Z-Brush," of understanding the x, y, z axis, of how to even operate the software itself. A whole other set of knowledge.

Then, there's the actual breathing of life into these objects. In an analog sense—how does a dinosaur, for instance, behave? Or, using a more mundane example, how is an Apache helicopter supposed to behave—and in what conditions, and under what circumstances? How do the blades connect to the rotor, the rotor to the engine, the whatever to the whichever? It's literally staggering how much has to be mastered and understood just to even build a single model. Entire departments are dedicated to doing just this. Other, entire departments are dedicated to bringing these objects to life.

Now, with all of that being said, there is a place where you can BUY many, many 3D objects/assets already created by a professional. There is a place, like a store, where you can go buy a model, like you might buy a model at a store, take it, import into a 3D software and do whatever you want with it. It's called TurboSquid, and you can visit and browse their entire selection—some of it free—at TurboSquid.com.

As far as the software you'll need to do these kinds of effects, here's a short list: 3ds Max, Cinema 4-D, Blender (which is free, by the way), Maya, and Houdini.

Not only are these software programs used to create assets, but they are necessary in order to breathe any kind of life into the asset itself. That is to say, make the blades on the helicopter spin, make the dinosaur walk, make the explosion go "boom," etc.

Which is why, if you want to utilize any kind of 3D object in your film, you must then learn one of the previously mentioned programs.

They are difficult programs. Do-able, to be sure. But difficult. If you do decide to learn them, or check one of them out, don't feel bad if you're at first blush intimidated by the layouts. These are not user-friendly programs created for the hobbyist.

But they can be learned. Many, many courses are available that demonstrate a step-by-step way of learning them. I highly suggest you follow the tutorials, steps, courses, and take the time to practice.

It can be done.

Special effects, especially visual effects, are like any of the skills mentioned in this book. They can be studied, they can be learned, they can be done. But it has to be done in that order. I promise: you can't just buy one of these programs, or any of these programs, and expect of yourself to jump in and, after a few hours, be utilizing the software to its fullest. That is a grossly unfair expectation to make on yourself. It's not like picking up a football and discovering you have a propensity for throwing it far distances (and I would argue being able to throw a football isn't exactly a plug-and-play affair either!).

If you are interested in effects, make a study of it. Again, seek out the works of Freddie Wong, Zach King, and most importantly, Andrew Kramer. Watch all of their videos, take the inspiration they will more than likely give you, and follow the steps they advise.

Then, practice.

The acquiring of special effects skills will ultimately give you a wider palette upon which you can not only make your movie, but ultimately save it.

22
EDITING

The assembling of all the video clips, the music, the special effects, the sound, will ultimately leave you with a massive blob of a movie. The big, massive blob that is the sum of everything you've achieved up until this point.

And it's going to feel, to you, like a blob.

Sure, there's stuff in there that looks good. In fact, there's a lot more stuff in that blob now, that looks good, that looks ten times better, than it did when you completed the so-called 'principal photography.'

But, the whole mass of it is still never the less a blob.

Now comes the actual editing! Which actually means to go back and refine—and sculpt down.

I caution, there is an element of madness at work in this phase. Material that seemed to work great on its own, now seems out of place or inconsistent. A piece of music doesn't fit with the rest of the tunes you've composed. A series of complicated sounds doesn't seem to gel with the vast majority of the other cues. A special effect shot that you created early on, one you were really, really excited about, now seems no longer up to par, considering how much practice all your work has accumulated for you.

There is a madness at work, and that madness is the very definition of insanity: doing the same thing over and over and expecting different results.

Sculpting your film down to a chiseled work of art will involve not only much subtraction, much extraction, but also a re-doing of all the previous elements.

EDITING

To begin the process, we must first return to the assembly.

To start, watch the whole movie. Yet another scary experience. But you will be seeing a different movie than previously. They'll be more colors, more sounds, different meanings, moments of sheer brilliance even! But already, you will start to see exactly where you need to—where you'll want to—cut.

To edit.

It is here where you start to throw material away.

If the axiom, "kill your darlings" ever applied, it's here, at this point of the process. And you will be killing a lot of your darlings. Because the very success of your film depends on which darlings you kill. You're going to be your own worst enemy with this too, holding onto things that, unto themselves, were once good, now only serve the creeping bloat.

As you sculpt and choose, know that your work entails thoughtful choices.

Thankfully, a lot of these choices will come naturally to you. For instance, when you watch the movie, you will already start to get a sense of what scenes to trim down, and what scenes to leave alone. This is why, when creating the initial assembly cut of the film, I wanted you to leave in so many redundant expressions, reactions, etc. Because as you watch, you will almost—intuitively so—know exactly where to pull the length of the shots back to.

So, when you go back through the movie, you will know, with huge confidence, with the confidence that can only be gleamed by working from such a high altitude, where exactly to make your choices.

Taking in the entire blob of the film, you really start to recognize how little of the movie resembles what it was you actually set out to do. Which can be a profoundly depressing experience. But only so because it's a process of your initial vision fading, and a new one emerging.

The new vision being what the movie actually is.

You will see "who" the movie really belongs to, which character seems to actually dominate the movie (you'll be surprised); you'll see which supporting characters are actually stronger than the other; you'll see themes that didn't exist before; messages that you didn't anticipate; emotional hues and cues you weren't even going for—but have somehow wormed their way into your production. This is the material that was all along trying to get out. These are the unearthed diamonds of your subconscious mind.

And it's only by circling the mass can you begin to see not only a true picture of the movie… but of yourself.

If there's any point in the movie production where you will really begin to see into yourself, it's here. It's what Robert McKee calls the great creative leap. But instead of one single leap, it will be a series of rapid choices, all leading up to the final, finished movie.

Perhaps at this point, the pacing feels off, scenes need reshuffling, or entire acts need to be shortened, or lengthened, or an entirely new scene needs to be shot because a plot point wasn't sufficiently explained. There's a reason movies have "re-shoots." And it's not because they didn't get it right the first time. It's because something in the working assembly told them contrary to what their instincts were telling them previously.

Music cues will have to be re-worked, perhaps even entirely overhauled. On an emotional level, the music isn't clicking; you feel, deep down, there's another level the music needs to tap into. A real high level procedure that, at this point, can still be done. On a more technical level then, you will need to dig down and re-time, re-work the music on a scene-by-scene basis, vis-à-vis re-opening the entire music production for that one scene (the file of that scene), and re-time your beats where you want to emphasize, and where you don't.

This is where the maddening part begins. Because once you start to tinker here, another piece of the film will start demanding something else. Deciding to insert the melancholic sigh of an oboe over the moment where a character realizes something profound about himself… will make you realize that there is a far deeper subtext to that particular person, and that you now have to go to other scenes and perhaps introduce a similar oboe sound.

This means editing down the assembled scenes, extending them back, flexing them forward, then backward, then pushing the 'edit' over to whatever music program you're using (or DAW, for the professional slang), re-assembling that music, then transporting it back with the 'edit' to the editing software, watching it, then…

Realizing that there needs to be some sort of special effect in that one shot.

Perhaps a sign still needs erased (and that can be done), perhaps you feel that establishing shot needs a totally new skyline—so, you shuttle that shot over to your compositing program, in whatever technical way the software demands, and you do that shot, then bring it back, then—

—Keep doing this over and over—back and forth—until the movie finally settles into place.

When you feel you have a "workable draft" of the movie, you print it back out to DVD or whatever solid media you're going to watch the movie on.

Let's take a breath here. This is a momentous occasion. I can almost promise you, it will be a very rewarding, pleasing experience. If there's any point of the filmmaking process where doom and gloom doesn't haunt, it's when you've assembled the real first draft of the "edit." The music is in place, the cuts are in place, the sounds are in place, the special effects have sealed up any noticeable cracks, etc. Because this is the movie that was always meant to be. This is what the movie is more than likely going to be.

You have to be feeling some sense of enjoyment, satisfaction, relief, and pride. You, after all, have done something that 98% of aspiring filmmakers haven't done—and more than likely… will never do. For what it's worth, you're in a club with very few members, amongst some of the most accomplished filmmakers.

It's something to relish.

I suggest you watch your movie alone, and enjoy yourself.

It's almost all over.

You more than likely will have some changes you want to make. Write down a long, long list of them.

Then, make the changes. Then, lock it down.

Now that everything is in place, let's go on to a few things you can do to really "punch up" the whole production. These are some of the things you can do to really give the movie an extra gloss!

23
FINISHING TOUCHES

Now that your movie is pretty much finished, I want to give you some ideas on how you can give the entire production a little extra punch. Just something to put it over the edge and really 'wow' your audience.

They are risky ideas. But they can pay off. If you do them right. And with caution.

ON COLOR CORRECTION

To be honest, I'm not sure what your ideas about "color correction" are, and what you think of when you see that phrase, "color correction." Personally, I knew almost nothing about color correction or that the 'look' of video could be significantly altered. It's one of those processes you don't know about Until You Know About It. Until someone points it out, or you happen to just stumble across it by accident.

Perhaps, like me, you've noticed on your editing software that there exists certain filters like "brightness/contrast," and "3-Way Color Corrector." Maybe you've experimented and found them, at best, puzzling.

I just know that once I found out about color correction, I really became aware of the fact that what you see in camera, what you get out of the camera, what you see on screen, is not necessarily what the picture will end up looking like.

If you haven't already noticed, some movies do 'look' different than other movies. Sure, a lot of that has to do with the "cinematography." But, past a certain point, this oblique notion of a movie's look, the "color" of a movie, settles right down into the color correction of a film.

A few examples to better understand. Look at the shots in any of the TRANSFORMERS movies. Then look at the shots in BLACK HAWK DOWN. Notice a difference? One seems… how should I put it…? Brighter, more "poppy," more colorful; the other gives off a "grittier vibe," a feeling of bleakness, of despair. Almost black and white. Almost. But not quite.

I want to point out this difference so we can to talk about it on the same page. Because it's important, and the distinction, this subject, what it's all about, holds a lot of potential power for you. And I want to be as delicate about it as possible because I'm almost 100% certain no one has ever tapped you on the shoulder about it. If you know what color correction is, fine. Bear with me. But I'm going to start the discussion from my own initial impressions and biases.

I was always keenly aware that my movies always ended up looking differently than the "big movies," the "real movies." Put another way, I was keenly aware of how I couldn't get my movie to look like a certain movie.

Because the difference between what my movie looked like, and what a big movie looked like, was always vast. The difference, ultimately, as I discovered through years of study, encompassed many facets.

A "movie's look" is made of many different parts. Color correction is a big part of that.

I can't remember any particular movie 'look' I wanted to emulate, but I would know the look when I saw it advertised as a certain 'look.' "Sepia-tone" always cast an old-time brownish hue to the picture, for instance. There was the "black and white" look. For a long time there was the so-called "blockbuster look," and I greatly, greatly admired that one. But "blockbuster" changes from time to time. At the risk of sounding dated, I will just go along with what was considered a "blockbuster look" when I started understanding color correction. It was actually a look that echoed the visuals of Michael Bay's TRANSFORMERS. With bright colors and stark levels of "contrast."

If you're not familiar with "color" terms, of what exactly "brightness" is, of what exactly "contrast" is, of what "hue/saturation" is, of what "RGB" means, of what "gamma" is, and a slew of other technical terms dealing with color correction, it's extremely difficult for me to really "get to the good stuff."

So, I'll just start with examples, and I'll try to encompass a wide variety of looks, and try to point you in the right direction of achieving them.

Know this: You may be under certain limitations in regards to color correction. As discussed earlier, most of the cameras you use, their recording methods, tosses a lot of the color away. You may actually "see" a certain color being reported, but I guarantee you not ALL of that color—or it's potential—is being recorded. Which is why finding a camera that sports a specification that reads something like "4:2:2" is so important. Most cameras will only have "4:2:0." Which is not good, and will tremendously limit what we're about to talk about. Usually the camera will only shoot in what's called 8-bit, which is, well, it's essentially, for our purposes, the same thing as 4:2:0. Without getting into what those numbers mean, or why they are the way they are, let's just say that those are the numbers that seriously determine how much of a look you can actually achieve.

So, if you really want to achieve the following looks, I seriously advise making sure the camera records in at least "4:2:2."

If you're unfamiliar with some of the titles I'm about to list, I highly recommend seeking them out and looking at some of the images. I guarantee, whatever year you're currently in, the look of that movie will catch you—and your admiration.

So with that...

BLACK HAWK DOWN

This is the BLACK HAWK DOWN look. It's from a 2001 war movie directed by Ridley Scott, about a squadron of soldiers who become embroiled in urban warfare with Somalian warlords. The mood of the film is desperate, grim, hopeless, brutal, and gritty. The look localizes around dark colors, sharp contrast, and highlights that almost look "bleary." It's a great look if you want a really, really depressing feel.

You might, if you were in possession of some color terms, believe that achieving the look is a matter of "de-saturating" the colors. And yet, if you were to try and simply turn down the "saturation" on your image, the effort would only slightly begin to echo the BLACK HAWK DOWN look.

To really get the look, to really "emulate it," you have to deploy a process called Bleach bypass. Never mind what the process actually is, or what it's referring to, or how it was once achieved—it doesn't matter.

FINISHING TOUCHES

How you achieve it does. And there are a few ways of doing that.

Without getting into a step-by-step explanation (it would be outdated by the time this reaches you), I'm going to give you a blow-by-blow, and do my best to hint at ways you can really achieve it.

First, take your clip. Find some way of "de-saturating" it by about 50%. Whatever tool you have at your disposal, find some way of cutting the color in half. Don't go "black and white," but just take about "half" of the color out.

Then, duplicate the image so that you have a copy of the same clip on top of the original. From that clip, remove whatever filter or tool you used to diminish the saturation. You want this clip to have "full color."

Then, I want you to find a setting—perhaps it's right beside the clip—perhaps it's in some menu somewhere, but I promise you, there is some setting that can "BLEND" the two images as if they are one. In After Effects, it's a menu under the heading "Mode." You'll know you've found it when you see the following options:

> Normal, Dissolve, Dancing Dissolve, Darken, Multiply, Color Burn, Classic Color Burn, Linear Burn, Darker Color, Add, Lighten, Screen, Color Dodge, Classic Color Dodge, Linear Dodge, Lighter Color, Overlay, Soft Light, Hard Light, Linear Light, Vivid Light, Pin Light, Hard Mix, Difference, Classic Difference, and so on.

These are important "modes." They supposedly represent all of the ways you can affect the color/brightness/darkness "modes" of whatever clip you're playing with. I recommend experimenting with this. You're bound to get some funky—and insightful—results.

But for this example, select "Hard Light." Instantly, you'll see the image in the timeline of your editing software, or your compositing software, will immediately start giving off a depressing, gritty vibe. Depending on your experience, this might be one of those moments where you're about to get lost in the wide, wonderful world of color correction. Because, by just doing this, you're seeing how profoundly the "color" of the image, the "look," a look that can be applied in post production, can completely change the FEEL of the image, of the movie it's a part of.

Personally, I rank "color correction" in importance almost right there with music.

To continue with this look, I would suggest finding some way of combining the two clips into one, perhaps adding what's called an "adjustment layer" above, and finding some way of brightening up the image.

However you have to do it, I suggest some way of brightening up the image. On my monitor, right now, as I do the effect, it looks a little dark.

But it's up to you. I just want to let you know the possibilities.

In fact, go back to the "Blending Mode," and change it from 'Hard Light' to 'Soft Light.' See how that changes the look? It probably looks… softer. Grayer. Try "Linear Light." Blegh! That looks way too dark. Try "screen." Hm, that's interesting. It looks brighter now; gritty still, but not as dark as the previous modes. In fact, try and affect the brightness/darkness of the entire image, using an adjustment layer, or however way you can combine the two clips. You find that by adding some more contrast that the image really "pops," and it's popping because the difference between the darkest part of the image and the brightest parts are extremely pronounced.

This is the essence of Bleach bypass. This is the essence of the BLACK HAWK DOWN look.

In fact, if you're feeling up to it, you can push it further. However you combine these two images, try finding a way to add a "glow," however your software might allow you to add that. Play with the settings. You'll see that depressing image on your monitor takes on an even more… dare I say… desperate look? A look of sickness? Of distance? Of bleariness? It makes one think of nuclear fallout.

Perhaps that would be a good look for your zombie epic.

Incidentally, there's a reason why this look is so popular with indie filmmakers. You can really NAIL it with very limited color information from the camera. If you don't have a camera that records 4:2:2, you can still really lock onto this look because the technique itself is based around very limited color getting through in the first place.

If you want your movies to resemble much of what David Fincher has done, what Ridley Scott has done, if you're doing a war movie, if you really admire the look of Steven Spielberg's MINORITY REPORT, look more into using the process of "Bleach bypass." You will really enjoy yourself.

THE BOURNE ULTIMATUM

The look of this film, a 2007 movie directed by Paul Greengrass, about a secret agent with amnesia taking on an array of conspiratorial forces, is really popular for spy/thriller kind of material. It's a hard 'look' to explain without the two of us being together, and pointing at it, or extolling a long list of adjectives like, "sleek," "bluish," "greenish."

But it's a look none the less. And it's a look I believe you'll have a lot of fun playing with. Because it will really make your movie feel "actiony" and "thrillerish."

This look is achieved by, again, first finding some way of de-saturating the image—but without really de-saturating the "yellows." On your saturation filters, adjusters, whatever they're called, you can isolate the various colors. You'll see there's a "yellow" color, a "yellow channel," as it were. Try to pretty much knock out all the other colors EXCEPT yellow.

You'll get a grayish kind of image, but with the skin color of whoever in the shot still looking... well... like... the same.

The key to this look, this "spyish," "technoish," type look, is isolating all of the other colors—except yellow—and de-saturating them, leaving the so-called "skin tones," the way they were looking before.

Then, once you've created a major difference between the skin color—i.e. the skin color looking as it were when you shot it—and the other colors—you're going to want to find some way of increasing the contrast slightly, and then color correcting only the green and blue channels of the video.

This sounds more complicated than it actually is, and it will require a great deal of experimentation on your part. But you'll begin to see what I'm talking about. Isolate the individual colors, and then color correct only those color channels.

The key to this look is found in retaining the skin tones, all the while majorly effecting the blue and green channels. And I promise you, on your software, on your whatever, there is a way of editing the different color channels—there's only three: red, green, blue. The key here, again, is just messing around with the green and red.

You'll begin to see where you can take this look, and how different it makes the footage feel.

Don't feel bad if you're not getting the exact look straight away. There are a lot of variables involved, and the experts who initiated this look, steeped deeply in color theory and years of practice as they are, probably experimented a great deal before they achieved it.

This is another look that can be obtained relatively well with a consumer camera.

TRANSFORMERS

TRANSFORMERS is a 2007 film directed by Michael Bay about an invasion of robots who can disguise themselves as trucks, cars, appliances, etc. The TRANSFORMERS 'look' is very colorful, contrasty, very "candy-like," and very "cartoon-like." However you describe it, if you're looking at the image, you will notice that the look of the movie is different from that of other movies.

It's full of color.

And it's a fairly difficult look to achieve. Filmmakers like to knock the look, but secretly, it's one of their favorites. Personally, I love how TRANSFORMERS, and its sequels, look. To me, it is the blockbuster look.

And you need a blockbuster camera to achieve it. More or less. But you can give it a 'go' even if all you have is a consumer camera.

The 'look' localizes around being able to make the blues really blue, the greens really green, and the skin tones look as if everyone has a really, really great orange tan. And it has to be done without just cranking up the saturation slider.

Put a 'color corrector' on your image, stretch out the contrast, put on a 3-Way Color Corrector, drag the blues more into the blues—then, in the "mid-tones"—these are your skin tones—crank up the dial on the yellows and oranges.

You'll begin to see the look take shape.

I only offer these three examples to get you started, to get you cognizant of the fact that the image you get out of the camera, can be seriously manipulated to make the viewer feel a certain way.

I highly, highly suggest making a major study out of "color correction," googling that phrase, and watching all of the videos you can on the subject matter. Make a list of movies whose look "catches" you, a look you really relish, and try to find out how it was done. More than likely someone else feels the same way and has been able to visually demonstrate a step-by-step fashion way to achieve it.

We're limited here by three things. One, I can't show you. Two, I have no idea what software you're using. Three, I have no idea how familiar you are with a lot of the terms.

I only want to make you aware that the process of "color correction" can seriously change the course of a film.

Use wisely, use smartly, and test, test, test. What you think looks awesome will probably look terrible to someone else. That really contrasty image, the image that really looks like something David Fincher shot? It will probably make Mom or Dad go, "Ohh, why's it so dark?"

So, again: use wisely, use smartly, and test thoroughly.

SOUND DESIGN

When I was in the final stretch of production on my film THE MOVIES, I stumbled across on the internet an audio disc series called *Pro Sessions*; subtitled, "sound + loop libraries." Now, before you jump to conclusions. We're not going to be talking about sound effects, which you think of as adding sounds that accent demonstrative actions on screen—gun shots, tire screeches, door slams—the chestnuts of sound effects. I'm assuming you're already well versed on those kinds of sound effects.

The sound effects I want to talk about are more of the psychological variety—more relating to the actual, emotional experience of watching the movie.

The *Pro Sessions* album I listened to had all these strange sounds—booms, bangs, whacks, smacks, drones—you name it. These were so-called "cinematic" sounds. And they did sound "cinematic." But why?

And why do I even bring this up?

These kinds of sounds, like the ones found in Jeff Rona's *Liquid Cinema*, are typically known as "cinematic impact."

Because the sounds create an impact that is… get this… cinematic.

In what way? By placing any of these sounds under any kind of "moment" that takes place on screen, the moment gets a certain "heaviness." It's the acoustical, aural equivalent of taking a yellow highlighter and underlining the moment.

Again, these sounds are typically low thuds, booms, bombs, whooshes, drones, slams, and otherwise ambient tones.

They are truly powerful sounds when placed up against any kind of moment on screen. Which is why it's easy to get carried away with them. When I loaded up *Liquid Cinema* for the first time and started experimenting with some of those sounds, I all of a sudden had 'whacks' and 'booms' and fire 'rushes' riddling the soundtrack, playing anytime someone was about to say or do something. I recognized the power of using these sounds, but I didn't know how to strategically place them.

I want you to find a "cinematic impact" library to purchase. Any of them will do; although, there are some excellent sources: Videocopilot.net, Boom Library (a favorite of mine—and most of Hollywood), 8dio, Liquid Cinema, and just about anywhere you can find some library of sounds that provide some sort of discernible accent.

Then, listen to these sounds. Note how some of them make you feel and what kind of impressions they give you. The 'whacks' tend to add a sense of finality, definition, clarity; the "booms" tend to add some weight, some heaviness; the "drones" seem to kind of fill up the soundtrack and render a certain mood, however oblique.

Few things will inspire you as discovering these sounds for the first time.

These sounds are not just random noises, but rather time-tested psychological triggers. They direct the mind's eye, the mind's ear, in one direction or another, shifting attention here, shifting attention there, and shaking you alert to something that's right in front of you. They are a kind of music, although they're mostly devoid of any melody.

Their purpose is to highlight the film's subtext. If a monster suddenly appears, and you want the audience to jump up—simply showing a picture of the monster won't do. This is why, in any horror movie, when a monster appears, say when a ghost appears on screen in INSIDIOUS, it's directly partnered with some loud crack, or boom, or some kind of sudden noise that's there to let you know: THIS IS A VIOLATION! The film's reality is being violated, and so, you need to be told that. If you need any proof that a movie is mostly about its sounds, look no further than a successful horror film. It's the sounds—not necessarily the visuals—that cue us to listen up relative to the rest of the supporting bits.

It's the sounds that turn the corners and propel along a story.

Simply showing something never, ever does the trick.

It's with these sounds, in all of their assortments, that you can truly unpack, and underscore, and underline the film's true subtext, the film's true meaning, the film's true effect. These sounds are a direct shortcut to manipulating the viewer's subconscious: PAY ATTENTION!

It works the same for moments even more subtle than a monster's face flashing on screen. In dramatic moments, when a character "realizes something," when a character's face begins registering that he indeed is realizing where the bomb actually is, suddenly realizing who the *real bad guy is, suddenly comprehending the bad guy's plan—there is usually some kind of low thud, boom, or bang present on the soundtrack.

Without the sound, it becomes immensely difficult for the audience to really understand what's happening.

Sound makes the invisible visible.

When you watch movies from now on, take note of how often you hear these "impacts." From some sound signifying a change in the story, to a sound gaining speed and then "whooshing" the audience into the next scene, keep your eye—and ear—open to various going-ons of the soundtrack.

Sometimes, the music does accomplish these accents. But mostly, it's the impacts that are the items driving the scene.

Buy a library, listen, and experiment. These sounds will take your movie—truly—to the next level!

MASTER THE SOUNDTRACK…..

For years, I wondered why, when I finally played my movie on TV, or on the computer, it always sounded worse than—or not as good as—professional TV shows and movies. Of course, I'd read about "mixing," and dutifully went about learning about it. I found nice results—i.e., lowering the volume so it doesn't drown out the mix. Yes, finding out how to appropriately "mix" the levels of the film's soundtrack, the film's sound is a must, is absolutely essential.

But there's one more packet of secret sauce that isn't often talked about.

The process is called "mastering." That is to say, the movie's audio track is "mastered." What does that mean? Well, let's first remove the whole notion that we're dealing with a movie.

Let's for a second pretend you are a singer and were instead in the process of creating a song that's meant to play on the radio. As a singer, mixer, all around engineer on this hypothetical song, you would "render" out the song—or "bounce" as the music people like to say—play it in iTunes or whatever software you use to play music, and then you'd compare it to other professional songs. You'd notice that the song, regardless of how well you "mixed" it in your editing software, just doesn't reach that certain level, doesn't have that certain, certain…dare I say, clarity?

It doesn't feel as "there" as the professional stuff.

You search and search for reasons why, but come up with repeated explanations about mixing, and about your failure to record good audio. That could be partly true, yes. But what you'll seldom hear about is the process of "mastering."

This process, simply, is the song being rendered out from the program, bounced out, placed in a single mp3 file or AIFF file, or some single file; then, an engineer takes that single file, places it back in some audio editor, then proceeds to still further add more filters, thereby giving it that fuller sound.

A similar process is used for movie trailers, and possibly, movies themselves.

Regardless of what they're doing, I want you to apply this "mastering" process to the audio track of your movie.

Here's what you do.

Before you print out the final cut of your movie, I want you to render out all three tracks of your audio—the dialogue, the sound effects, the music—into one stereo track. Then, take that file and put it back into whatever audio editing system you're using. That may very well be the editing system you've used to edit the movie. It might be Logic Pro, it might be Pro Tools, it might be whatever. But once you put it into that program, I want you to seek out a few filters.

I have no way of knowing what the filters will be called on your end, but I can describe what kind of filters you should put on your audio track—if only to give it that "extra punch."

At the very least, at the bear minimum, look for some kind of audio filter that is called something like "compressor." What it is, what it does—well, again. Another book. But seek this little tool out. Apply it to the file. Perhaps, if you're lucky, there will be presets. Dial those presets to something having to do with "vocals," "voice," or "tools." And as you do so, you will notice an immediate change in the sound of your audio. Perhaps that change may not be desirable. You'll have to experiment. You'll have to investigate more into what compressors are, and what they do. At the very least, I just want you to hear that some kind of change is possible.

Because you might just like the sound. You may notice, after applying the compressor (and this is not to be confused with Apple's Compressor, which has to do with file sizes), that the dialogue of the movie seems to come through a lot more clearly.

Really what's happening is that all of the louder sounds of your soundtrack are being lowered to the average level of the track, enabling you to raise the entire volume without making the loud sounds too loud. At least, this is the best benefit it can offer you. If you've watched your movie with friends or family, and there are those moments when the character's talking seems to kind of fade—and then suddenly everything gets loud, and gee, you'd hate to lose the "impact" or the loudness of those sounds that are supposed to be loud and in your face, so, gee, you don't want to turn down the volume—then this tool, "the compressor," is for you.

So, you apply a compressor.

Then, you find some way of applying what's normally called a "limiter." It'll be called something like that (you know how companies like to get cute with these names). If there are no presets, then look for what's called an "Output Level." This controls the so-called "legal" limit of what's allowed to be played on TV. Practically, this means setting a limit so that the speakers don't start crackling. Which is an unpleasant sound. Beneficially, this caps the volume of your film at, say, -1db, or wherever you should set it at. The key is that this is the *official volume of the film, and no other sounds will be getting in over that limit. Why this is, why you need to do this, don't worry. It's kind of like putting a lid on a steaming cup of coffee.

But then here's the good part.

While you are setting the "output level," you can also go to another setting and increase what's called the "gain." Turn it up. Play your audio, and you will immediately notice how everything is much, much louder—but that, technically, it's still only at a certain level.

This the essence of mastering.

It's louder without blowing out the speakers.

Play with the gain, adjusting it to your heart's content.

Now, this isn't to say that you can just keep cranking up the volume and live happily ever after. At some point, the recording begins to sound bad. It's losing what's called "dynamic range," which just means the difference between the quiet and the loud sounds. Or, more specifically, that means the audience is still leaning forward when the girl is creeping around the corner—and then still being surprised when that loud BANG signals the monster behind her! The quiets are quiet, the louds are still surprising.

Thankfully, there's an even easier way to try this process. If you have access to the right software.

For instance, in Logic Pro X, you can go to the "Stereo Out" channel, go to the top of the channel strip, click "Setting"—a menu drops down—drag your mouse over "Factory," and click on any of the many settings that come up. Hint: try "Broadcast Ready." The software will automatically apply a series of the correct filters—and a few more for fine tuning abilities.

Then, if you want to spend a little money, look up "iZotope Ozone." I can't know what number they'll be up to by the time you read this, but I can promise that by just putting your audio through their software, it's going to sound about five times better. Just putting it into the software, just selecting one of the hundreds of presets, will create a profound difference in the quality of your audio.

A difference for the better.

At the very least, experiment with all of this stuff.

PART 5

GETTING THE MOVIE OUT THERE

24
THE NEXT PHASE...

"How do I get distribution?" This question is usually asked when there isn't even a movie to distribute. It's kind of the equivalent to the "author" who has never written a book asking, "How do I get published?" Of course, the question betrays a deeper anxiety: why bother going through all the hard work of actually creating the book, the movie, the album, the whatever, if it's just going to end up sitting on the shelf?

A self-defeating attitude that leads to idling in wait.

But, you may not have that attitude. Provided this is your second or third read, AND you've finished your first feature film (or even your first short, for that matter), you will actually have a reason to "get distribution." And not only that, but you will have braved the waters of creating the product that is to be distributed. You deserve a major congratulations on that. You're like Bruce Wayne in that one scene from BATMAN BEGINS where, after a brutal, punishing journey through the mountains, the Liam Neeson character, Wayne's trainer and mentor, greets him with an unsympathetic kick to the stomach.

While you too may feel like keeling over, exhausted from your journey, you're also in for a similar surprise: you've only just begun.

Of the total effort that goes into producing a motion picture, you've maybe, so far, done about 30-40% of the work. That's being generous. In filmmaking, the actual making of the film counts for very little of all the work that will go into making a film. This is a big, tough pill to swallow.

Reading this section of the book, you're going to discover one single truth:
You are not a filmmaker.

You are not a filmmaker, a "moviemaker," a movie director, a writer, an actor, an editor, a whatever that has to do with the actual creation of a movie.

Because you are NOT in the movie business. Your friends and family may think you are. Your teachers may think you are. Your colleagues might believe they themselves are. But they're not.

And neither are you.

You are, now and forever, <u>in the marketing business</u>.

Read that sentence again:

You are in the marketing business.

If there's any "red pill" to be swallowed in this field, it's that the business of making movies is actually the business of marketing.

All notions about quality, about creativity, about "finding a voice," about "saying something new," about anything having to do with creation or inspiration or whatever that goes into actually making anything… has to go right out the window. The movie you've completed, whether it's good or bad, is <u>nothing more</u> than what's called "a deliverable." It is the item that will ultimately be "delivered" over to the customer. It is the thing that money is exchanged over. Nothing more. Nothing less.

Really, "the deliverable" could be anything. If you were a programmer and you made web sites, the web site would be the deliverable. If you made widgets, then the widget itself would be the deliverable. Whether that widget is an iPhone, a fidget spinner, a pet rock, a glass of beer, a song, a whatever. It's simply, whatever it is, a deliverable.

And you need to attenuate yourself to that thinking. In fact, you need to attenuate that to the point that you see your movie as nothing more than a deliverable—but also blind yourself from recognizing another terrible truth: **from the standpoint of efficiency, a movie is a terrible deliverable.** An expensive, high budget movie even more so. Both require untold amounts of resources to achieve something that could otherwise be achieved with something like a pet rock.

Because if you took it a step further, you would see you're not even in the marketing business—you're in the money business.

And once you see both of these concepts together; well, it may be difficult to continue as a filmmaker.

Of course, you're saying, "but I'm not doing this for money." That's now, on film number one. That's now, in the spring of your aspirations. Because when you actually make a few films, when you actually complete

THE NEXT PHASE...

and sell some work, when you actually—and I mean REALLY—drop into that mission-creep of making a real movie, and you see all your friends prospering at normal jobs, buying cars, homes, finding wives, creating families, pleasing their families, receiving acceptance from society; when you really start to feel the shackles of actually producing a movie, you'll realize one painful fact: "No man but a blockhead ever filmed except for money."

Samuel Johnson said it about writing, but it applies to filmmaking just as well.

You're going to wretch at this notion more than anything, and you're going to do all in your mental powers possible to persuade yourself that I'm wrong, and that this isn't true. But if you can understand this, wrap your mind around it, master the tenants and skills involved with it, you <u>will be</u> the next Steven Spielberg, the next George Lucas, the next Christopher Nolan, the next Quentin Tarantino, the next whoever you really enjoy as a filmmaker.

Because the downtown truth about all of your favorite artists, favorite filmmakers, favorite whoever, is that they are successes due solely to the marketing. Of course, talent is involved. And these are talented people. But what, after all, is talent? What, in its raw state, is this thing called talent? Is it something tangible? No.

What you and I call talent is based <u>solely on results</u>.

Talent is the sum total of what has actually been done and demonstrated—i.e., the deliverable. To the uninitiated, Steve Job's and Bill Gates' genius resided in the ability to make computers. To you, after you fully and truly understand these ideas, you'll see that their genius resided in their abilities to sell computers. I highlight these two men to clarify a point beyond moviemaking. When you think of these two men, you think of computers, of tech stuff—and yet, neither one of them actually made the computers they're famous for. They didn't sit down and invent whatever it is that ultimately makes you call them a genius. In other words, they didn't make a better mousetrap. They SOLD a better mousetrap. That it's better has nothing to do with anything.

Now, I understand this goes against literally everything you believe about moviemaking, about art in general, about commerce in general. But it's the truth. If you need more convincing, let's look at athletes, at the ones who earn $20+ million dollar contracts while their colleagues make not even a fraction of that. Are those highly paid athletes statistically that much better than their lesser-paid team members? Are they that many times more talented than their team members? No. The highest paid athletes are paid less for their skill—lots of good athletes out there—and based more on their "name." In example, the ability to get people in the stands, the ability to get butts in the seats, the ability to generate more eyeballs—i.e., money! Which is the whole reason the NFL, the NBA, the MBA, all those industries, even exist in the first place. The money!

Does this sound familiar? Why do you think movie stars make upwards of $40 million dollars a film? Because they're that much more talented then their minimum wage counterparts? You know that's not the truth. They're paid that much more because of their name. They're paid that much more because their name has already been successfully positioned to the general public, and that the positioning of that name will give investors some sense of comfort in going forward with producing the movie itself. The actors or actresses are paid that much more for purely marketing purposes—not some innate talent or intangible sense of magic.

Those actors and actresses are paid that much more because there's a semi-reasonable expectation that they'll attract audience members—in other words, more money!

If you want to increase your odds of becoming the next Steven Spielberg, the increasing of those odds are to be found in the marketing. Not the filmmaking.

Yes, Steven Spielberg has a ton of talent, and is a really good filmmaker. But he only became Steven Spielberg <u>AFTER</u> JAWS. And JAWS only became successful after producers Richard Zanuck and David Brown turned the Peter Benchley BOOK into a best-seller, only after every copy of the BOOK (JAWS is based on a book, by the way) had the film's logo on it, only after the hardcover of the BOOK was sent out to all the major influencers of the day, only after Spielberg and co toured 11 cities, only AFTER a picture of a huge shark with the words 'Jaws' appeared on the cover of TIME magazine, only AFTER Universal Pictures spent what their publicity director at the time, Clark Ramsey, called "the largest expenditure on advertising of a release in the history of the company," only AFTER Universal bought tons and tons of 30 second commercials spots in the days leading up to the movie's release.

Of course, JAWS is a good movie. I imagine the movie SHARK! starring Burt Reynolds, another movie about a killer shark, is also a good movie. No way of saying, because neither one of us have ever seen it, or heard of it. Although, it does exist. And it came out years before JAWS.

At the end of the day, it's all about the "getting of the customer"—and the making of the dollar. That only happens—only ever happens—through marketing.

This is where we depart movie-land, and enter the wide, wonderful world of trying to convince people—other people—real people—to watch our movie. Think for a moment of that scene in THE WOLF OF WALL STREET where the DiCaprio character, a salesman, tests his friends by asking them to sell him a pen. They try the usual "it writes nice," "it's really great," "it's an awesome pen." But none of them are able to make the sale. Then, his last friend, holding the pen and looking at DiCaprio, gets it. He simply says, "I want you to write your name down."

The point of the exchange, the point of the entire film, is that selling is all about creating demand. Our goal, at this point, is to create demand.

A tough climb. Because, I can realistically assume, there is no demand for your movie. Which is OK, because that's pretty much anyone in Hollywood, or anywhere else, who ventures to do an actual, original movie. If there's any reason why Hollywood keeps making sequel after sequel, remake after remake, reboot after reboot, it's mostly because they're too afraid or too lazy to do the actual work of marketing something new to the masses. It has nothing to do with an inability to come up with new ideas. Hollywood, when trying to launch an original movie that no one has ever heard of, has to go through the same exact process you're about to go through too.

WHO YOU'RE COMPETING AGAINST

Of course, Hollywood has more capital—and not just in terms of money. Their main resource, other than a vast war chest of funds to spend on an assault-like campaign of high-profile media buys (TV, radio, newspaper, internet, etc), are the vast tentacles to jack in and jam out any and all other competing films opening on that opening weekend or on that Tuesday home-video release. Space is limited. And "visible" space—i.e., space that is visible to a paying customer—whether that's in a movie theater, at a cineplex, or in the virtual space of iTunes, Amazon, Netflix—is even more limited. Only a handful of films can dominate the limited attention of the paying customer at any given time.

The ability to wrestle and control this limited scope belongs, and will continue belonging, to a handful of what are called "conglomerations." The Merriam-Webster dictionary defines "conglomeration" as a "mixed mass or collection." In practice, the word points to a business entity that controls many business entities.

For us, it means a media landscape controlled by—as of 2017—six—count em' six—companies: General Electric (yes, lightbulbs/refrigerators), News-Corp, Disney, Viacom, Time Warner, and CBS. All of these companies should be familiar to you. They have only been shaping, molding, and crafting everything you've seen and read since president Bill Clinton signed the "Telecommunications Act of 1996."

6 companies control 90% of what you read, watch, and listen to.

For instance—take Disney. They own ABC, ESPN, Pixar, and Marvel. That means... if Marvel is releasing yet another AVENGERS movie, it won't be happening on the day another STAR WARS is coming out. They're both properties owned, ultimately, by Disney. They do not step on one another's toes.

Or, in a more dynamic situation: When yet another Batman movie arrives on the scene, you can almost be certain it will receive, at the very least, delicate consideration from CNN, Time magazine, and then ultimately be exhibited on HBO. Time Warner owns all of them—including Batman.

This delicate consideration works—or should work—in all of the other companies too. Universal Pictures releases a movie, the stars will be on *The Today Show*. Or, they better. General Electric owns both. If 20th Century Fox releases a movie, the New York Post should—in theory—give it some decent reception. When the same studio releases a sequel to DIE HARD, Bruce Willis will—will—appear on *The O'Reilly Factor*. Or, he would, if O'Reilly were still in the employ of News Corporation.

The "delicate consideration" in the industry is known as "synergy." Which is another great word: it means all of the parts of a conglomerate working together... to create something even bigger.

Synergy.

This is something you should know about if you're trying to sell your movie.

It means that you are up against a vast set of interlocking corporations all marching to the same drumbeat. And you can be sure... that beat doesn't include you.

Of course, it wasn't always like this.

Whereas six companies now own 90% of the media, that same 90% was once owned by fifty different companies, all of which were no more powerful than sum total of their own parts.

That was 1983.

Do you believe it's any coincidence that this was around the time movies—and TV—in general started going down hill? I'll leave that for you to ponder.

The point is: you're up against a lot more than you've been previously led to believe.

THE NEXT PHASE...

You have been led to believe that you're living through a "democratization of technology." Which is the notion that more and more power is falling into the hands of more and more people—via technology. For filmmakers, this was the notion that the cheaper cost and wider availability of cameras, camera technologies and media, meant a liberation of sorts from the corporate interests that dominate and control the flow of media.

But, just because videocameras became wildly available in the 1990s, doesn't mean the business you and I are in is any more democratic.

Whereas corporations could once reasonably sort through a limited set of available movies, music, TV, artists, and filmmakers, the limited channels that now exist—the ones controlled by the conglomerates—are now completely clogged by sewers of people giving movies "a go."

Put in another way, when you compete today, you aren't JUST competing with these six companies, you're competing against millions more trying to find their way into that very apparatus—millions who have also been so-called "liberated" by cheap video cameras.

You see, the six corporations exist at the behest of the consumer.

SOMEONE has to sift through all of the garbage.

And the American people, the people of planet Earth, have—whether knowingly or unknowingly—elected a corporatocracy, a panel of gatekeepers—real gatekeepers—all powerful gatekeepers—to sort and control everything you see, feel, hear, touch, and experience.

More content means more need for gatekeepers.

But, you say, what about YouTube? What about Google? About Amazon and Netflix? If you're reading this in 2019, your brain is already reaching for those companies. And with good reason. For now, they are private companies, all traded on Wall Street.

For now.

But, what else, you might ask, do those companies have in common?

The internet.

They all exist solely... purely... on the internet.

And they only exist on the internet.

This is important, for you, for me, for all filmmakers. Because the internet, really, is the last frontier.

For now.

Because I promise you, sooner or later, the internet will fall under firm control of either the US government, or, perhaps some larger, global entity. Whether through a lattice of anti-obscenity laws, the merging of the conglomerates (as I write this, AT&T is trying to merge with AOL), national security, whatever, the internet will come under the direct control of some larger, controlling force.

The notion that we're living through any kind of democratization of technology is an illusion created by the very companies trying to distract you from their increasing power. If there is any kind of democracy in our art, any kind of freedom, it exists only in the creation of that art, and only exists in the creation… of that media.

And you are not in the creation business.

<u>You are in the marketing business</u>. Because that's the very business the conglomerates are in. Disney, GE, News-Corp, Viacom, Time Warner, CBS. Producing content is not their problem. Distributing it is. Which is why they've angled themselves into controlling 90% of the available means of communication.

Which is why so many filmmakers ultimately fail.

Filmmakers believe, in their heart of hearts, that they are—at best—only up against Steven Spielberg, only up against—at best—the masters they greatly admire. They believe that succeeding in this business is merely a matter of getting really, really good at making movies, making better movies, and navigating the art to the next level.

It. Is. About. No. Such. Thing.

I empathize with the misunderstanding. When I was younger, the film PULP FICTION represented the lightning rod of independent filmmaking. Its greatness important and inspiring to filmmakers—including me—because its maker had started out as a video store clerk. So I personally set that movie as my bar. That if I could just get as good as Quentin Tarantino, then all such doors following would open, and I could be free to express myself as an artist.

What I failed to understand, was that Quentin Tarantino was able "to get with," of all places, Disney! Kevin Smith, Ben Affleck, Matt Damon, all of the indie darlings of the 1990s, the filmmakers I admired as a teen, were all Disney men. More power to them. They understood the game.

The films of Quentin Tarantino, to again use him as an example, are known to you not because of their quality—although, make no doubt, they are quality films—but because of the vast distribution powers of The Walt Disney Company.

If you find this difficult to believe, do yourself a favor and seek out all of Roger Ebert's reviews of Quentin Tarantino's movies (If you're not familiar with Roger Ebert, he was *the top film critic from the 1980s until his death in 2013. A great, raving review from him could cement the success of a movie).

His review of Tarantino's "debut" movie RESERVOIR DOGS: 2 ½ out of 4 stars.

THE NEXT PHASE...

Not so hot.

Thumbs down. That was 1992.

Then, look at Ebert's review for PULP FICTION: 4 stars. Best movie of the year. One of the greatest movies of the decade! A thumbs up.

What changed?

Better movie, right?

Maybe.

If we were just talking movies, we'd leave it at that. But we're not. We're talking about your career, your livelihood, your life.

What changed was that everyone got their ducks in line.

You have to understand, Ebert, in the day, did BOTH written and televised reviews—the televised ones making him infinitely more visible and famous than the written ones. If you remember him as giving the "thumbs up," or "thumbs down" decree, it's because of the show. Not the written reviews. It was the show, in other words, that really mattered.

The show, by the way, was owned and distributed by Buena Vista.

Buena Vista was and still is owned by...

Disney.

Tarantino's RESERVOIR DOGS? Not a Disney movie.

PULP FICTION? A Disney movie.

This is what's called "delicate consideration."

To be fair, Ebert did have major enthusiasm for Quentin Tarantino. Because, yes, Tarantino is a great moviemaker, and Ebert did know a great movie when he saw it.

But alas...

Tarantino's DEATH PROOF / GRINDHOUSE?

Ebert's review: 2 ½ stars.

Not a Disney movie.

DEATH PROOF / GRINDHOUSE truly was an independent movie in that it was the first movie after the Weinsteins (Tarantino's producers for the past two decades) left Disney over a disagreement over—you got it—a faux pas in 'delicate consideration'; which was over a film called FAHRENHEIT 911, a movie that violated the most delicate of considerations: criticism of a then-sitting president of the United States.

If you want to see how it is for a *truly, actual high budget independent movie, look to the movie GRINDHOUSE / DEATH PROOF. A great movie, by the way (it's one of those movies that really, really inspired me personally). Loved by fans, admired by critics (most, except Ebert). But a total bomb at the box office. 3 hours in runtime, sure. But INGLORIOUS BASTARDS, Tarantino's next film, a movie that grossed over $300 *million dollars, was over 2 ½ hours long.

The difference is that GRINDHOUSE had to navigate the treacherous mote outside of the conglomerations, while INGLOURIOUS BASTARDS, Tarantino's next and—then—highest grossing film, was a production from General Electric. Yes, the lightbulb company.

If PULP FICTION has dropped off the commercial radar in recent years, it's because PULP FICTION, along with all the other 90s and early 2000s Miramax films, was sold off from The Walt Disney Company in 2010. The film, along with all the other Miramax movies, is now owned by… Al Jazeera. Quentin Tarantino's great film, and therefore the marketing prowess behind him, is literally in the hands of the Qatar government, which owns Al Jazeera.

Therefore, you're not in competition with Quentin Tarantino. You're in competition with the government of Qatar. Although not GE or Viacom, you can be sure the Qatar government has some serious resources behind it. The key is power and leverage and control of what everyone sees, hears, and reads.

This is important because you have to know who you're competing against—or who you may want to ultimately work with.

I go through all these pains of describing this process to get your mind out of the whole Hollywood/Indie nonsense. There's no such thing. There is only…GE, News Corp, Disney, Time Warner, Viacom, or whoever in the future it is that owns all of the marbles.

Knowing this levels the playing field—for you. It will help you make smart, informed choices. Knowing these truths keeps you from being distracted from the bigger truth:

You are in the distribution / marketing business. Not the moviemaking business.

Let me say upfront that I'm very passionate about marketing/distribution, if you haven't already picked up on that. Most likely because I used to be so passive about it. You see, I believed in what professional marketers like to make fun of called the, "If you build it, they will come" myth. There's that one, and then there's the "build a better mousetrap" thinking (ask your parents about that one and they'll know you're starting to grow up). I would finish a movie, then I would release the trailer, then I would schedule a screening somewhere, then I would show the movie—and then, lights out. Nothing ever came from it.

In other words, I viewed marketing and distribution—if I viewed it at all—as something that's done AFTER the completion of the film.

Of course, in this book, I've placed the marketing section after the making of the movie. But that's only because I didn't want to confuse any expectations you had of the whole process of filmmaking. I didn't want you expecting to read a book about filmmaking and find the entire first section on marketing.

Truth is: marketing is something that should be going on the entire time you're making the film. Like a parallel universe that exists as a project separate and apart from the movie itself, you continually, for the months or years it takes to make the movie, get the word out there about the movie, continuously creating and exploiting marketing "events" (like the release of a trailer or the getting on of the radio program), continuously cultivating an interest—a demand, really—in finally seeing your movie.

In fact, it's this very demand by the time you're ready to "release" your movie that makes you all but totally sick of the entire enterprise of the making of this particular movie. If you do your job right, and you create enough demand, and do it all the while making your movie, you should have people constantly asking you, "When's the movie going to be finished?" When is the movie going to be finished?

Like an albatross trolling a boat, this question will follow you everywhere you go—if you're doing the marketing right. Of course, it will drive you insane, and will create more and more pressure on you, and it will push you to becoming a hermit by the end of producing the film, and it will make you never again want to talk about your movie with anyone—but this is the lifeblood of not only your movie itself, it is the very lifeblood of your livelihood.

Because it's here you'll see—if you're doing it correctly—which I'm going to show you how—that your real job as a movie maker is, as Kevin Smith talked about in one of his excellent books, a "presenter." A "host." A carnival barker. You're PT Barnum, you're Kim Kardashian, you're Mama June (OK, we won't go that far), you're Gene Simmons of KISS, you're Ryan Seacrest, you're Carson Daly.

This is truly the job of making movies. It's in not making movies, but in being a personality that people are passionately interested in.

If you do the marketing of your movie correct, you will see a painful truth that only about .0001% of filmmakers ever see, and even fewer, actually grasp:

People are more interested in you…then they are your movie.

If you want to make a quantum leap forward in understanding the movie business, in having major success in the movie business, it's in seeing that audiences *should be more interested in YOU, than they are in the actual content of the movie. This is where you'll find Spielberg, Scorsese, Nolan, Fincher, Tarantino, all of your favorites. This is also Eli Roth, M. Night Shyamalan, Michael Moore, Oliver Stone, Tom Six, David Lynch, and, you're favorite of them all, Stanley Kubrick. It's no coincidence that these directors are usually labeled as "controversial." They're not.

They're just really, really good at promoting their films.

They are MASTERS at promoting their work.

You don't go see their movies because of the content, but to see what THEY'RE doing with the content. You go see it because it's a "so-and-so film." I'd personally never go see a movie about gangsters. But I was first in line the night Scorsese's THE DEPARTED opened. I'd never see a martial-arts / slasher movie about a bereaved bride taking not one, but TWO films to seek revenge on her killers. But you can be sure I was first in line for KILL BILL 1 AND KILL BILL 2.

Let's say it again. "People are more interested in you, than they are in the movie."

Yes, I did say it is all about the marketing and not the movie. What I didn't say was that the marketing you will be doing is ultimately NOT about the movie—but about you.

Success as a filmmaker depends on how much you can make YOUR work… about you.

Truth be told, the movie itself is kind of incidental.

It's a movie about YOU. Not whatever it's about.

Knowing that, you begin the marketing for the movie long before you even make the movie. Marketing for the movie, really, should be a never ending job of marketing yourself.

THIS is creating demand to see your movie.

With those truths, we can then begin to assemble some sort of cogent plan.

25
MARKETING

But what is marketing? Is it running around slapping movie posters on the wall? Is it "getting the word out" in any way possible? Is it going to a film festival? Is it the making of the poster? Is it the making of the trailer? How about the "showing" of the trailer? How will you even get people to see the trailer? Is that marketing?

I would argue that everything you do from the time you decide to become a filmmaker, to the moment you die, is the marketing.

And the best place to start marketing, at least at this point, is by establishing what you actually want. What do you want out of your movie? Be honest. Do you want accolades? Do you want money? Do you want people to just see your movie? And there's noting wrong with that. In fact, that might be an easier goal. It's what I did for many years: I wanted people to see that I was making a movie, I wanted feedback on whether the movie was good or not, and I wanted to get a pat on the head. That was that.

Then, I got a little older.

And I started to have vague ideas about making money.

Money complicates things.

If you want to make money, then there are different strategies.

If you want to make a lot of money, then you really, really need a different strategy.

For our purposes in this book, let's assume you want everything. You want the pat on the head, the pat on the back, the great feedback, you want EVERYONE to see the movie, you want to get the awards, you want to get the great reception, and you want the money!

And of course… the ultimate. The thing that's even better than the money.

You want to be discovered.

Isn't that what has been behind all of your effort thus far? To be discovered. Or, put another away: to be noticed.

To gain exposure.

Ostensibly with the notion that you'll be picked out of the crowd and groomed for a far easier ride on the next-go-around.

THE BEST PLACE TO START…

The best place to start with your major marketing efforts is by showing the movie to someone. That someone will most likely—or should be—someone in your family, or one of your close friends. It should be someone close to you.

This is the first person, other than you, who will watch the movie.

Of course, marketing should have been taking place long before you ever do this—but we'll get to that. For now, I want you to show the movie to a friend or loved one. You can watch it with them, or you can not. It's up to you. I personally always liked to drop it off with a friend or loved one, then go on a long, long drive, then return and get the verdict.

Is it bad? Is it good?

Everything you've been doing has led up to this moment. Here is a loved one, a friend, sitting there with your movie, completely unabated by you, and they're supposed to ascertain a point of view about it.

Most times, truthfully, their reaction will be one of three things. One and two, most obviously, will be whether it's good or bad. The third option, the more likely option, is that their reaction will be one of reserved indifference.

Who, whom, you show your movie to in these initial stages is fairly critical—and the people you select will instinctively know this. They will know how much work you've put into it, how much effort, how much of your heart and soul you've sunk into this massive artifact, and they likely won't know how to react.

Think about it. Even when you go see a movie in the theater, one you're not even involved in, don't you often walk away—in all truth and integrity—with mixed emotions about whether or not it was a GOOD… or a BAD movie? How many times have you walked out of a movie raving, only to awaken the next day feeling a little more chilled?

How many times have you walked out of a movie, absolutely aghast, absolutely disgusted, only to awaken a month later, suddenly to discover that it was actually a GREAT movie?

Now, imagine a loved one made that movie in question.

Imagine how you'd react. With great hesitancy and caution.

This is why you pick a loved one to watch the movie first. They know the responsibility.

At this stage of the game, at this nascent crevice of the marketing section, you have to really ease your way into what's going to be a rough and bumpy road of how the audience—all the people "out there"—will receive your film. And that starts with exposing the movie to people who are going to take the duty with some responsibility and care.

You don't want snap judgements at this point.

In fact, you just want to have the movie seen by at least one person. Frankly, I always liked to show it to two people, simultaneously, in different locations. One person—most likely my Dad—would receive a copy, then, simultaneously I'd drop a copy off at my friend's house. I'd go for a drive, then return after the film's runtime.

Comparing the two independent reactions is what's really crucial.

Because it's in comparing reactions where you'll best understand what it is exactly you have on your hands.

Everyone reacts to a movie differently. But people, in general, tend to react to a movie in one way or another. Sure, there are "mixed" reactions, sure there are polarized reactions, but there is usually, ultimately, an aggregated sense of whether a movie is good or bad. Put more simply, if two independent people are saying the same exact thing—you can bet there's something to it.

The key here is trust.

You don't want people who are going to rush out and lambast the movie in public.

Because it's here, in this early stage of the marketing, that you're more than likely going to have to go back and open the movie up again and make changes.

Because part of marketing is changing the movie.

Not in big, drastic ways. But, in small, seemingly inconsequential ways.

Because after this loved one or friend, or both, have watched the movie, I want you to find someone—maybe even the same person—to watch the movie WITH. Because if anything will make time slow to a stand-still, if anything will make your movie's runtime last an eternity, it will be the first time you watch your movie with SOMEONE ELSE.

I won't lie: this is a horrifying, terrifying, exciting, emotional roller coaster. Watching the screen with one eye, peaking over at the friend or whoever with the other, constantly observing the person's reactions, constantly readying to explain whatever is actually happening, constantly bracing for the nervous breakdown…

BECAUSE YOU MADE A TERRIBLE MOVIE!

If there's any point when you'll feel you failed as a filmmaker, it'll be here, when you're finally watching the movie with someone else.

You will interpret their silence as boredom, their boredom as rapture.

And everything you think will be mostly wrong.

But it's crucial to have this experience—because it will essentially be YOUR first time watching the movie. The experience will literally rip you away from whatever preconceived notions you had, and tear away any hopes or unrealistic expectations you had. It's like kicking a rock over and exposing everything beneath it to the blazing light of the sun.

After this truly first, truly humbling experience, you will go back and make the necessary changes to the movie. You don't have to make each and every change people suggest. You just have to get a sense—and by a sense, I mean, "what keeps getting said over and over again." It's really amazing how an aggregate of people can figure out what's actually wrong with the movie. Listening to—and interpreting—these suggestions is an art all unto itself.

Then, the movie is done.

Well, kind of. Movies are never really done, as the adage goes, they're abandoned. But let's say, for our purposes, the movie is done.

The next thing to do is lock away the digital "print" of the movie. This is the not wanting the movie to be pirated—because, once you do create some demand for your movie, once you do register your movie with the proper channels, the pirates will be out to copy your film and pump it out to their own distribution methods. Meaning, they get paid. You don't. And once the movie is out there, it's out there. For now, put the movie on a few DVDs, and file the digital print away for later on down the line. The DVDs are excellent because they're not 'master' quality, and you can keep an accounting of them very easily. Whoever you lend this movie to, make sure you trust them, or, at the very least, that they don't have skills to 'rip' the DVD onto their computer and upload it to the internet. Use common sense, OK?

Now. That covers everything with the movie and wraps it up nicely. In the next chapter, we're going to really delve into the business of actually marketing. Of not just marketing, but creating the marketing materials that will be absolutely essential in carrying out your campaign. I want you to prepare yourself. You're going to be doing some serious work!

26
MAKING A POSTER

Before you do anything else, you have to create a series of assets for your movie marketing. These are obvious assets—but their creation is anything but, and the reason for creating them, their real purpose, is generally never understood. What to do with the assets, also, is a whole other story.

The first marketing asset we'll deal with is the poster.

A poster, of course, is crucial. You will need to create one, and create a good one. It will need to not only look nice, but it will have to fulfill certain expectations and create enough interest for someone to look a little further into your movie. No easy task.

Of course, your inclination with the poster's design will be to do something different, creative. And I urge you away from that. It's hard enough to make a compelling poster without trying to get cute about it. Fussing about originality when it comes to posters, or any marketing materials, will derail your efforts and thwart your goals.

A movie poster is made up of many different elements—pieces, as it were—all stitched together. When I was a kid, I used to think that movie posters were literally just one picture. They aren't. They're many different pictures "Photoshopped" together, the phrase "Photoshopped" referring to the image editing program Adobe Photoshop. The poster is made up of what are called "elements." A poster-artist in making a poster, will hunt down hundreds of images—elements—just to make a single poster.

Below is an original poster for AMERICA HAS FALLEN when it was still titled RISING FEAR. It's of the film's main character—me—guarding the city. Behind everything, a fireball 'rises.'

The domestic poster for RISING FEAR (AMERICA HAS FALLEN).

The various elements in the poster then are as follows: the picture of me holding the gun, the bridge, the city behind, the building, the American flag hanging on the building, the fireball behind the building, the sky, and the helicopter. These are all different pictures stitched together—different "elements."

The poster was assembled in this way.

First, I took a picture of me holding the gun:

MAKING A POSTER

I dressed up in my outfit, grabbed a few guns (for different variations of tone—big gun, epic—small gun, thriller—etc.), set up my DSLR camera on my porch, and took upwards of a hundred pictures. Holding the shotgun, not holding the shotgun, holding a machine gun, holding a handgun, wearing the jacket, not wearing the jacket, SOMETIMES wearing the jacket with the shotgun, sometimes not wearing the jacket and going with the handgun, on and on on. You don't just take one picture. You take hundreds. Each combination says something different. And everyone will have a different opinion about what works best.

When taking pictures for the poster, take hundreds. You'll need the options for later.

Second. The picture behind me is from iStock.com. I searched endlessly for a picture that captured both the essence of Pittsburgh, and something relevant to the story I wanted to tell. I tried many pictures. After going through literally every picture of Pittsburgh on public record, I settled on the one with the bridge leading to the city's skyline. It looks like the drawbridge to a castle. Symbolically, it's to evoke a "barbarians at the gates" feeling—an empire in need of protection. The symmetry of the bridge's suspension provided a kind of direction that would lead to the picture of the tall building, which was later added behind the skyline, as that building in real life, the Mellon building, isn't that big (in comparison to the other buildings), and can't be seen in relation to the skyline that symmetrically.

The big building in the background was taken separate from the bridge / skyline photo. During the "pre-production" and "production" of RISING FEAR, I visited the streets surrounding the Mellon building and took upwards of 200 photographs, all from different vantage points, all with different focal lengths (that is to say, I zoomed in sometimes, sometimes I zoomed out and made the building look wide). I cut out the sky from the picture I ultimately chose, then stretched out the bottom portions of the building to make it seem as if it were taller and bigger.

This is a good place to say that you should, while making the movie, while writing it even, while editing it, indeed the entire production, always, always, always be taking high quality photos with a decent DSLR camera. These photos will come in handy later when it comes time to produce more marketing materials.

Third. The flag on the building. It's actually a picture of a flag hanging from a pole, flapping in the wind. I couldn't just use any American flag. Here again I searched through endless photos. The flag flapping, the flag at a stand-still and sagging, the flag shot from below, from above, the flag up, down, sideways, all around. The challenge being to find one that was just in the correct "pose." I ended up having to flip the chosen picture, and stretch the bottom edges to make it more in perspective with the building.

Fourth. The picture of the explosion in the background. That's actually just a picture of a fireball exploding in the middle of a desolate field.

All of these "elements" are stitched together in a pattern that, while invisible, is actually guiding your eye: The gun leads to me, the bridge's supports direct you to the building, then up to the flag—which is the heart of the image.

A poster is about captivating attention, charting it, and then directing that attention. All posters are designed around this principle. If you were to take any movie picture and draw straight "directional lines," you would see real quick that the elements of the poster weren't stitched together in a hap-hazard way, but rather in a manner to direct the viewer's eye from point 'a' to point 'b' to point 'c.'

AN EXERCISE

I want you to round up at least ten movie posters for movies like yours. If you're doing an action movie, track down the posters for those kinds of movies. Either download or print them out. Then, look at all these posters side by side, just taking them in, studying them, looking at what commonalities they share. Looked at long enough, you'll begin to see similar patterns. For example, horror movies tend to favor an oblique picture of the monster, action movies tend to show the hero engulfed by chaos, romance movies tend to show the "lovers" in some kind of embrace.

These are examples of "what worked."

Looking at the ten posters you've collected, I want you to break down their various elements. If you have before you, say the poster DIE HARD, the various elements would break down like this:

A picture of Bruce Willis, the Nakatomi building, a helicopter, some fire, and a city background.

It's a relatively simple "poster" to create.

The artist or artists had what's called a "publicity still" of Bruce Willis—that's just a picture of him, on set, looking worried or whatever. They de-saturated the picture—i.e., turned it black and white—cut out the background of the still, then placed it on a blank canvas.

Then they took a picture of Nakatomi Plaza (actually the 20th Century Fox building) and cut out the background. Placed that on the canvas, then placed it half over the picture of Bruce Willis.

Then, they found a picture of an explosion. Cut the explosion out of the picture, pasted it on top of the Nakatomi building.

Of course, how does one cut out the picture of an explosion?

In fact, how do you "cut" out any of these elements from their initial pictures? How does one "cut" up a picture? I'm not sure how they did it back in the DIE HARD days. But I can tell you it's all done now on a computer, with software like Adobe Photoshop. You use the digital equivalent of an X-Acto knife, and cut where you want to cut. The tools for doing this have improved amazingly in the past 20 years.

Before you begin, however, I want you to see what you're really doing when you create a movie's poster. Your first inclination might be to go out and measure an actual movie poster. You'll discover it's 27 x 40 inches. And so, either you or someone you hire will open up a Photoshop document and create a 'canvas' of 27 x 40, then proceed to construct the poster within those confines.

Do not. Do not. I repeat, do not do that.

Because what we're REALLY talking about is the movie's "graphical art." That is to say, not only will you NEED a poster, but you will also need many sizes and variations of that movie poster. It's much easier to start from something bigger and re-size as necessary, then make up a 27x40 inch poster, and then try to constantly have to re-structure the elements when you re-frame for the DVD, the t-shirts, the backgrounds, the whatever you want to create.

You're creating the film's graphical art.

As such, when you select a canvas to build your poster (your artwork), you do so on a much larger, more expansive canvas. You don't think in terms of actually creating a poster—i.e., fiddling around with where the fonts go. You first construct the actual artwork on a large canvas, then have that single piece of artwork available to be re-scaled for any and all uses.

This is called "KEY ART." You create that, THEN you re-scale everything to fit the size of not only a movie poster, but whatever demands should crop up.

27
MAKING THE TRAILER

If there's anything necessary for a movie, if there's anything MORE important than the movie… it's the film's trailer. You must—I repeat—MUST have a trailer. And it's got to be a great movie trailer. Not an idling collection of video clips spliced with some vague text.

My friend is really fond of saying, "It's all about the trailer."

It is.

Because it's not just a matter of having something that will convince your target audience out there to see your movie. It's more a matter of convincing the most important person involved with a movie's success: the buyer. "The buyer" is someone who can make things happen for you. Someone within the system. An agent, a producer, an executive. Someone versed in the ways of marketing, who has the knowledge of marketing, and can recognize a fellow traveler. Because while you may have trouble digesting the idea that a movie is all about its marketing, this someone, or group of someones, lives and dies by that understanding. In fact, they see it more clearly than any of the filmmakers: Money is not made by people watching the movie, it's made by people paying to see the movie. A trailer is what spurs that. It is the hook, the line.

This someone, this important person who will pay you a lot of money for your movie (or broker a sale for a lot of money) will constantly, and I mean constantly, be in need for and on the lookout for something tangible that has all the elements in place and ready for an easy sale.

It's a professionally made trailer that attracts someone who can open doors for you. It's a professionally made trailer that can help you, in many ways, penetrate that very 90% of media we were talking about. If you make the trailer right, and you have a semi-decent movie, and a buyer actually sees that trailer, they will reach out to you, ask to see the movie, offer you money, and invite you in.

Which is how someone makes it in world of professional moviemaking.

They are invited in.

The best way to conjure up this invite is with a professionally made trailer.

A PROFESSIONAL TRAILER

Of course, a professionally made trailer is the one thing starting filmmakers never get right. A typical trailer from a first-time filmmaker, armed with a film, is usually patterned after a trailer for a Wes Anderson or Stanley Kubrick film. Just some random shots of people looking vague and dumb, haphazardly stitched together over esoteric music. Ironic, opaque, and stupid. You've seen the kind of trailer before. It's replete with "art" type movies—which is, chiefly, why art movies seldom make any money. The director was given control of the advertising either through his professional power, or by default (re: low-budget), and the result is a trailer that turns off all but the most die-hard moviegoers. Directors flock to this kind of trailer-design because it's, one, a design used by a director they admire, and two, because it's really, really, really easy.

When you watch a trailer for a professional movie, a Hollywood movie, a REAL movie, one with lots of money behind it, you'll notice that the edits of the trailer are tight, quick, and fast. The music is on point. The titles are crisp and pertinent. The entire video is no longer than 2 minutes and thirty seconds. More importantly, the trailer imparts valuable, intriguing information in an extremely structured way. Because not only does a trailer have to raise interest, but it has to pique curiosity. This creates a need for the two-handed trick of providing a lot of information—while at the same time creating mystery. It's a common complaint with movie trailers that they "give away" too much. Robert Zemeckis (director of BACK TO THE FUTURE, CAST AWAY, and WHAT LIES BENEATH) however, puts it well: "The reason McDonald's is a tremendous success is that you don't have any surprises. You know exactly

MAKING THE TRAILER

what it is going to taste like. Everybody knows the menu."

People want to know what they're getting into.

So, how do you turn the trick? How do you let people know 'what they're getting into,' all the while conjuring up mystery, and more importantly, a demand to see the movie?

Further more, how do you go about actually crafting these ideas into a finely tuned, tightly wound Hollywood-like movie trailer.

For one, you could get in touch with me at **tom@tomgetty.com**. I've been editing trailers for almost twenty years and know how to structure them, create the assets, the edits, the sound design, and the music that make up a professional trailer, for a reasonable fee.

But, if you want to chance it going at it alone, you perform the below exercise.

The first thing you do is go and find the trailers to at least five of the movies that are like yours. The more recent, the better. Because while the principles are the same, you want to get current with what's selling now—or very recently.

Get a huge stack of 3x5 notecards. Note each shot—image—in the trailer. Yes, that's each shot. Say you're studying the trailer for a RESIDENT EVIL movie. If there's a shot of Milla Jovovich as Alice walking at the camera, gun at the ready, you note "Alice walks at the camera, gun at the ready." Then you count how many frames that shot lasts for. Not seconds. Because seconds are too large of a measure of a trailer shot's duration. It must be measured in frames, by clicking through frame-by-frame, counting. It's in getting a sense of how many frames a typical trailer-shot lasts that will lead you to crafting a professional—and therefore precise—trailer.

I can't stress how important this precision is!

Go through the entire trailer noting and describing each shot. Yes, this is a lot of work. Because trailer making, while only ultimately a 2 ½ minute video, is one of the hardest of jobs in show business. It's brevity is what makes it so difficult.

When you're done going through all the shots, go back to the beginning. It's time to write down each line that's spoken—or heard by the viewer—on its own notecard. That means, when Alice's voice in RESIDENT EVIL voice booms onto the soundtrack, "My name is Alice," you write that down on a separate notecard. You mark whether it's only heard on the audio, or whether it's also shown being spoken by the character on screen.

You do this for each line that is spoken.

Again, a tremendous amount of work. And it is.

But doing this will show you a pattern:

A trailer is not crafted out of shots and music, as is often the practice of filmmakers making their first trailers, but rather, **a professional trailer is crafted—and therefore, motivated—by the lines of dialogue.**

Because it's in the dialogue where you'll find the most clarified demonstration of the film's plot. And it's within curating the plot points of the film where you will best allow the audience to know what they're getting into—while at the same time retaining mystery.

Knowing this cuts through a lot of blind alleys, like trying to craft a message through visuals.

In trailer editing, indeed in any kind of commercial editing, it's the audio that motivates the visuals. You'll begin to see this as you study and compile all the other trailers for the movies that are like yours.

It'll look like this:

> Card 1—Alice: "I've been fighting my whole life."
> Card 2—Alice: "I've lost all my friends."
> Card 3—Alice: "I've lost all my loved ones."
> Card 4—Alice: "I have only my enemies."
> Card 5—Alice: "My name is Alice."

You'll have all of these on separate notecards, and you'll notice a pattern, and immediately you'll begin to SEE the actual progression of the trailer:

Alice: "I've been fighting my whole life." — BAM, BAM, shots of Alice punching a zombie — Alice: "I've lost all my friends." — BAM, BAM, shots of Alice's friends screaming, sliding into a pit of zombies — Alice: "I've lost all my loved ones"— BAM, BAM, BAM — shots of some guy getting blown up — Alice: "I now have only my enemies." — BOOM (you might hear that power-down sound)—a shot of Alice confronting some suited-boss of the Umbrella corp.

After you compile all of these notecards, you then go through the audio portions, the snippets of dialogue, and examine how they are "stacked," so to speak; you note which snippets of dialogue were chosen, and in what order they were placed, to create the intellectual effect of the trailer, the mental space where the trailer wants to position the viewer.

It's in the film's dialogue that a trailer can truly be crafted in a professional manner.

So, knowing that. You go through your own film, you listen for—not *look for*—trailer-worthy dialogue. What's "trailer-worthy?" Anything that pertains to the prior status of the story's world. That would be

MAKING THE TRAILER

something like a character in the movie saying, "The mainland has been under attack for 3 months," or "Our supplies are dwindling," or "The soldiers are growing restless."

In other words, exposition. Facts that are stated about the world of the movie. Collect those, write them down on a notecard.

Then, find snippets of dialogue that seem to pertain to the film's "inciting incident."

> Card 1: "We're under attack!"
> Card 2: "They've breached the perimeter."

It's here where you reveal the plot points without revealing how they unfold. Because it's in revealing plot points—not concealing them—that creates the intrigue. The surprise isn't that something in a movie will happen—it's in HOW it will happen.

This is the case with Christopher Nolan film DUNKIRK. You know *what's going to happen. History has already so-called "spoiled" the film for you. In fact, the trailer for that movie begins *with a spoiler: "What has happened is a colossal military disaster." It's those very words that set up the main thrust of DUNKIRK.

It's not how the event will turn out—it's how the event will unfold.

So, as you study your trailers, search for dialogue that seems to support any means of the character taking action to close the gap opened by the film's inciting incident. This will be found in the character talking about how they'll go about restoring the balance of their world.

In the DUNKIRK trailer, it's more of the one character reading the Churchill speech: "We shall never surrender." Because that's what the main note of the movie is, the main action. It is about men fighting to get off a beach. It says, "This movie is about soldiers fighting to survive." You then look for dialogue that supports this. In the DUNKIRK trailer, there's a line where the one solider shouts, "The ship's about to leave!"

Then, when you find something like that line, you go in the other direction and hunt down any dialogue that seems to oppose that particular effort of the character.

In the DUNKIRK trailer, no sooner does the one soldier announce, "The ship's about to leave," someone else screams, "TORPEDO!" And KA-BOOM.

Tit for tat.

Which is what makes for a "dynamic," dramatic trailer.

Continuing with the DUNKIRK trailer...

"They need to send more ships; every hour the enemy pushes closer."

The answer to this?

"They've activated the civilian boats."

That's an action taken by the good guys.

But then, some words in opposition to that piece of action:

"Civilians!? We need destroyers!"

In other words, the action they plan to take may or may not work out. That is the drama. How will they got off that beach?

Build up a goodly amount of lines from your movie that seem to contradict one another.

Then, using the notecards, sort everything out until you start to "see" the trailer develop before you. Lay the cards out: what line best defines the the big problem? What lines escalate that conflict? What lines oppose that escalation?

You will very clearly "see" the actual structure of your movie trailer.

From that, all of the titles, the sound effect "hits," and music will fall in line.

Because it's between the opposing lines of dialogue where you intersperse the sound effects, the transitioning sounds, the "stingers," the titles that may juxtapose, that may further clarify the ideas presented.

Then, finally, beneath it all, you place the music.

Amazingly enough, you don't even really need an actual song.

A trailer's construction, beyond the structure of the lines, is determined by meter and time. Tap, tap, tap. The beat, the rhythm. Tempo. From the RESIDENT EVIL trailer: "Ah, Alice, you think you can defeat the Umbrella corp?"—BOOM—BOOM — Alice: "I know I can defeat the Umbrella corp."

In other words, you make your own song out of the sound "impacts," the sound "hits," the "BOOM—BOOM" that cranks in after every line.

From there, you massage your edits to an invisible rhythm—or, if you prefer, put in what's called a "click track." A "click track" is what musician's use to keep time and rhythm—it's set at a certain "beats per minute"—or BPM—which sets the tempo.

A trailer's tempo is always found in the structuring of these lines.

If you follow this advice, and if you really treat the making of the trailer as serious business, I guarantee you will create a piece of marketing that will be sure to attract not only a buyer for your product, but thousands of curious moviegoers.

If you fail at this, if you you don't follow my advice, you might as well burn the movie and just become a dentist.

No pressure!

MAKING THE TRAILER

When you have your poster, your key art, and your trailer ready to go, it's really time to get to work. Truth be told, this is the material you have to worry about distributing—not the movie itself. Shortly, you're about to find out that marketing is all about marketing the marketing materials themselves. Not the movie. Like an INCEPTION dream-within-a-dream, it can sometimes seem as if the layers of marketing never penetrate or end. For instance, say you're able to get on a radio program to talk about the film. Great. But, that's not enough. Because then you have to market not only the airing of the radio program segment, but the announcement that you're going to be on that radio program, the traveling to the radio station (an Instagram pic of you outside the station or—better—at the microphone itself), the actual airing of the radio program, and then the making available of the interview for all of the people who missed the original broadcast. That's real marketing. You don't just go on the radio program. You make an announcement out of even getting on the program. You make an announcement of, "Getting psyched for being on such-and-such DJ this morning—don't forget to watch!" You take a selfie at the station. You get a picture with the DJ, the host, the receptionist at the station. Everyone likes a picture of themselves. So much the better if you're in it!

And yes—I will tell you how to get on a radio show.

Frankly, there's no end to how far you can penetrate and perpetuate into a single marketing event. But that's what you have to see it as. "An event." Not just the final opening of the movie, but each and every marketing "event" that occurs.

To begin, you need to create some kind of localizing stage where you send everyone interested in your movie. This could be a website, a Facebook or Twitter page, or an Instagram account, or whatever kind of social media market you're using there in the future. Just create some sort of place where you can sign up everyone who is interested, and in the future deliver them updates on the making of the movie and its release. You want not only a place that can deliver messages to a mass of people, but also a place that will show how many people are indeed "massing" for your film. On Facebook, this would be the number of 'likes' the page is getting. On Twitter, the number of followers. On a website, some kind of counter or sign that says, "This movie has *this many people waiting to see it." Anything really that can demonstrate what's called "social proof." That being something that shows other people, "Hey, you don't want to miss out on this thing everyone is gathering around." Ideally, this page should have been created once you started filming the movie.

You post to this page—or whatever it is in the future—regularly. You post updates, the trailer, the poster, the making of stills, the updates, all of that. The idea, obviously, is to create "buzz." Whatever it takes, get this page—or whatever it is—out in front as many people as possible. Take out Facebook ads if you have to. Or whatever kind of ads. Drive traffic there.

Every marketing event will spring from here.

The first major marketing event then, of course, will be the debut of the film's poster. Make a big deal out of this. I mean, a really big deal. Once you subscribe enough followers to your film's site—again, wherever it should be—then you start letting out hints that the poster is coming shortly. You want to really maximize the debut of this amazing, awesome poster. And it better be an amazing poster. Not just a still from the film with some text. It needs to be "Wow." It needs to be like the poster below, which is the is the first one I debuted for AMERICA HAS FALLEN when it was still called RISING FEAR. It, along with a few well placed ads, brought in almost 4,000 people who 'liked' the film's page.

The original poster for RISING FEAR.

MAKING THE TRAILER

The creation of this poster, not to get back into the making of a poster again, was not taken lightly. I studied Photoshop for many, many years, and spent hours—days, really—articulating all of the details in the photo, making it pop and grab attention. Because not only did it grab attention, it did exactly what a movie poster does: it called people to action. The poster grabbed their attention, then directed the viewer to the Facebook page. That's what your poster needs to do. Grab their attention—and then get them to do something.

That's the difference between an amateur poster and a professional poster. One is just… there; the other inspires action on behalf of the consumer. To illustrate the distinction—and not to unduly critique my 15 year-old-self—take a look at the below poster I created for my film UNBELIEF.

Pictured above: poster I did at 15 for my 2003 film UNBELIEF. Not my best poster. But one of my favorite films. It was an ambitious, epic production!

It is NOT a poster that would grab attention and inspire someone to action. Artistic, maybe. Cool for a 15 year old. I applaud my 15-year-old-self for the initiative and even knowing to make a poster. But it's not ready for prime time. It says nothing. It does nothing.

If you feel your poster will end up looking like the above poster for UNBELIEF—that is to say that while it might look cool, it won't get anyone to do anything—or, it might just look worse—then I want you to get in contact with me via **tom@tomgetty.com**. For a reasonable fee, I will look at your poster, make suggestions—or, if you want, I will just outright make the poster for you. If you've got your film this far, I don't want you to throw it all away just because you've never really done a poster before. Believe me, I've seen that happen!

Once you debut the poster, you proceed to get it out there in anyway you can. Put it on your Twitter, your Instagram, your LinkedIn, wherever—and anywhere. In fact, order up a few 11x17s of the poster from a print shop, sign a few, and offer to give them away free to anyone who does something for you in regards to getting the marketing out there. Yes, that means mailing a bunch of 11x17 posters. It will pay off. It is a way of getting people involved.

28
GETTING MEDIA ATTENTION

First. Prepare some kind of media booklet in digital form. It will include a synopsis of the film, a list of the cast and crew, behind-scenes-stills, stills from the movie, an interview with yourself that sheds some insight into who you are and why you made the film, and whatever other information you would like to include. The purpose of this little media booklet will be revealed in a second.

Next, you make a list—however short—of all the media outlets in your local region. This includes newspaper, radio, magazines, TV news, blogs, and any other various publications within a 20 mile radius of where you live—or, wherever you were brought up. Start with a list of the various radio shows that may be produced in this area. Then, get in touch with the hosts of the show, or the host's producers. You can do so via email or letter. Simply tell them your story. You're a young, aspiring filmmaker; you've JUST finished mounting a production, and you want to share it with the world. Be humble, be enthusiastic, and be nice. No attitude. I repeat, NO ATTITUDE. Just because attitude seems to sell for rappers and Beyonce does not mean it will get you anywhere of value in this world. If you feel you might have an attitude problem, or you're not quite yet adjusted to getting passed the "resting bitch face" that's become so embraced by young girls in recent years, pick up a copy of Dale Carnegie's *How To Win Friends And Influence People*. Read it once. Read it twice. Read it three times. Carry the book everywhere, thankful that someone wrote such an enlightened book, and that you've been shown the correct—and productive—way to think and behave.

The producer or host for the radio program, hungry for content, will happily have on a local, entrepreneuring, creative young person. Send this producer or host your media booklet and a thumbnail (jpeg or png) of your poster. You will most likely be given upwards of an hour to not only talk about your background, who you are, your local area, but your movie and why it's going to be the most amazing thing since sliced bread.

Once you've secured the slot and sent along all of your materials about the movie and yourself, you go on your Facebook, your wherever, your everything, and you announce—like you just got your dream job (you'll soon see this is indeed the truth)—that you're going to be on the show. Then, the day of the interview, you show up 15 minutes early armed with a few copies of your 11x17 poster and two—two—what are called DecoColor Premium 3 Way Chisel Point pens that are either silver or gold. These are essentially "paint pens" that make signing virtually anything easy and official. The posters will be big and awkward to carry, and so the people you encounter on your way to the station, inside the station, will be interested; and so, you'll hand them a copy of the poster—happily—and, if it's a good poster, they'll look at it and be really impressed and see that you're the real deal (which is why it's so important to have such a good poster). Then, you'll offer to sign it with your gold paint pen. Their day will be made.

Then, you go in for your interview with the host. You express your gratitude for being there, shake hands; being respectful, humble, and knowingly appreciative of someone else even giving you the chance to talk about your movie.

Then, sit before the microphone and go at it. Sure, you'll be terrified. If this is your first time, you'll be horrified. Nervous, sick, paralyzed. But just ease into it and let er' rip. You'll discover those negative feelings slipping out the backdoor as your natural enthusiasm for your product bubbles up and takes over. An hour of talking will seem—and I promise—WILL SEEM—like 5 minutes before it's over. You'll be thrilled you did this, the host will be thrilled he or she has a live wire, and the audience, normally accustomed to rants and raves about the local community, will be infected by your excitement, enthusiasm, good cheer, and honesty. Trust me, trust me on this. Even if you think stage fright or nerves will be the death of your career. They won't. I can with 100% accuracy promise, when the interview concludes, you will feel like you did on the last day of school.

When the interview concludes, ask if you can get a picture with the host. Truth be told, you'll actually be in that good of a mood to take a picture with someone, and won't just want to take the picture for publicity reasons. You'll actually want a picture with this very kind person. Immediately upload the picture of the two of you to your social media network, your website, wherever, using whatever tagging tools to link the picture to the radio host and his or her fans. In the description, you tell everyone when the broadcast will be (if it wasn't already live), and when they can hear the re-play.

Then you go home, you find the re-play, wherever it is, and you post it again on your page.

Then, you do all of the above for all the other media publications in your area. Are there any speciality magazines or monthlies related to your current region? They always like content that highlights and promotes the area. In trying to solicit an invitation to be interviewed by their publication, go on their site and look for articles/stories that are of some similar content to what you're doing. In example, take note of any stories that are written about local artists or musicians or local businesses. You'll notice that those articles are usually written by the same reporter, as that reporter tends to gravitate to those stories. Get the reporter's email address.

Then, before you write to them about writing a story about your film, you sit down, take a breath, and get ready to become a reporter yourself. Seriously. Most people, when what's called "querying" a media publication, just write off a few lines to the publication or author, pitching what it is they're all about.

Not good enough.

I want YOU to write the article you're wishing to see in the publication. I want you, yes you, to sit down like you're in the 11th grade again, and write the article as if you were a reporter for the publication writing about your story. It'll take a lot of work, I know. It'll take a lot of time, I know. But it will accomplish two things. One, it will show you how hard reporters and writers at publications work, and two, how pressed they are for time. While you're writing this story, you will understand how long it actually takes to write a story. Now, imagine if you had to manufacture 10 of those articles—and on a deadline for next Tuesday. You'll fully realize the stress, pressure, and headache the modern reporter feels on a daily basis.

Now, here you are with the article written up, ready to go, crystal clear, already untangled and presented with a "hook." Because that's what you're going to have to come up with. A "hook." Why is THIS story a relevant story for the publication? Usually it's something like, "Local filmmaker does good." The hook will get more complicated as you extend out to more and more publications in areas further away.

Writing the article will force you to whittle everything about you and your movie down to something that would be of relevance to this publication. Achieving this, writing the article, will present the author or reporter with what I call a "slam dunk."

When they see the article and can recognize "the hook"—usually found in the headline—and then, better, see there are pictures included (because you've sent them your poster, the behind-the-scene stills, the media booklet), they'll usually respond back happy to do a story on you. Of course, they're not going to use the article you've spent so much time typing up. 99.9% of reporters are hard working, serious people, and so they will have their own questions for you, they will do their own research, and then they will write up their own article.

When the article "runs," get a copy, scan it, and upload it to your social media accounts with the same verve you did with the radio broadcast.

Additionally, you also start a scrapbook of sorts. This is a vast collection of all your "press clippings." Any mention of you or your movie in the media, clip it out, put it in this booklet. It doesn't have to be a real physical booklet; it can be a pdf collection on your computer. You even go beyond "press clippings," and look for any tangible evidence that you made a media footprint. Pictures with the host, Facebook posts about the event, etc.

Now, after a certain point, you will cap out and find it difficult to go beyond your regional area.

That's fine at this point. And expected.

A marketing campaign isn't built in one deft swoop. It's accrued in erratic movements. A mention here, a mention there, an article in this publication. It starts to add up.

In other words, this won't be like how major movies are marketed. Which is to just completely saturate the market with ad buys and press coverage leading right up to the epicenter of the film's release. Really, truth be told, that's not how a movie should even be marketed. If you ask me, one of the big problems Hollywood has is its marketing, and how it goes about ramming a movie down the public's throat. Whereas today Hollywood will explode open a movie on a set date, used to be they "rolled out" the release, opening in a few select cities, then allowing the production to grow "legs" through word-of-mouth.

That's the strategy you're going to use. The old fashioned system Hollywood used in the 1960s, 1970s, and the system Miramax leveraged throughout the 90s and 2000s.

You start small—in your case, regionally. Then you leverage out, proving to people that your movie, your thing, whatever it is, actually has some kind of relevance to the moment.

That's how a movie is released.

By convincing others of its relevance, and doing so in ever widening concentric circles.

So, don't feel bad if you have but a measly $1.98 for advertising/marketing. You don't need money. You just need hard work, time, and a really great attitude.

Then, when there's some interest in your movie, when people in your region are talking about it—and they will be talking about it if you go through the steps I've outlined above—then, and only then, do you go about dropping hints that you're going to release the trailer. You show pictures of the various edits of the trailer on the timeline in your editing software; you talk about how well the edits, the sound, the graphics, are coming together, how this trailer is going to be the trailer to end all trailers. And it is going to be a great trailer, right? You've gone around sparking interest and curiosity in people, here's the chance to really skyrocket the enterprise. A great, great trailer.

Because when it "drops," there are going to be a lot of interested people.

And if it's a great trailer, they'll feel moved to start sharing it with their friends and colleagues. They will start chatting it up even more so, and have something of tangible proof—an awesome trailer—to show others that there is indeed "something to talk about."

Because it's here, if you have a great trailer, where you start to really capitalize on the talk.

It's here, where you launch.

29
LAUNCH

You post the trailer everywhere, appropriating it with the relevant "tags," so that Google, or whatever panopticon in the future that is watching all of us, begins to move your movie's title up in the search engines, on social media, etc. You contact all of the movie trailer websites like TrailerAddict.com and ComingSoon.net, all of them, every last one of them, each with a personalized note (yes, it'll take a while), asking if they'll graciously include your movie trailer with the rest of the top-flight trailers.

This is why, and I repeat, this is why you need—absolutely NEED—to have a GREAT trailer. It has to "fit in" with all the rest of the professional trailers that Hollywood, at that point, will be assaulting the American public with. If you don't have a great trailer at this point, forget it. Just forget everything you've read in the book, everything you've done up till this point. **It's on the strength of the trailer that all of your study, all of your work, all of your blood and sweat, will be gauged and judged**.

It's on the trailer whether or not you will be given admittance into the wider realms of society.

Not the movie.

Let's repeat it again.

It's the trailer. Not the movie. Because the movie is still just locked in your drawer waiting to be seen.

The value has to be in the trailer, which should be out there being seen and admired by the American—and global—public.

Because it's here, somewhere in here, where the movie pros hang out and look for what's going on. Agents, producers, people in the movie industry, hang around in this realm. They're looking for what's going on in their industry, what the competition will be in the coming months, and most importantly, checking for anything that may have, just may have, just maybe, maybe, maybe, slipped through their hands. Something like the *next PARANORMAL ACTIVITY or the next BLAIR WITCH PROJECT.

Of course, those are extreme examples. But they do happen, and no one in Hollywood, in the movie industry, wants to be the person who let it slip past. Just think, PARANORMAL ACTIVITY was this no-budget movie that found its way up the ranks, all the way to Steven Spielberg.

But in that case, it wasn't Spielberg who found it. And that's important because you don't have to initially signal it all the way up to Spielberg. You only have to get it to someone in the industry who is hungry. With PARANORMAL ACTIVITY, it was producer Jason Blum, who at the time did not yet have the following credits to his name: SINISTER (and its sequel), PARANORMAL ACTIVITY (and its sequels), THE PURGE (and its sequels), INSIDIOUS (and its sequels), GET OUT (and its, as of now, assumed sequels), and too many more to mention.

It was Jason Blum who understood the business side of Hollywood, who understood the movie industry in general, who came across PARANORMAL ACTIVITY, and recognizing its potential, fought like hell to get it into the Paramount marketing/distribution system.

That is the person you want to signal. Because, for a moment, remember, while he didn't yet at the time have all the above-listed credits, he had the hunger to someday GET those credits. And you only do that through successful moviemaking. Therefore, someone like Jason Blum—and I'm talking about Jason Blum then—not now—is the someone you need to see your trailer and recognize its potential. I'm talking about a man or woman who is hungry, hungry, hungry for success in the movie business.

While I have no way of knowing, I can only speculate what he saw with PARANORMAL ACTIVITY: a high quality low-budget film with huge marketing potential (high concept preceded by a similar phenomenon that could work even better in the age of social media—i.e., here is the next BLAIR WITCH PROJECT, but with better marketing tools to move the goods). But there was something else I imagined he saw: no over-head. PARANORMAL ACTIVITY only cost $11,000. And while that's not so much important in and of itself, it suggests a fellow traveller who truly grasps the whole concept of the movie business. He saw that Oren Peli, the director and creator of PARANORMAL ACTIVITY, wasn't some liberal-arts major looking to re-invent the wheel. He saw—and I can only speculate, of course (however informed that speculation is)—Oren Peli truly understood and lived the movie business: it's not in the movie, IT'S IN THE MARKETING!

With PARANORMAL ACTIVITY, Oren Peli made a high quality movie for virtually no money with even higher quality marketing potential—and then found someone who could capitalize on that potential.

I believe Jason Blum recognized a fellow traveller in Oren Peli and his film.

I want the same for you.

You need to make a no-budget movie with huge marketing potential, and then find someone, anyone, anywhere—maybe it will be Jason Blum—maybe it'll be me (send me a copy if you should get this far, by the way)—who has a hunger, a lot of openness, an understanding of the business, and a profound sympathy for what it is you're trying to do:

BE A MAJOR SUCCESS!

If you find this person, if they find you, success—if not at the PARANORMAL ACTIVITY level, then some level you'll find agreeable—will be all but assured.

All but assured.

There's no reason it shouldn't be.

No reason.

Because truth be told, of all the films that are produced and make it to fruition each year, for the thousands upon thousands of films that flood the festivals and the transoms of anyone who is anyone in Hollywood, 98% of them are really, really terrible. Either incompetent in story or production. Of that 2% that can actually tread water—and I'm even talking the work that makes it to the theaters, Netflix, Amazon, etc—most of it, the vast majority of it, is just art house crap that no one will ever watch. Read: this is even stuff with big name stars in it! You hear that? Big stars—and no one in the industry, no one buying movies, not even the movie goers, will even touch it.

The vast majority of movie product produced on any given year has no marketable value.

And out in Hollywood, they're all desperate for anything with marketable potential. This is PARANORMAL ACTIVITY, this is SAW, this is BLAIR WITCH PROJECT, NIGHT OF THE LIVING DEAD. Yes, the list happens to all be horror movies. But that doesn't mean there aren't other films that were ushered from virtual obscurity to box office success: ROCKY, NAPOLEON DYNAMITE, MAD MAX, AMERICAN GRAFFITI, LITTLE MISS SUNSHINE, OPEN WATER, EL MARIACHI. All great movies with marketable potential. All ultimately found and curated by someone with the knowledge to spot and exploit that potential.

If you've made a commercial movie—AND a GREAT—and I mean, GREAT—trailer—one that screams you know a lot—and I mean, a lot—about marketing—then someone "out there," someone in an office somewhere, someone hungry and wanting a career in the movies, will see the trailer, will recognize there's no officially recognized studio or production company logo at the front of the trailer, and will reach out to you.

Of course, it goes without saying that you should also have SOME way of getting in touch with you. But you've already thought of that, right?

When they do get in contact with you, when this someone does reach out to you, I want you to be your usual professional, conservative self. None of this talk about keeping the movie's integrity or putting the movie first. You're as open as a 7-11 when it comes to your product.

You. Just. Want. To. Succeed.

Of course, table these calls if you receive many. Weigh and compare offers. Money counts!

But truth be told, you probably WON'T be flooded with calls from distributors, agents, and executives, and people like Jason Blum. Because contrary to what I've just pounded into your head about movies being all about the marketing, few, if any in Hollywood—especially anyone with any ambition—will actually GET that, and therefore be activated to action by it. I know. You've heard all your life about how business oriented Hollywood is, and how it's filled with MBA business grads, and how it's all about the "bottom line." But it's not true. If it were, movies would be a lot better. The harsh truth is that Hollywood—and I'm talking about the decision makers, not the craftspeople—is 98% crammed with people all vying and looking to seek command over the 2% of people who actually do care about movies, and who actually want to make a fortune at them. Yes, shocking. That 98%? They're looking for prestige, to drive a nice car around, to have more power, and lord over all the lemmings pouring across the southern Californian border.

Bureaucrats, in other words.

If you want to understand Hollywood, you need only look to Washington D.C. Hollywood is a virtual mirror of our nation's capitol. A deep state controlled by generations of people who have no leadership skills or business sense. Don't let the MBA and law degrees fool you. The decision makers in Hollywood have very little business sense—let alone a sense of moviemaking. They are as out of touch as our "leaders" in D.C.

If there's any big problem with Hollywood, it's this. Very few people "out there" take it as seriously as the select few who are actually dedicated to practicing and forwarding the art form.

Which is why, again, you will receive few, if any, calls from someone with power in Hollywood. Your existence, your movie, your wanting to be there, is an instant threat to the cozy bureaucracy they stake so much of their identity in.

This is why I cite Jason Blum as the type of person I hope gets in touch with you. That is to say, the type of person who is both business-minded... AND an artist, passionate about staking out new territory in the industry and making an actual mark. Not someone who is just looking to drive a leased Beamer down Sunset Blvd.

I want you to find—or be found by—A Jason Blum circa 2006, hungry and serious about the business.

Someone who can recognize actual, BANKABLE talent.

Well—what if that person doesn't get in touch with you? What if NO ONE calls?

That's fine.

I've been there, and it means very little—if anything.

What you do then is what I did when I came home from college with my first official feature EMULATION and was looking to forward my career. I sat down in my room and I made a list of every single film that was vaguely like EMULATION. Then, from that list, I made another corresponding list of every single decision-maker / producer involved with those movies. This included directors, writers, producers, executives, and agents. This also included any of the production companies that produced those films.

So therefore, I want you to sit down and do the same. Make a list, look for the contact information. It takes some work, but you can find the information, believe it or not. Most of it can be found on the Internet Movie Database's Pro service, for a fee.

Then I want you to write a personalized letter to each and every one of those people. And this isn't a mass mailing either. This is sitting there, looking at, say, the producer's list of credits, looking at their movies, thinking about how you felt about those movies, finding that those films more than likely had some major impact on your film (after all, your film IS like theirs), thinking about how their work inspired yours. This means researching the producer, director, writer, the whatever, reading articles that have been written about them, reading their words, reading up on what they're involved in now. Then, armed with all of that, you write them a really personal letter, something you'd write to someone you admire (because you do, after all), telling them what their work means to you, telling them about your situation, and what you hope to do with your film—the kind of film they've had much success in making and distributing.

This, by the way, is what Jason Blum did when he was trying to find funding for his first major production, KICKING AND SCREAMING. He reached out to comedian Steve Martin, articulated his own situation and goals for the film, and miraculously (keep in mind, this is Jason Blum circa 96') received a letter of recommendation back from the PLANES, TRAINS, & AUTOMOBILES star himself! This opened a lot of doors and lead to the funding of Jason Blum's film.

Of course, you might be a little intimidated about this as these are some very powerful and famous people. But, look, you have to understand you're not approaching them *as the casual Dick, Harry, or Sally on the street looking to just get a selfie and an autograph. You're approaching them as someone who is serious, sober, and earnest. In this, they will recognize themselves when THEY were just like you, starting out, unknown and untested. Believe it or not, these are human beings. And if they are as successful as their credits show, then they'll most likely be thoughtful enough to return correspondence at some level. Whether that's wanting to talk to you, or a simple "thank you, no thank you," or the "can't take unsolicited material," one of them, someone, WILL take you seriously enough to at least acknowledge your efforts.

If this yields no leads or no sales, that's fine.

It simply means you have more work to do.

After you've released the trailer, and buzz is building for your movie, you'll have to pick some kind of "distribution" plan. I use the word "distribution" for a lack of a better word. Really, you're going to figure out how you will show this movie to the public—and monetize those showings, however those showings should occur.

As you may already know, there are many, many options to "distribute" your movie. But while there are many options, you want the one that's going to maximize your exposure and the amount of money your film brings in (i.e., how much money you make).

If no direct leads come from the release of the trailer—and again, that very well may be the case—and no one offers to take the movie off your hands, then you dig deeper.

30
FILM FESTIVALS

You've probably already been asked the question: "You sending it to any festivals?" Film festivals. Should you submit your film?

Few things make me feel less festive… than a film festival.

So, I'm a little biased.

Suffice to say, I am not fan of "travel." Seriously—what is it with people scouring the globe's tourist traps? Perhaps I'm odd, but I just don't look forward to expending the major resources it takes to get to the festival, and even less so, the resources it takes to get into the festival.

For one, just submitting your film is a pricey ordeal. Each festival submission will run you somewhere in the neighborhood of $50 to $200 dollars, depending on the nature of the subsequent deadlines. Non-refundable. Meaning, it really stings when you don't get in. You fire down $90 bucks for a film festival you've never heard about; six months later hear back, "Lots of great films this year—your's ain't one of them. Thanks!" For the small price of almost $100 dollars you get the privilege of receiving a sorry-not-sorry note.

I can't help but think of that old painful adage about, "The only people who ever got rich in the gold rush were the people selling shovels." Not the pikers picking for gold! That reads: you and me. Of course, no, you and I aren't just fools whacking away for gold.

But you'll sure feel like one when you submit your movie to film festivals.

I understand and empathize with the desire to get into film festivals. And the pressure everyone will put you under to enter. The promise of the whole festival meme is irresistible. For a small fee, submit your movie, wait, hear back, get accepted, show up, get shown, get seen, BE DISCOVERED! So many low-budget / no-budget movie success stories begin with film festivals, it all but seems a necessity to run "the circuit," as they say, and get into as many as possible. If you don't, then you're going to hear a lot of the, "Oh, you gotta' believe more in yourself" from friends and family. A lot of the, "You have to get exposure!" "You have to be seen!" "You gotta' get it out there somehow!"

But as someone who has run the film festival "circuit" with two feature films, I can offer some more sobering—and practical—insights.

Take, for instance, the Sundance Film Festival. Held annually every winter in Park City, Utah, attended by almost 50,000 people, it is* the gold standard in film festivals. Sundance, Sundance, Sundance. Countless indie hits began their ascensions here. Acceptance to this film festival means not only high visibility for your movie, but a high visibility for you. This is where famous, lucrative careers are made.

And yet, according to Backstage magazine, in an article by Sara Fenton, the Sundance Institute, in 2013, received 4,057 features and feature documentaries. In any given year, only a hundred films-or-so will be accepted.

Do the math and you realize these numbers give you about a 1 in 40 chance of making it. Favorable odds, actually. Not to mention, your movie is actually really great. And you know, and I can assure you (in all seriousness), that 90%, maybe even 97% of the 4,000 features submitted... are going to be terrible.

But quality is not the problem.

The real problem... is time.

Figure the average feature is 90 minutes. If you take that number and times it by 4,057 you get...

365,130 minutes. Read: that's way over a quarter of a million minutes that must be expended by someone, somewhere, or some combination of people.

That's time. Something that is non-negotiable.

Think of it this way: each year, the Sundance Institute must sit through almost 400,000 minutes of film!

That's...

That's over 6,000 hours of movies to watch!

That's 250 days worth of movies to watch.

Every year, Sundance, as an institute, "must" review 250 days worth of movies.

If submissions for Sundance opens on May 1, and the festival happens the following January 19th, that's, according to Planetcalc.com, approximately....

263 days.

That's 263 days to watch 250 days worth of movies. Round the clock.

Alright, I hear you say, "They have more than one person watching the movies."

OK, sure. The Sundance Institute website, in fact, lists 21 "programmers."

So... among them, they must all watch 6,000 hours of content. Divided up evenly: they must all watch 285 hours worth of content.

That amounts to, roughly, 140 movies. So, within a span of 263 days, each member of the programming team at Sundance, must watch 140 movies.

That's—roughly—2 movies a day.

Of course, that is still a reasonable enough number—

Until you figure we're only accounting for the feature films.

According to the same Backstage article, Sundance receives—in addition to the 4,000 feature films—8,000 shorts! 8,000!

Sure, they have people dedicated to just watching those 8,000. The Sundance website lists 9 people as holding the title of "shorts programmer."

So, that leaves... 11 people... to watch 250 days of movies. That's 250 days straight, of non-stop movies, running round the clock.

That of course is assuming they get a steady stream of entries, and not a big rush toward the fall deadline. And that would never happen, right? Creative people are known for doing things on time, right?

Because if they didn't, then the programmers would have to start watching <u>four or five films a day</u>.

How would you feel having to sit through upwards of four or five movies of questionable quality, day after day? Happy? Cheerful? Ambivalent?

Of course, up to this point, we're making the generous assumption that the selected programmer is actually watching the whole movie. You paid an honest fee with the honest expectation that your movie is actually going to be watched by an expert, judged thoughtfully and carefully, right?

—C'mon!

They're under absolutely no legal or moral obligation to have eyeballs glued to your movie for its entire duration. I imagine, at best, they're watching 10 minutes. Why should they watch any longer? If, after 10 minutes, the movie isn't grabbing them, why bother? It's not going to get any better.

The programmers at Sundance have to sit through a lot of movies.

And who are the programmers? More importantly, what would "qualify" someone to program—or, the more apt word: curate—a film festival? I can't imagine the work of watching movies pays all that well. Or maybe it does? Your guess is as good as mine.

The question is whether or not you think—or believe—they'll give your movie a credible shot. Perhaps they will. There's always a chance. Personally, I'd rather play the lottery. Because with the lottery, you're only dealing with astronomical odds that are at least backed by a mathematical certainty: there will be a 'winning' number, and that the number will be chosen at random.

At least with the lottery, you're not dealing with human beings. Because with human beings, you're dealing with a bag of biases—of which I imagine the people at Sundance are not immune to.

None of us are.

Sundance, and the majority of film festivals, lean toward a very rigid edifice of content. They like the movies they like. What these movies are is beyond the scope of this book. People are allowed to like what they like. It's only worth noting because their preferences may not gel with your film. Or worse, of who you are.

Or aren't.

Of course, I don't want to come across as "lamenting" about film festivals. There are good ones. The trick is in recognizing them. Here are some questions you should ask. How many years has the festival been in operation? Yes, the longer the better. But, also, who seems to be running the festival? Is it the founder? There's the Bare Bones Film Festival in

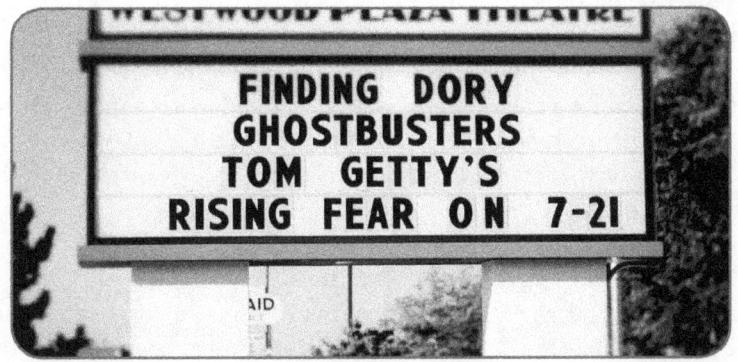

Pictured: the marquee for a 2016 showing of RISING FEAR. Note what movie was coincidentlly also playing! A happy moment, and a journey full circle.

Muskogee, Oklahoma, run by a lovely couple who legitimately care about the well being of their community. They treat attending filmmakers like royalty. If your aim is to find a warm, positive environment—check out the Bare Bones Film Festival.

Or is it a festival where the founder has long since abandoned his vision and abdicated the festival duties to a hire? Or, worse, has it just been a succession of hires? Or, even worse, is it a "non-profit" with a board of trustees? Seriously, if something has a "board of trustees," than that means the festival has become so lucrative that it can pay a whole host of people to do what it is people on a trustee boards do: nothing.

What kind of movies does the festival seem to accept? There are ones that aim for content more in line of what actual "indie" moviemakers are likely produce. Take the Action on Film Festival run by the wonderful Del Weston. While specializing in action, he and his team are very welcoming to filmmakers who produce movies like the one you're about to produce.

Then there are festivals that seem to gravitate—I would say, hover over—material that… is… "of the times." Politely put, these are the movies about "the issues." These are the movies that are "daring" and "bold," "courageous" and "honest." These are the movies that no one in their right mind would watch. Acceptance here is more pleasing to one's vanity, than to any practical need.

Here's a crucial question. Who goes to the festival? Filmmakers? Celebrities? DeNiro? Matt Damon? Ben Affleck? Good rule of thumb: if Kate Upton and Taylor Swift are going, then you won't be.

Film festivals are ultimately what they are. A place where films are shown. The quality of one can be judged on a single thing: how many venues are showing movies? That means, at any given time, how many movies are being shown?

The more, the worse.

If a film festival has one theater, one screen, and only shows one movie at a time—then it's a great film festival. The attendees are funneled from one film to the next via the fact that the movies are all playing on the same screen. To the degree a film festival sticks to this model is to the degree of its quality.

Otherwise, what's the point?

"To get shown," I can hear an advocate say.

Then, if all you want is to "get shown," I would suggest renting some screen somewhere, and advertise—in whatever way you can—the screening itself.

Because you're going to do this anyways. Go to any film festival in the world—and you'll discover you're on your own in terms of getting people to show up at the screening. As it should be. That's your job, promoting your film. Of course, hundreds of filmmakers doing this at the same place and time—as is what happens during a festival—renders an environment more akin to a middle eastern bazar than a bohemian gathering of like-minded artists. I don't care how good of a marketer you are—it's hard work to promote in an environment littered with thousands of postcards for thousands of films showing in a thousand different locations at a thousand different times. Quiet desperation is always a tough tempo to dance with.

Look, if you really want to be shown, do this. Pick a theater, any theater, meet with the theater owner, describe your situation, and see if he or she will be agreeable to showing your movie on a weeknight. That's a weeknight. You explain that you'll be promoting the hell out of the screening, contacting the papers, the TV stations, the magazines, and you'll bring in a lot of people. The owner, being a smart business owner, will see your enthusiasm and realize he or she can get an attendance spike on an otherwise slow Thursday night.

If that's a successful screening, then see how far you can push it. Can you expand out regionally? To other theaters? Could you do this in the nearest city? Maybe, maybe not. Sounds like a lot of work. And it is.

But it's work you would have to do anywhere if you were "lucky" enough to get accepted into a film festival. Realizing that makes your situation real clear. When you apply to Sundance—or any festival—really what you're applying for is a chance to have your movie beamed onto a wall in a room somewhere up there in Park City, Utah. That's it. That's all. Sure, you may catch some loose traffic.

But remember, that loose traffic is probably going wherever Kate Upton and Taylor Swift are. "Important" people don't go to film festivals to see the movies. They go to be seen by other "important" people.

Whichever you decide to do in regards to a film festival, know this: it's no shortcut to getting your movie seen.

That is up to you!

31
WHEN NO ONE COMES KNOCKING…

OK, so say you get five months out from making your film—and none of your efforts have worked. I mean, like, nothing. No one important or famous wrote you back. No agents are calling. You didn't get into any festivals. You couldn't arrange any screenings. Instead, you're laying on the floor, clutching the rejection letter from Sundance, wiping tears with a "we don't take any unsolicited material" letter from Universal, realizing no one in the world cares about this product you so put so much work into!

What then?

First, have a milkshake. Or a cheeseburger. Or a really, really good meal.

I want to congratulate you. You've done something few souls on the planet ever do: you've actually made a real movie.

While the world doesn't seem to be lining up at your doorstep, I can personally, truthfully, and in all honesty, confirm that you've done something impressive. Nah—wait—forget 'impressive.' You've done something amazing.

You ARE amazing.

Which is why you can just go ahead and brush off all the rejection and hard feelings. While you will feel bitter that the world and the industry have met your Herculean-efforts with indifference, I can assure you this is NOT the end.

For one, you are in possession of an asset that will only GROW in value—not lessen. While it may feel like your movie is becoming more and more irrelevant with each passing day, it's actually going in the opposite direction. You may be a nobody today—but when you do "make it," when you do become a huge director—and you will, if you give it everything and really want it enough (not so easy)—then audiences will flock back over your resume to find any prior work. Not all, but some. Enough to generate a sizable royalty check, wherever it should come from. While some people strive for what's called "residual income" in real estate or the stock market, you've been fortunate enough to create an asset that can possibly generate income for you in the future.

Which is why you don't go out back and burn the movie. Or do something crazy like give it away for free.

And by "it," I mean the film's rights.

Never, never, but never, just "give away" the film's rights to an agent, a producer, a movie star, anyone. Never, never, never. I can't say it enough. Never!

If they pay, sure. Of course.

But don't think that just because the movie wasn't a "hit" on release then it's forever a dud. This isn't Hollywood! We're not in their convoluted, artificial bubble where art is treated like a trash commodity if it doesn't 'hit' in its first 72 hours. You have something completely different. You own 100% of the rights to a film's 'negative.' That is the kind of thing most—if not all—successful movie directors NEVER see. In fact, Alfred Hitchcock was ecstatic with owning even 60% of the movie PSYCHO (although 60% of $50 million is something to get excited about).

Sure, a 100% of nothing is nothing. You're right.

But that's today.

And you're in a business where a 100% of nothing can be a 100% of a fortune overnight. There's literally no rhyme or reason to what makes money, and even less correlation between quality and its future rewards.

Quality, in this business, means very little.

What does matter, as you already know, is marketing.

Here's what you do. You shake off all that depression and hang-ups about having made a bad movie, and you go and make a DVD of your movie with high quality menus, a trailer, maybe an interview with yourself, a commentary; you re-size that poster into a DVD cover, you write up an appealing summary for the back; you go to Discmakers.com, you get the DVD REPLICATED. That's replicated, not duplicated. The difference being much better, much more official quality. Yes, that means you'll have to order a 1,000 copies. It'll cost maybe a thousand-or-so dollars. That's a dollar a DVD. Then, you get the DVDs, and you hand them out to friends, family, and anyone who will give you the time of day.

Then—you get an Amazon Vendor account. Read: not Createspace. You're not getting off easily. You get the Amazon Vendor account so you can be a real business person and have a real, actual Amazon page that will put you on a level playing field with everyone else.

Then—you ship the DVDs off. You do this to wherever you can get the film placed.

The goal is to be seen. And to be seen means people seeing your DVD "out" and "about," at actual, real stores whether online or offline. You work at that. Believe me, you'll have the time.

Then—you look into all of the streaming services like Amazon Prime, iTunes, etc., and you get your movie up online, where it will sit and receive anyone who should happen upon it.

You, all the while, retaining the rights to the film.

At the very least, even if you are sick of the film business by this point, you will learn invaluable skills about business and marketing that will translate to any field imaginable. Wherever your paths should take you, that movie will always be available for others to find it. Lightning may strike! Stranger things have happened. Tom Clancy became Tom Clancy—that is, a hit—because then-president Reagen called *The Hunt For Red October* "my kind of yarn."

It's called a lucky break.

And "luck," as the old saying goes, "is when preparedness meets opportunity."

Be ready.

32
CONCLUSION

The sun is setting on our time together. Our walk coming to a close. This was a long journey; and one I hope you will return to again and again. There is much more to absorb in this book than just a single reading will yield. I suggest going back, reading it again; this time, making notes.

There is a lot in this book to take in. And frankly, none of it is complete. It'll never be. I'm personally learning new things daily—and I hope the same for you. I hope I've at least given you a comprehensive view.

Of course, there is still much, much more to learn. There are subjects far beyond story writing, recruiting, camera equipment, production, editing, special effects, marketing, and general morale. Delving deeper into the abyss of those subjects, alone, promises comprehension and wisdom still unknown to you—and everyone else.

And yet, that's what will continue to light your inspiration throughout the years. The learning. Continually realizing that there is still just one more skill, or tool, or chip of knowledge, or tidbit, or insight that can press your craft a fraction of a percent forward.

That's what inspires me.

I'm in awe of what a single insight can accomplish in terms of forwarding one's abilities to make film.

So therefore, we're not finished. Not with your education, nor with mine. I hope you will continue to check in with me as I continue to make available similar insights to the one found in this book. Insights that will do you a wealth of good for you in your pursuit of filmmaking achievement and stardom.

I can be located in many ways.

First, visit **TomGetty.com**. Where I will post updates, new tutorials, and other gems to forward your goals. A simple Google search of the name "Tom Getty" will reveal wherever I currently am, the social media networks I am on, and any other updates. I am on Facebook. Friend me or 'like' me, or whatever should be the option when this finds you. Subscribe to my YouTube channel at TomGetty88, where you can check out a myriad of my work, tutorials, and other content that will be of great help to you. Follow me on Twitter **@tsgetty**. Follow me on Instagram **@tsgetty**. I float around on all those platforms posting a wide range of content that should be helpful and inspiring to you. Use whatever means on any of those platforms.

And of course, email me at **tom@tomgetty.com**. Sometimes direct communication is the very best.

In addition to offering a lot of movie services (poster making, trailer making, story fixing, special effects), I am sure I can be of major help to whatever jam you should find yourself in. I'm very easy to get inspired about moviemaking—and I never feel more inspired than when I think about trying to solve the movie problems I faced when I started out.

Especially with what I know now.

With that, I wish you nothing but encouragement, support, and luck for your future endeavors. Whether you should seriously invest in becoming the next, greatest filmmaker of your time, or you wish to do something involved with filmmaking, or you'd ultimately like to just move on to something else in life, know this: The greatest gift moviemaking can offer an aspiring filmmaker is the key it holds to life, and living it. Most people, while alive and breathing, never find their way to actually living the life they have before them. They've tuned in AND dropped out, content with an endless parade of reality TV and the interminable dirge of a 9-5 job. What they lack, however, is not ambition—but rather, an interest.

Thankfully, that is what God or whomever has blessed you with. Yes, your filmmaking aspirations will seem at times very burdensome. Even painful. It WOULD be easier if you didn't care about moviemaking and the impossible dream it promises.

But it's not the end of your journey that will be rewarding. It is the journey itself, and the simple experience of hitting the road—wherever it should lead—and engaging the conflicts that arise.

Your interest in movies is the fuel for that journey.

Where it should take you, whether to Hollywood stardom, or a total abandonment of the entire field itself, the journey along the way will reward you with riches that will benefit you long beyond this journey.

Never worry about "making it" or "not making it," and whether or

CONCLUSION

not your time invested in this endeavor of becoming a great filmmaker or making a feature film is "worth it in the end." You will be better for having taken the journey.

Whether you abandon your dreams, or achieve them, or take up some other hobby; whether you actually make it to Hollywood or stay in your little town, or you take off for Wall Street, or K street, or you venture to find a mate, settle down and have a family, THIS journey will bring out the noble and wise man or woman within you.

Your interest in this subject matter is a catalyst for your trek on the "unexpected journey."

Perhaps, like Bilbo Baggins, you may be surrounded by people who have no use for adventures, and you may as well cautiously worry—and sense—that "adventures are nasty, disturbing, uncomfortable things—things that will only make you late for dinner."

True. But I promise…

You won't be late for dinner.

Best of luck.

Tom Getty,
January 6, 2019.

TOM GETTY
FILMOGRAPHY

FLOWERS FOR ALGERNON (2001)

PROJECT 205 (2001)

PREDICTABLE (2002)

UNBELIEF (2003)

AMERICAN WRITER (2004)

THE MOVIES (2005)

EMULATION (2010)

RISING FEAR (AMERICA HAS FALLEN) (2016)

INDEX

3.5mm jack, 129–131
3-D graphics, 252–254
3ds Max, 254
3-point lighting, 142
28 Days Later, 11, 45, 51, 54, 187
28 Weeks Later, 45, 51, 54
2001: A Space Odyssey, 101
"Blair Witch Project" scenario, 195
Directing Actors, 205
Today Show, The, 280
"Soap opera" look, 110

ABC, 280
Acting, 163–167
Action on Film Festival, 324
Actors, 202–204
After Effects, 110, 249–251, 263
After Hours, 34–35, 37
Agfa, 111
Algar, Garth, 106
Alien, 16, 29, 56
Aliens, 56, 58
Al Jazeera, 284
All The Money In The World, 35
Amazon, 14, 95, 130–131, 210, 251, 279, 281, 316, 328
America Has Fallen, 14, 183, 293, 306

American Graffiti, 316
American Writer, 175
Anamorphic, 40, 41, 85, 134, 135, 138
Anderson, Paul Thomas, 40
Anderson, Wes, 15, 300
AOL, 281
Aperture, 138, 141, 143–146, 207, 211
Apocalypse Now, 42
Apple, 93, 144, 250, 270
Aronofsky, Darren, 33
ARRI, 85
Art majors, 159
AT&T, 281
Audience, 25, 27, 42–44, 47, 50, 53, 64, 67–71, 73, 112, 121, 137, 172, 191, 203, 225, 231, 231–232, 238, 260, 268, 271, 278, 289, 299, 302, 310
Audience reaction, 25
Audio
    recording, 120–127
    slate, 127
Audio mastering, 269–271
Avatar, 252
Avengers, The, 27
Aykroyd, Dan, 246

Backing up files, 116
Back To The Future, 16, 300

Bad Taste, 32, 33
Bardem, Javier, 203
Bare Bones Film Festival, 323–324
Barnum, PT, 285
Barrymore, Drew, 72, 73
Batman, 19, 27, 60, 60–62, 70, 222, 224, 242, 275, 280
Batman Begins, 19, 61, 62, 275
Bay, Michael, 261, 265
Beautiful Mind, A, 24, 97
Being John Malkovich, 16
Beltrami, Marco, 45
Benchley, Peter, 278
Best Buy, 93, 95, 114, 122, 134, 136
Beyonce, 309
B&H, 91, 94, 114, 142
Billups, Scott, 112
Birds, The, 56, 196
Black Hawk Down, 252, 261–262, 264
Blackmagic, 91
Blade Runner, 11
Blair Witch Project, The, 12, 195, 315, 316
Bleach bypass, 262–264
Blender, 254
Blend modes, 263
Blues Brothers, The, 11
Blue screen, 247
Blum, Jason, 315, 316–319

335

Blurry look, 135–136, 148–149
Bond, James, 27, 71
Boogie Nights, 11, 40
Bourne Ultimatum, The, 264
David Bowie, 40, 41
Braff, Zach, 36
Brando, Marlon, 42, 161
Budget, 35, 36
    above-the-line, 30
    below-the-line, 32
    Hollywood, 30–31
Burden of Dreams, 196
Burton, Tim, 15

Caldwell, Curtis, 183
Camera
    a7RII, 91
    Alpha a7s, 91
    C100, 91
    C200, 91
    C300, 91
    C500, 92
    Genesis, 94
    GoPro, 92
    HVX200a, 141
    HXR, 91
    Panavision, 94, 138
    PWX-FS7, 91
    (RED) Dragon, 91
    (RED) Raven, 91
    (RED) Scarlet, 27, 91, 93
    (RED) Weapon, 91–93
Camera jobs, 211
Camera movement, 209–212
Camera requirements, 101–107
Cameron, James, 15, 56, 69
Campbell, Neve, 73
Canon, 87, 91, 94, 103, 104
Carnegie, Dale, 310
Carpenter, John, 33, 45, 229
Carrey, Jim, 26
Casino, 16, 40, 241
Cast Away, 300
CBS, 282
CGI, 248, 249, 250, 253
Change, 67–68
Chapman, Michael, 97
Character goal, 73
Cheap lights, 150

Cinema 4-D, 254
Circuit City, 122, 134
Citizen Kane, 177, 229
Clancy, Tom, 328
Clerks, 32, 33
Cliffhanger, 247
Climax, 43, 72
Clinton, Bill, 280
Clooney, George, 28
Cloverfield, 58
CNN, 280
Codecs, 117, 118, 243
    AVCHD, 112
    H.264, 118
    MPG-4, 112
    ProRess, 118
    XF-AVC, 118
Color correction, 260–266
Color information, 118–119, 262
Competence, 29–30
Compositing, 249–252
Compression, 117–119
Condrick, Christian, 66
Conglomeration, 279
Content, 27, 37, 64, 136, 145, 159, 177, 193, 196, 237–238, 271, 281, 282, 285–286, 310, 311, 322, 323, 324, 330
Coppola, Francis Ford, 15
Coverage, 207–208
Crackling microphone, 212–213
Crazies, The, 54
Creating inertia, 172–178
Cube, 233

Damon, Matt, 28, 282, 324
Dark Knight Rises, The, 24, 70, 71, 72, 222, 224
Dark Knight, The, 11, 24, 29, 33, 50, 70, 71, 72, 96, 222, 224, 238, 241, 242
Dark Star, 32, 33
Dawn of the Dead (1978), 45, 50–55, 58
Dawn of the Dead (2004), 45
Day of the Dead, 45, 51, 56

Dazed and Confused, 43, 44
Deakins, Roger, 97, 98
Death Proof / Grindhouse, 283
De Bono, Edward, 38
Deer Hunter, The, 11, 104
De Palma, Brian, 33
Desperation, 169
Dialogue, 78
Diary of the Dead, 45, 51
Die Hard, 11, 64, 69, 124, 241, 280, 297
Die Hard 3, 11
Directing actors, 204–205
Directing Actors (book), 205
Directing practice, 213
Disney World, 57, 89
Distribution, 49, 275, 282, 284, 290, 315, 319
    Posters, 292–298
Distributors, 14, 242, 317
Donnie Darko, 11
Drive, 11, 306
Dunkirk, 11, 15, 303

Earthquake, 56, 246
Ebert, Roger, 44, 282
Editing, 256–259
Edwards, Gareth, 33
El Mariachi, 316
El Mariachi, 32, 33, 316
Empire Strikes Back, 247
Emulation, 14, 59, 60, 115, 184, 186, 243, 318
Enemy of the State, 48
Equipment
    Camera, 18
Eraserhead, 32, 33
Erin Brockovich, 28
ESPN, 280
ET, 241
Evil Dead, The, 16
Expectation, 69, 99, 104, 231, 255, 278, 322
Exposure, 143

Fahrenheit 911, 283
Fate of the Furious, The, 24
Fear and Desire, 32, 33
Fields, Verna, 228
Fight Club, 11, 47, 48, 49, 60
Film festivals, 320–325
Filming For Your Life, 34

INDEX

Film school, 176
Film stocks, 111
Final Draft (software), 80
Fincher, David, 15, 46, 47, 48, 156, 264, 266
Finishing touches, 260–271
First assembly, 232–239
Fitzgerald, F. Scott, 175
Fleetwood Mac, 40
Flowers For Algernon, 62
Following, 32–38
Ford, Harrison, 59, 229, 242
Forrest Gump, 96, 247
Frame rates, 109–111
Friedkin, William, 98
F-stops, 146–147
Fugitive, The, 48, 50, 59, 241–242
Fujimoto, Tak, 97
Fun with Dick and Jane, 25

Game, The, 48, 59
Gangs of New York, 97
Garden State, 36
Gauntlet, The, 38
GE, 282, 284
General Electric, 279, 280, 284
Genre, 49, 55, 58, 59, 60, 231
Get Out, 315
Getting media attention, 309, 309–313
Getting permission, 191–193
Getty, Tom, 3, 4, 14, 121, 330, 331
Ghostbusters, 11, 14, 19, 96, 241, 245, 246, 249
Gibson, Mel, 26
Giger, H.R., 26
Gladiator, 12
Goblin, 45
Godfather, The, 12
Godzilla, 56, 57
Go Fund Me, 35
Goldman, William, 30
Goodfellas, 11, 34, 40, 96, 97, 225, 241
Good Girl, The, 25
Google, 12, 24, 144, 251, 281, 314, 330
Goyer, David S., 71, 72
Greengrass, Paul, 264
Grindhouse, 284
Group projects, 174–176

Gyllenhaal, Jake, 19

Half-way mark, 221–226
Halloween, 11, 229
Hamiliton, Jake, 247
Hangover, The, 25
Hanks, Tom, 247
Herzog, Warner, 196
Hidden Fortress, The, 55
Hitchcock, Alfred, 15, 156, 196, 327
Houdini, 254
Howard, James Newton, 241, 242
How Do You Know, 26
Huffington Post, 32

I Am Legend, 45, 55
I Am Legend (novel), 45, 55
Ideas, 27–29
Idiocracy, 43
Inception, 11, 50, 121, 305
Independence Day, 26, 247
Inglorious Bastards, 12, 283–284
Insidious, 268, 315
Insomnia, 28, 60
Inspiration, 44–58
Interchangeable lens, 135
Internet Movie Database Pro, 318
Interstellar, 12, 19
Invading, The, 75
iStock.com, 296
It's Murder!, 32
iTunes, 269, 279, 328
I Wish I Was Here, 36

Jackson, Peter, 15, 33
Jaws, 49, 228, 229, 278
Job of director, 198–199
Johansson, Scarlet, 27
Johnson, Samuel, 277
Jones, James Earl, 229
Jovovich, Milla, 301
Jurassic Park, 11, 15, 57, 58, 213, 241, 246, 247, 253
JVC, 87, 91, 94, 95

Kardashian, Kim, 285
Keitel, Harvey, 28
Key art, 298
Kicking and Screaming, 319

Kickstarter, 25, 35, 36
Kill Bill, 97, 286
Kill Bill 2, 286
King Kong, 15, 56–57, 246
King of Comedy, The, 34
King, Zach, 251, 255
Kodak, 91, 111
Kontakt, 243
Kramer, Andrew, 242, 251, 252, 255
Kubrick, Stanley, 15, 33, 286, 300

Land of the Dead, 45, 54
Land of the Lost, 57
Last Temptation, The, 34
Launch, 314–319
Lawrence, Jennifer, 27
Lawrence of Arabia, 96
Lean, David, 15
Ledger, Heath, 242
Lee, Spike, 15
Lennon, John, 240
Lenses, 134–139
 24mm, 136
 50mm, 136, 138
 70mm, 136
Linklater, Richard, 33, 43, 44
Linson, Art, 48
Little Miss Sunshine, 316
Lord of the Rings, 11, 19
Los Angeles, 13
 living in, 13
Lost World, The, 124
Lugosi, Bela, 54
Lynch, David, 15, 33, 286
Lynda.com, 251

MacGyver, 38, 113–116
Mad Max, 316
Mama June, 285
Manchurian Candidate, The, 49
Marketing, 275
Marketing business, 276–279
Marley & Me, 25
Marshal, Neil, 56
Martin, Steve, 319
Marvel, 280
Mascagni, Pietro, 240
Matheson, Richard, 55
Matrix, The, 12
Maya, 254
McClane, John, 69, 71

McConaughey, Matthew, 19
Mckee, Robert, 37, 49, 58–59, 65, 258
Meaningful change, 68–70
Mean Streets, 240
Media interviews, 310–311
Memento, 11, 49, 50, 137
Memorization, 200–207
MIDI, 243, 244
Mindset, 230–231
Minimizing variables, 194–196
Minority Report, 48, 264
Mona Lisa Smile, 24
Monsters, 32, 33
Moore, Michael, 285
Movie producer, 197–199
Movie production plans, 170–171, 174
Movies, The, 267
Movie trailer, 299–306
Codecs
    MPG4, 118
Multiple shoots, 183–185
Murphy's Law, 106, 189
Music, 10, 30, 40, 41, 42, 47, 199, 226, 227, 228, 229, 230, 231, 232, 238, 240, 241, 242, 243, 244, 256, 258, 259, 263, 268, 269, 270, 281, 300, 301, 302, 304
Music software
    Ableton, 244
Music Software
    Garage Band, 244
    Logic Pro, 244, 270
    Pro Tools, 244, 270
My Best Friend's Birthday, 18, 32

Nakatomi Plaza, 297
Napoleon Dynamite, 316
Netflix, 14, 251, 279, 281, 316
News article, 311–312
News-Corp, 282
New York, New York, 34
Night of the Comet, 45
Night of the Creeps, 45
Night of the Living Dead, 12, 26, 45, 51, 54, 55, 56, 57, 316

Night of the Zombies, 45
Nikon, 91
No Country For Old Men, 97, 203
Nolan, Christopher, 15, 16, 17, 28, 33, 46, 49, 50, 61, 70, 71, 97, 121, 156, 157, 277, 303
Nolan, Jonathan, 71
North By Northwest, 16, 49, 156
Norton, Edward, 48

Ocean's 11, 28
One Hour Photo, 137
Open Water, 316
Opportunity, 34
O'Reilly, Bill, 280

Pacino, Al, 28, 34
Panasonic, 87, 91, 92, 94, 95, 105, 109, 135, 141
Paranormal Activity, 12, 315–316
Pareto principle, the, 35
Peanuts Movie, The, 24
Pearce, Guy, 49
Peli, Oren, 315, 316
Pfister, Wally, 137
Photoshop, 90, 292, 297, 298, 307
Pi, 32–33
Picking actors, 31
Pink Floyd, 170
Pitching, 27, 47–49
Pitt, Brad, 28, 48
Pixar, 280
Planes, Trains, & Automobiles, 319
Planet Terror, 45
Platoon, 16
Poseidon Adventure, The, 56
Poster creation, 307–309
Poster making exercise, 297–299
Post-production, 127, 221, 226, 228, 229, 230, 231, 232
Predator, 122, 124
Preparation, 179–186
Pre-production, 171–174, 221
Prescott, Sidney, 73
Prestige, The, 16, 50

Process, 100
Professional actors, 163
Project justification, 177
Prometheus, 29
Prowse, David, 229
Psycho, 156, 327
Public domain, 244
Pulp Fiction, 16, 282, 283
Purge, The, 315

Qatar government, 284

Raging Bull, 34, 241
Raiders of the Lost Ark, 11, 50, 245, 246
Raimi, Sam, 15, 33
Ramsey, Clark, 278
Reading, 179–181
Reagen, Ronald, 328
Rear Window, 48
Recording media, 111–117
Recruiting, 155–167
    family, 158
    friends, 158
    students, 158–161
Recruit, The, 48
RED (camera), 41, 85, 86, 91, 92, 93, 94, 97, 99, 102, 106, 107, 129, 130, 131, 136
Red Digital Cinema Camera Company, 93
Reitman, Ivan, 246
Reservoir Dogs, 17, 28, 282
Resident Evil, 29, 30, 45, 51, 54, 58, 301, 304
Resident Evil: Apocalypse, 29, 30, 58
Residual income, 327
Return of the Living Dead, The, 45, 51, 56
Revenant, The, 11
Reynolds, Burt, 278
Richardson, Robert, 97
Rising Fear, 14, 183, 293, 296, 306, 323
Rocky, 316
Rodriguez, Robert, 16, 17, 33, 127
Rolling Stones, the, 40
Romero, George A., 45, 55
Rona, Jeff, 267
Roth, Eli, 285
Royal Tenenbaums, The, 11

INDEX

Royalty check, 327
Rudd, Paul, 26

Saw, 316
Scene folders, 235
Scheduling, 181–188
Schoonmaker, Thelma, 225
Scorsese, Martin, 15, 16, 33, 34, 46, 97, 98, 156, 225, 240
Scott, Ridley, 15, 29, 262, 264
Scott, Tony, 48
Scream, 11, 56, 72, 73
Screen Actors Guild, 163
Screening the movie, 288–291, 324–325
Screenplay, 63, 64, 65, 74, 75, 78, 79, 180, 181
Scripting, 74–80, 179–184
Seacrest, Ryan, 285
Secret Window, 60
Set-ups, 170–171
Seven, 11
Seven Samurai, The, 55
Sex and the City 2, 24
Shakespeare, 71
Shark!, 278
Shawshank Redemption, The, 97
Shining, The, 16
Shooting permits, 192–194
Shooting with cameras, 206–216
Showing up, 162
Shutter Island, 34, 49, 97
Shyamalan, M. Night, 15, 17, 285
Signing autographs, 310
Signs, 26, 29, 97
Silence of the Lambs, The, 12, 97
The Silence of the Lambs, 12, 97
Simmons, Gene, 285
Sinister, 315
Sixth Sense, The, 16, 27, 29, 49
Skyfall, 97
Slacker, 32, 33, 43, 44
Smith, Kevin, 33, 282, 285
Soderbergh, Steven, 28
Soloist, The, 25
Sony, 87, 91, 94, 95, 113
Sound design, 267–269

Sound stage, 247
Special effects, 245–255
Spector, Phil, 240, 241
Spielberg, Steven, 15, 16, 33, 49, 57, 97, 107, 156, 157, 228, 246, 264, 277, 278, 282, 315
Stallone, Sylvester, 247
Stars
   value of, 31
Star Wars, 15, 55, 229–230, 241, 245–246, 252, 280
Stepford Wives, The, 24
Stoker, Bram, 57
Stone, Oliver, 285
Stranger Things, 39
Subconscious, 188, 189, 215, 233, 234, 237, 238, 257, 268
Subject matter, 40–42
Subtext, 236
Sundance Film Festival, 41, 321, 322, 323, 325, 326
Survival horror, 57
Swift, Taylor, 324, 325

Taking pictures, 295
Talent, 30, 31, 32–33, 44, 100, 125, 161, 162, 204, 277, 278, 318
Tarantino, Quentin, 15, 17, 32, 277, 282, 283, 284
Taxi Driver, 11, 34, 202, 203
Teaching the scene, 200
Terminator 2, 11, 24, 246
Texas Chainsaw Massacre, 28
Theater majors, 159–161
The Departed, 34, 241, 286
There Will Be Blood, 11
The Walking Dead, 46, 54
Thing, The, 16, 49, 73, 93, 127, 149, 180, 253, 276
Three Days of Condor, 48
THX-1138, 163
Time magazine, 280
Time Warner, 282
Titanic, 15, 16, 24, 69, 203, 241
Towering Inferno, The, 56
Train to Busan, 45

Transformers, 261
Transportation, 173
Transformers, 265
Tremors, 58
Twilight, 25

Unbelief, 307, 308
Unbreakable, 12
Upton, Kate, 324, 325
USC, 176

Vader, Darth, 229
VHS, 113, 114, 115, 116
VideoCopilot.Net, 251, 252
Village, The, 97
Virtual instruments, 243–244

Wahlberg, Mark, 35
Waking Life, 43, 44
Walt Disney, 282, 284
Wan, James, 15
Washington, Denzel, 49
Waveform, 127
Wayne, Bruce, 19, 61, 70, 71, 72, 224, 275
Wayne's World, 106
Welles, Orson, 177, 229
Weston, Del, 324
Weston, Judith, 205
Wexler, Haskell, 97
What Lies Beneath, 300
When Time Ran Out, 56
White Zombie, 54, 55
Williams, Robin, 137
Willis, Bruce, 280, 297
Wilson, Owen, 26
Witherspoon, Reese, 26
Wolf of Wall Street, The, 24, 34, 202, 279
Wong, Freddie, 251, 255
World War Z, 24, 45
Writing description, 76–78
Writing ideas, 40

XLR input, 128–130

YouTube, 12, 240, 242, 244, 249, 281, 330
You've Got Mail, 24

Zimmer, Hans, 45, 241, 242
Zodiac, 19, 39

www.ingramcontent.com/pod-product-compliance
Lightning Source LLC
Chambersburg PA
CBHW030636150426
42811CB00077B/2166/J